Earl Shinn

The New Hyperion

From Paris to Marly by way of the Rhine

Earl Shinn

The New Hyperion
From Paris to Marly by way of the Rhine

ISBN/EAN: 9783337370275

Printed in Europe, USA, Canada, Australia, Japan

Cover: Foto ©Andreas Hilbeck / pixelio.de

More available books at **www.hansebooks.com**

FROM PARIS TO MARLY BY WAY OF THE RHINE.

BY

EDWARD STRAHAN.

WITH OVER THREE HUNDRED ILLUSTRATIONS FROM DESIGNS BY GUSTAVE DORÉ AND OTHERS.

PHILADELPHIA
J. B. LIPPINCOTT & CO.
1875.

Entered according to Act of Congress, in the year 1874, by

J. B. LIPPINCOTT & CO.,

In the office of the Librarian of Congress, at Washington.

NOTICE.

THIS volume, committed to scenes connected with Mr. Longfellow's celebrated romance of *Hyperion*, travels over ground already made the common property of various authors, native and foreign.

Among the best of these is M. Boniface, who in 1861 wrote a book of *Hyperion*-like adventures under his usual pseudonym of X. B. Saintine. Where the pathway of this work coincides with his (and especially in cases when the pictures by Doré made a special style of description imperative, in which cases the frankest resemblance will be found) a very grateful obligation is acknowledged by " The New Hyperion." Toward what author could there be an obligation so agreeable, or lying so light, as toward the author of *Picciola ?*

CONTENTS.

PART		PAGE
I.	PREAMBULARY	7
II.	THE TWO CHICKENS	19
III.	THE FEAST OF SAINT ATHANASIUS	36
IV.	A DAY IN STRASBURG	49
V.	IN PURSUIT OF A PASSPORT	62
VI.	SHALL AULD ACQUAINTANCE BE FORGOT?	78
VII.	THE SEDUCTIONS OF BADEN-BADEN	96
VIII.	THE MUSIK-FEST AT ACHERN	115
IX.	ASTRAY IN THE BLACK FOREST	130
X.	A WALK TO WILDBAD	144
XI.	THE NECKAR REVISITED: OLD FRIENDS AT HEIDELBERG AGAIN	155
XII.	CONFLICTS AT HEIDELBERG	166
XIII.	ON WITH THE OLD LOVE	180
XIV.	AN AGREEABLE DUET AT FRANKFORT	194
XV.	EN ROUTE AGAIN	205
XVI.	EMBARKATION AND VOYAGE FROM MAYENCE	211
XVII.	THE CURRENT OF FATE	229
XVIII.	THE DIFFICULTY OF CATCHING UP	237
XIX.	TYING UP THE CLEWS	251

THE NEW HYPERION.

FROM PARIS TO MARLY BY WAY OF THE RHINE.

PART I.

PREAMBULARY.

HE behavior of a great Hope is like the setting of the sun. It splashes out from under a horizontal cloud, so diabolically incandescent that you see a dozen false suns blotting the heavens with purple in every direction. You bury your eyes in a handkerchief, with your back carefully turned upon the west, and meantime the spectacle you were waiting for takes place and disappears. You promise yourself to nick it better to-morrow. The soul withdraws into its depths. The stars arise (offering two or three thousand more impracticable suns), and the night is ironical.

Having already conquered, without boasting, a certain success before the reading public, and having persuaded an author of renown to sign his name to my bantling, my Expectation and Hope have long been to surpass that trifling production. You may think it a slight thing to prepare a lucky volume, and, tapping Fame familiarly on the shoulder, engage her to undertake its colportage throughout the different countries of the globe. My first little work of travel and geography had exceeded my dreams of a good reception. It had earned me sev-

EARLY FAME.

eral proposals from publishers; it had been annotated with "How true!" and "Most profound!" by the readers in public libraries; its title had given an imaginative air to the ledgers of booksellers; and it had added a new shade of moodiness to the collection of Mudie. The man who hits one success by accident is always trying to hit another by preparation. Since that achievement I have thought of nothing but the creation of another impromptu, and I have really prepared a quantity of increments toward it in the various places to which my traveling existence has led me. That I have settled down, since these many years past, at the centre and capital of ideas would prove me, even without the indiscretions of that first little book, an American by birth. I need not add that

THE MECHANIC IN GREEN.

my card is printed in German text, 𝔓aul 𝔉lemming, and that time has brought to me a not ungraceful, though a sometimes practically retardating, circumference. Beneath a mask of cheerfulness, and even of obesity, however, I continue to guard the sensitive feelings of my earlier days. Yes: under this abnormal convexity are fostered, as behind a lens, the glowing tendencies of my youth. Though no longer, like the Harold described in Icelandic verse by Regner Hairy-Breeches, "a young chief proud of my flowing locks," yet I still "spend my mornings among the young maidens," or such of them as frequent the American Colony, as we call it, in Paris. I still "love to converse with the handsome widows." Miss Ashburton, who in one little passage of our youth treated me with considerable disrespect, and who afterward married a person of great lingual accomplishments, her father's late courier, at Naples, has been handsomely forgiven, but not forgotten. A few intelligent ladies, of marked listening powers and conspicuous accomplishments, are habitually met by me at their residences in the neighborhood of the Arc de Triomphe or at the receptions of the United States minister. These fair attractions, although occupying, in practice, a preponderating share of my time, are as nothing to me, however, in comparison with that enticing illusion, my Book.

The scientific use of the imagination in treating the places and distances of

Geography is the dream of my days and the insomnia of my nights.

Every morning I take down and dust the loose sheets of my coming book or polish the gilding of my former one. It is in my fidelity to these baffling hopes —hopes fed with so many withered (or at least torn and blotted) leaves—rather than in any resemblance authenticable by a looking-glass, that I show my identity with the old long-haired and nasal Flemming.

Yet, though so long a Parisian, and so comfortable in my theoretic pursuit of Progressive Geography, my leisure hours are unconsciously given to knit-

TRIUMPH OF APRIL.

ting myself again to past associations, and some of my deepest pleasures come from tearing open the ancient wounds. Shall memory ever lose that sacred, that provoking day in the Vale of Lauterbrunnen when the young mechanic in green serenaded us with his guitar? It had for me that quite peculiar and personal application that it immediately preceded my rejection by Miss Mary. The Staubbach poured before our eyes, as from a hopper in the clouds, its Stream of Dust. The Ashburtons, clad in the sensible and becoming fashion of English lady-tourists, with long ringlets and Leghorn hats, sat on either side of me upon the grass. And then that implacable youth, looking full in my eye, sang his verses of insulting sagacity:

> She gives thee a garland woven fair;
> Take care!
> It is a fool's-cap for thee to wear;
> Beware! beware!
> Trust her not,
> She is fooling thee!

Meeting him two or three times afterward as he pursued his apprentice-tour, I felt as though I had encountered a green-worm. And I confess that it was part-ly on his account that I made a vow, fervently uttered and solemnly kept, never again to visit Switzerland or the Rhine. Miss Ashburton I easily forgave. The disadvantage, I distinctly felt, was hers, solely and restrictedly hers; and I should have treated with profound respect, if I had come across him, the professional traveler who was good enough to marry her afterward.

But these bitter-sweet recollections are only the relief to my studies. It is true they are importunate, but they are strictly kept below stairs.

Nor would any one, regarding the stout and comfortable Flemming, suspect what regrets and what philosophies were disputing possession of his interior. For my external arrangements, I flatter myself that I have shaped *them* in tolerable taste.

My choice of the French capital I need not defend to any of my American readers. To all of you this consummation is simply a matter of ability. I heartily despise, as I always did, all mere pamperings of physical convenience. Still, for some who retain some sympathy with the Paul Flemming of aforetime, it may be worth while to mention the particular physical conveniencies my soul contemns. I inhabit, and have done so for eight years at least, a neat little residence of the kind styled "between court and garden," and lying on the utmost permissible circumference of the American quarter in Paris—say on the hither side of Passy. For nearly the same period I have had in lease a comical box at Marly, whither I repair every summer. My town-quarters, having been furnished by an artist, gave me small pains. The whole interior is like a suite of rooms in the Hôtel Cluny. The

METAMORPHOSIS.

only trouble was in bringing up the cellar to the quality I desired and in selecting domestics—points on which, though careless of worldly comfort in general, I own I am somewhat particular.

No gentleman valets for me — rude creatures presuming to outdress their masters. What I wanted was the Corporal Trim style of thing—bald, faithful, ancient retainer. After a world of vexation I succeeded in finding an artless couple, who agreed for a stipulation to sigh when I spoke of my grandfather before my guests, and to have been brought up in the family.

But I am wandering, and neglecting the true vein of sentiment which so abounds in my heart. All my pleasure is still in mournful contemplation, but I have learned that the feelings are most refined when freed from low cares and personal discomforts. I was going to cite a letter I wrote to my oldest friend, the baron of Hohenfels. It was sketched out first in verse, but in that form was a failure:

"15th MARCH.

"The snow-white clouds beyond my window are piled up like Alps. The shades of B. Franklin and W. Tell seem to walk together on those Elysian Fields; for it was here (or sufficiently nigh for the purpose) that in days gone by our pure patriot dwelt and flirted with Madame Helvetius; and yonder clouds so much resemble the snowy Alps that they remind me irresistibly of the Swiss. Noble examples of a high purpose and a fixed will! Do B. and W. not move, Hyperion-like, on high? Were *they* not, likewise, sons of Heaven and Earth?

"I wish I knew the man who called flowers 'the fugitive poetry of Nature.' That was a sweet carol, which I think I have quoted to you, sung by the Rhodian children of old in spring, bearing in their hands a swallow, and chanting 'The swallow is come,' with some other lines, which I have forgotten. A pretty carol is that, too, which the Hungarian boys, on the islands of the Danube, sing to the returning stork in spring, what

THE LYRE OF HYPERION.

time it builds its nests in the chimneys and gracefully diverts the draft of smoke into the interior. What a thrill of delight in spring-time! What a joy in being and moving! Some housekeepers might object to that, and say that there was but imperfect joy in moving; but I am about to propose to you, as soon as I have taken a little more string, a plan of removal that will suit both us and the season. My friend, the time of storms is flying before the pretty child called April, who pursues it with his blooming thyrsus. Breathing scent upon the air, he has already awakened some of the trees on the boulevards, and the white locust-blossoms in the garden of Rossini are beginning to hang out their bunches to attract the nightingales. He calls to the swallows, and they arrive in clouds.

"He knocks at the hard envelope of the chrysalis, which accordingly prepares to take its chance for a precarious metamorphosis—into the wings of the butterfly or into the bosom of the bird. How very sweet!

"Strange is the lesson, my friend, which humanity teaches itself from the larva. Even so do I, methinks, feed in life's autumn upon the fading foliage of Hope, and, still feeding and weaving, turn it at last into a little grave. A neat image that, which, by the by, I stole from Drummond of Hawthornden. Do you recollect his verse?—but of course I should be provoked if I thought you did—

For, with strange thoughts possessed,
  I feed on fading leaves
  Of hope—which me deceives,
And thousand webs doth warp within my breast.
And thus, in end, unto myself I weave
A fast-shut prison. No! but even a Grave!

"To pursue my subject: April, having thus balanced the affairs of the bird and the worm, proceeds to lay over the meadows a tablecloth for the bees. He opens all the windows of Paris, and on the streets shows us the sap mounting in carnation in the faces of the girls.

"My dear Hohenfels, I invite you to the festival which Spring is spreading just now in the village of Marly. My cabin will be gratified to open in your honor. May it keep you until autumn! Come, and come at once."

Having signed my missive, I tucked it into an envelope, which I blazoned with my favorite seal, the lyre of Hyperion broken, and rang for Charles. In

INFIRMITIES OF AGE.

nis stead, in lieu of my faithful Charles, it was Hohenfels himself who entered, fresh from the Hôtel Mirabeau.

"Look alive, man! Can you lend me an umbrella?" said he briskly.

I looked out at the window: it was snowing.

The moment seemed inopportune for the delivery of my epistle: I endeavored to conceal it—without hypocrisy and by a natural movement—under the usual pile of manuscript on my table devoted to Progressive Geography. But the baron had spied his name on the address: "How is that? You were writing to me? There, I will spare you the trouble of posting."

He read my sentences, turning at the end of each period to look out at the snow, which was heavily settling in large damp flakes. He said nothing at first about the discrepancy, but only looked forth alternately with his reading, which was pointed enough. I said long ago that the beauty of Hohenfels' character, like that of the precious opal, was owing to a defect in his organization. The

baron retains his girlish expression, his blue eye, and his light hair of the kind that never turns gray: he is still slender, but much bent. He went over to the fireplace and crouched before the coals that were flickering there still. Then he said, with that gentle, half-laughing voice, "Take care, Paul, old boy! Children who show sense too early never grow, they say; by parity of argument, men who are poetical too late in life never get their senses."

"I have given up poetry," said I, "and you cannot scan that communication in your hand."

"But it is something worse than poetry! It is prose inflated and puffed and bubbled. You are falling into your old moony ways again, and sonneteering in plain English. Are you not ashamed, at your age?"

"What age do you mean? I feel no infirmities of age. If my hair is gray, 'tis not with years, as By—"

"If your hair is gray, it is because you are forty-eight, my old beauty."

"Forty-five!" I said, with some little natural heat.

"Forty-five let it be, though you have said so these three years. And what age is that to go running after the foot of the rainbow? Here you are, my dear Flemming, breathing forth hymns to Spring, and inviting your friends to picnics! Don't you know that April is the traitor among the twelve months of the year? You are ready to strike for Marly in a linen coat and slippers! Have you forgotten, my poor fellow, that Marly is windy and raw, and that Louis XIV. caught that chill at Marly of which he died? Ah, Paul, you are right enough. You are young, still young. You are not forty-eight: you are sixteen—sixteen for the third time."

Hohenfels, whose once fine temper is going a little, stirred the fire and suddenly rose.

"Lend me an umbrella!" he repeated imperatively.

"Are you in such a hurry to go? That is not very complimentary to me," I observed. "Have you done scolding me?"

What is called by some my growing worldliness teaches me to value dryness in an old friend as I value dryness in a fine, cobwebbed, crusty wine. It is from the merest Sybaritism that I surround myself with comrades who, like Hohenfels, can fit their knobs into my pattern, and receive my knobs in their own vacancy. My hint brought him over at once into the leathern chair opposite the one I occupy.

"Paul, Paul," he said, "I only criticise you for your good. What have you done with your three adolescences? You are getting stout, yet you still write poetically. You have some wit, imagination, learning and aptitude. You might make a name in science or art, but everything you do lacks substance, because you live only in your old eternal catchwords of the Past and the Future. You can sketch and paint, yet have never exhibited your pictures except in ladies' albums. You profess to love botany, yet your sole herbarium has been the mignonette in sewing-girls' windows. You are inoffensive, you are possessed of a competency, but in everything, in every vocation, you rest in the state of amateur — amateur housekeeper, amateur artist, amateur traveler, amateur geographer. And such a geographer as you might be, with your taste for travel and the Hakluyt Society's publications you have pored over for years!"

This chance allusion to my grand secret took me from my guard. Hohenfels, blundering up and down in search of something to anathematize, had stumbled upon the very fortress of my strength. I deemed it time to let him into a part of my reserved intellectual treasure—to whirl away a part at least of the sand in which my patient sphinx had been buried.

"I have indeed been a reader," I said modestly. "When a youth at Heidelberg, I perused, with more profit than would be immediately guessed from the titles, such works as the Helden-Buchs and the Nibelungen-Lieds, the Saxon Rhyme-Chronicles, the poems of Minnesingers and Mastersingers, and Ships of Fools, and Reynard Foxes, and Death-Dances, and Lamentations of Damned Souls. My study since then has been in German chemistry from its renaissance in Paracelsus, and physical science, including both medicine and the evolution of life. Shall I give you a few dozen of my favorite writers?"

"Quite unnecessary," said the baron with some haste. "But I fancied you were going to speak of geographical authors."

AMERICAN!!

"Are you fond of such writings yourself?" I asked.

"Immensely—that is, not too scientific, you know," said the baron, who was out of his element here. "Bayard Taylor, now, or some such fellows as the Alpine Club."

"My dear baron, the republications by the Hakluyt Society are but a small part of the references I have taken down for my Progressive Geography. You admire Switzerland?"

"Vastly. Steep jump, the Staubbach."

"But the Alps are only hillocks compared with the Andes of Peru, with the Cordilleras, with Chimborazo! Ah, baron, Chimborazo! Well, my dear boy, the system I elaborate makes it a matter of simple progression and calculation to arrive at mountains much more considerable still."

"Such as—?"

"The Mountains of the Moon!"

I then, in a few dexterously involved sentences, allowed the plan of my newly-invented theory to appear—so much of it, that is, as would leave Hohenfels completely in the dark, and detract in no wise from the splendor of my Opus when it should be published. As science, however, truly considered, is the art of dilapidating and merging into confused ruin the theories of your predecessors, I was somewhat more precise with the destructive than the constructive part of my plan.

"Geographical Science, I am prepared to show, is that which modern learning alone has neglected, to the point of leaving its discoveries stationary. It is not so with the more assiduously cultivated branches. What change, what advance, in every other department of culture! In geology, the ammonite of to-day was for Chalmers a parody facetiously made by Nature in imitation of her living conchology, and for Voltaire a pilgrim's cockle dropped in the passes of the Alps. In medicine, what progress has been made since ague was compared to the flutter of insects among the nerves, and good Mistress Dorothy Burton, who died but in 1629, cured it by hanging a spider round the patient's neck "in a nutshell lapped in silk"! In chemistry, what strides! In astronomy, what perturbations and changes! In history, what do we not owe to the amiable authors who, dipping their pens in whitewash, have reversed the judgments of ages on Nero and Henry VIII.! In genealogy, what thanks must we pay to Darwin! Geographical Science alone, stolid in its insolent fixity, has not moved: the location of Thebes and Memphis is what it was in the days of Cheops and Rameses. And so poor in intellect are our professors of geodesic lore that London continues to be, just as it always was, in latitude 51° 30′ 48″ N., longitude 0° 5′ 38″ W., while the observatory of Paris contentedly sits in latitude 48° 50′ 12″ N. and longitude 2° 20′ 22½″ E. from the observatory of Greenwich! This disgracefully stationary condition of the science cannot much longer be permitted."

"And how," said the baron, "will it be changed?" and he poked the fire to conceal a yawn. Excellent man! his time latterly had been more given to the investigation of opera than of the exact sciences.

"Through my theory of Progression and Proportion in geographical statistics, by which the sources of the Nile can be easily determined from the volume and speed of that current, while the height of the mountains on the far side of the moon will be but a pleasing sum in Ratio for a scholar's vacations. Nor will anything content me, my dear Hohenfels, till this somewhat theoretical method of traveling is displaced by bodily progression; till these easy excursions of the mind are supplemented by material extensions; till the foot is pressed where the brain has leaped; and till I, then for the first time a traveler, stand behind the lunar rim, among the 'silent silver lights and darks undreamed of!'"

"I am unable to appreciate your divagations," humbly observed Hohenfels, "though I always thought your language beautiful. Meantime, my hat is spoiled in coming hither, and you have the effrontery to write bucolics to me during the most frightful weather of the year. Once for all, do you refuse me an um—"

He did not finish his sentence. A world of sunshine burst like a bomb into the chamber, and our eyes were dazzled with the splendor: a sturdy beam shot directly into the fireplace, and the embers turned haggard and gray, and quickly retired from the unequal contest. I opened the window. A warm air, faint with the scent of earth and turf, invaded the apartment, and the map-like patches of dampness on the asphaltum pavement were rapidly and visibly drying away.

"I'm off!" said Hohenfels, with a rapid movement of retreat.

"But you are forgetting your—"

"What, my gloves?"

"No, the umbrella." And I presented him the heaviest and longest and oldest of my collection. He laughed: it was a hoary canopy which we had used beside the Neckar and in Heidelberg—"a pleasant town," as the old song says,

LUNAR!!!

THE SILVER RIM.

"when it has done raining." We sealed a compact over the indestructible German umbrella. I agreed to defer for a fortnight my departure for Marly: on his side he made a solemn vow to come there on the first of May, and there receive in full and without wincing the particulars of my Progressive Geography. As he passed by the window I took care that he should catch a glimpse of me seated by accident in a strong light, my smoking-cap crowded down to my spectacles, and my nose buried in my old geographers.

For the next few days the weather supported the side of Hohenfels. It scattered rain, sunshine and spits of snow. At last the sun got the upper hand and remained master. The wisterias tumbled their cataracts of blue blossoms down the spouts; rare flowers, of minute proportions, burst from the button-holes of the young horsemen going to the Bois; the gloves of the American colony became lilac; hyacinths, daffodils and pansies moved by wagon-loads over the streets and soared to the windows of the sewing-girls. Overhead, in the steaming and cloud-marbled blue, stood the April sun. "Apelles of the flowers," as an old English writer has styled him, he was coloring the garden-beds with his rarest enamels, and spreading a sheet of varied tints over the steps of the Madeleine, where they hold the horticultural market.

This sort of country ecstasy, this season at once stimulating and enervating, tortured me. It disturbed my bibliophilist labors, and gave a twang of musty nausea even to the sweet scent of old binding-leather. I was as a man caught in the pangs of removing, unattached to either home; and I bent from my windows over the throngs of festal promenaders, taciturn and uneasy. I fancied that wings were sprouting from my brown dressing-robe, and that they were the volatile wings of the moth or dragon-fly. But to establish myself at Marly before the baron, would not that be a breach of compact? Would he not make it a *casus belli?* Luckily, we were getting through April: to-morrow it would be the twenty-eighth. On that memorable morning the sun rose strong and bright, and photographed a brilliant idea upon my cerebellum.

I would undertake a pedestrian attack upon Marly by winding my way around the suburbs of the capital. What more appropriate, for a profound geographer and tourist,

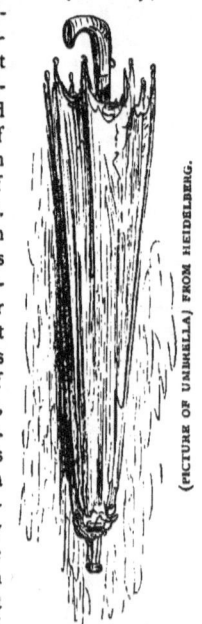

(PICTURE OF UMBRELLA) FROM HEIDELBERG.

A THEORETICAL GEOGRAPHER.

than to measure with my walking-stick that enormous bed of gypsum, at the

INCREDULITY.

centre of which, like a bee in a sugar-basin, Paris sits and hums?

The notion gained upon me. Perhaps it was the natural reaction from the Mountains of the Moon; but in my then state of mind no prospect could appear more delicious than a long tramp among the quiet scenes through which the city fringes itself off into rurality. Those suburbs of blank convent walls! those curves of the Seine and the Marne, blocked with low villages, whose walls of white, stained with tender mould and tiled with brown, dipped their placid reflections into the stream! those droll square boats, pushing out from the sedges to urge you across the ferry! those long rafts of lumber, following, like cunning crocodiles, the ins and outs of the shallow Seine! those banks of pollard willows, where girls in white caps tended flocks of geese and turkeys, and where, every silver-spangled morning, the shore was a landscape by Corot, and every twilight a landscape by Daubigny! How exquisite these pictures became to my m i n d as I thought them forth one by one, leaning over a grimy pavement in the peculiar sultriness of the year's first warmth!

"Quick, Charles! my tin botany-box."

I could be at Marly on the first of May at the dinner hour as punctually as Hohenfels — before him, maybe. And after what a range of delicious experience! How he would envy me!

"Is monsieur going to travel all alone?" said keen old Charles, taking the alarm in a minute. "Why am I not to go along with monsieur?"

The accent of primitive fidelity was perfect. I observed casually, "I am going on a little journey of thirty-six hours, and alone. You can pack everything up, and go on to Marly as usual. You may go to-morrow."

"Shall I not go along with monsieur, then?" repeated Charles, with a turn for tautology not now for the first time manifested.

"What for? Am I a child?"

"Surely not—on the contrary. But, though Monsieur Paul has a sure foot and a good eye, and is not to say getting old, yet when a person is fifty it is not best for a person to run about the streets as if a person was a young person."

It was Josephine who did me the honor to address me the last remark.

I confess to but forty-five years of age; Hohenfels, quite erroneously, gives me forty-eight; Josephine, with that raw alacrity in leaping at computations peculiar to the illiterate, oppressed me with fifty. Which of us three knew best? I should like to ask. But it is of little consequence. The Easterns generally vaunt themselves on not knowing the day of their birth. And wisdom comes to us from the East.

I decided, for reasons sufficient to myself, to get out of Paris by the opposite

STARTING.

side. I determined to make my sortie by way of the Temple Market and the Belleville abattoirs. On the thirtieth of April,

FAREWELL!

at an ambitiously early hour, wearing my gardening cap, with my sketch-book sticking out of my pocket, my tin box in one hand and my stout stick in the other, I emerged among the staring porters of the neighboring houses, and it was in this equipment that I received the renewed lamentations of Charles and Josephine.

"Will you dare to go along the Boulevard looking like that, sir?" said Josephine.

"A gentleman in a cap! They'll take you for a bricklayer—indeed they will, sir," said Charles; "or rather for a milkman, with his tin can. I can't stand that: I will carry it rather myself, though I feel my rheumatics on these damp pavements."

"Monsieur Paul must take a cab—at least to the barrier: it will not be pleasant to make a scandal in the street."

"Who will tend Monsieur Paul these two days, now?" This was uttered with manly grief by Charles.

"And whoever will cook for him along the road?" It was Josephine who asked the question with a heavy sigh.

To make an end of this charming scene of Old Virginia faithfulness, I put my best leg out and departed with gymnastic sprightliness. An instant after I turned my head.

Charles and Josephine were fixed on the doorstep, following me with their regards, and I believed I saw a tear in the left eye of each. What fidelity! I smiled in a sort of indulgent and baronial manner, but I felt touched by their sensibility.

Come on! It is but a twenty-four hours' separation.

Go forth, then, as I remember saying long ago, without fear and with a manly heart, to meet the dim and shadowy Future.

PART II.

THE TWO CHICKENS.

THE FLOWERS OF WAR.

"THOU art no less a man because thou wearest no hauberk nor mail sark, and goest not on horseback after foolish adventures."

So I said, reassuring myself, thirty years ago, when, as Paul Flemming the Blond, I was meditating the courageous change of cutting off my soap-locks, burning my edition of Bulwer and giving my satin stocks to my shoemaker: I mean, when I was growing up—or, in the more beauteous language of that day, when Flemming was passing into the age of bronze, and the flowers of Paradise were turning to a sword in his hands.

Well, I say it again, and I say it with boldness, you can wear a tin botany-box as bravely as a hauberk, and foolish adventures can be pursued equally well on foot.

19

Stout, grizzled and short-winded, I am just as nimble as ever in the pretty exercise of running down an illusion. Yet I must confess, as I passed the abattoirs of La Villette, whence blue-smocked butcher-boys were hauling loads of dirty sheepskins, I could not but compare myself to the honest man mentioned in one of Sardou's comedies: "The good soul escaped out of a novel of Paul de Kock's, lost in the throng on the Boulevard Malesherbes, and asking the way to the woods of Romainville."

Romainville! And hereabouts its tufts of chestnuts should be, or were wont to be of old. I am in the grimy quarter of

THE INVADERS OF ROMAINVILLE.

Belleville. Scene of factories, of steam-works and tall bleak mansions as it is to-day, Belleville was once a jolly country village, separated on its hilltop from Paris, which basked at its feet like a city millionaire sprawling before the check apron and leather shoes of a rustic beauty. Inhabited by its little circle of a few thousand souls, it looked around itself on its eminence, seeing the vast diorama of the city on one side, and on the other the Près-Saint-Gervais, and the woods of Romainville waving off to the horizon their diminishing crests of green. A jolly old tavern, the Ile d'Amour, hung out its colored lamps among the trees, and the orchestra sounded, and the feet of gay young lovers, who now are skeletons, beat the floor. The street was a bower of lilacs, and opposite the Ile d'Amour was the village church.

Then the workmen of the Paris suburbs were invaders: they besieged the village on Sundays in daring swarms, to be beaten back successfully by the duties of every successive Monday. Now they are fixed there. They are the colorless inhabitants of these many-storied houses. The town's long holiday is over. Where the odorous avenues of lilacs stretched along, affording bouquets for maman and the children and toothpicks for ferocious young warriors from the garrisons, are odious lengths of wall. Everything is changed, and from the gardens the grisettes of Alfred de Musset are with sighing sent. Their haunts are laboratories now, and the Ile d'Amour is a mayor's office.

I, to whom the beer-scandals of the Rhine and the students' holidays of the Seine were among the Childe-Harold enormities of a not over-sinful youth, was sadly disappointed. Thinking of the groves of an Eden, I ran against the furnaces of a Pandemonium. For a stroll back toward my adolescence, Belleville was a bad beginning. I determined to console myself with the green meadows of Saint-Gervais and the pretty woods of Romainville. Attaining the latter was half an hour's affair among long walls and melancholy houses: at Saint-Gervais, a double file of walls and houses — at Romainville, houses and walls again. In the latter, where formerly there were scarcely three watches distributed amongst the whole village, I was incensed to find the shop of a clockmaker: it was somewhat consoling, though, to find it a clockmaker's of the most pronounced suburban kind, with pairs of wooden shoes amongst the guard-chains in the window, and pots of golden mustard ranged alternately with the antiquated silver turnips.

Before the church I found yet standing a knotty little elder tree, a bewitched-looking vegetable. A beadle in a blouse, engaged in washing one of the large altar-candles with soap and water at the public pump, gave me the following history of the elder tree. I am passionately fond of legends, and this is one quite hot and fresh, only a hundred years old. Hear the tale of the elder of Romainville.

The excellent curé of Romainville in the last century was a man of such a charitable nature that his all was in the hands of the poor. The grocer of the village, a potentate of terrific powers and inexorable temper, finally refused to trust him with the supply of oil necessary for the lamp in the sanctuary. Soon the sacred flame sputtered, palpitated, flapped miserably over the crusted wick: the curé, responsible before Heaven for the life of his lamp, tottered away from the altar with groans of anguish. Arrived in the garden, he threw himself on his knees, crying *Meâ culpâ*, and beating his bosom. The garden contained only medicinal plants, shaded by a linden and an elder: completely desperate, the unhappy priest fixed his moist eyes on the latter, when lo! the bark opened, the trunk parted, and a jet of clear aromatic liquid spouted forth, quite different from any sap yielded by elder before. It was oil. A miracle!

The report spread. The grocer came and humbly visited the priest in his garden, his haughty hat, crammed with bills enough to have spread agony through all the cottages of Romainville, humbly carried between his legs. He came proposing a little speculation. In exchange for a single spigot to be inserted in the tree, and the hydraulic rights going with the same, he offered all the bounties dearest to the priestly heart—unlimited milk and honey, livers of fat geese and pies lined with rabbit.

The priest, though hungry—hungry with the demoniac hunger of a fat and paunchy man—turned his back on the tempter.

One day a salad, the abstemious relish yielded by his garden herbs, was set

STORY OF AN OLD MAN AND AN ELDER.

on the table by Jeanneton. At the first mouthful the good curé made a terrible face—the salad tasted of lamp-oil. The unhappy girl had filled a cruet with the sacred fluid. From that day the bark closed and the flow ceased.

There is one of the best oil-stories you ever heard, and one of the most recent of attested miracles. For my part, I am half sorry it is so well attested, and that I have the authority of that beadle in the blouse, who took my little two-franc

MERCHANDISE IN THE TEMPLE.

piece with an expression of much intelligence. I love the Legend.

The environs of Paris are but chary of Legend. I treasure this specimen, then, as if it had been a rare flower for my botany-box.

But the botany-box indeed, how heavy it was growing! The umbrella, how awkward! The sun, how vigorous and ardent! Who ever supposed it could

FATHER JOLIET.

become so hot by half-past eight in the morning?

Certainly the ruthless box, which seemed to have taken root on my back, was heavier than it used to be. Had its rotundity developed, like its master's? I stopped and gathered a flower, meaning to analyze it at my next resting-place. I opened my box: then indeed I perceived the secret of its weightiness. It revealed three small rolls of oatmeal toasted, a little roast chicken, a bit of ham, some mustard in a cleaned-out inkstand! This now was the treachery of Josephine. Josephine, who never had the least sympathy for my botanical researches, and who had small comprehension of the nobler hungers and thirsts of the scientific soul, had taken it on her to convert my box into a portable meat-safe!

Bless the old meddler, how I thanked her for her treason! The aspect of the chicken, in its blistered and varnished brown skin, reminded me that I was clamorously hungry. Shade of Apicius! is it lawful for civilized mortals to be so hungry as I was at eight or nine in the morning?

At last I saw the end of that dusty, featureless street which stretches from the barrier to the extremity of Romainville. I saw spreading before me a broad plain, a kind of desert, where, by carefully keeping my eyes straight ahead, I could avoid the sight of all houses, walls, human constructions whatever.

My favorite traveler, the celebrated Le Vaillant, to whom I am indebted for so many facts and data toward my great theory of Comparative Geography, says that in first reaching the solitudes of Caffraria he felt himself elated with an unknown joy. No traced road was before him to dictate his pathway—no city shaded him with its towers: his fortune depended on his own unaided instincts.

I felt the same delight, the same liberty. Something like the heavy strap of a slave seemed to break behind me as I found myself quite clear of the metropolis. Mad schemes of unanticipated journeys danced through my head; I might amble on to Villemonble, Montfermeil, Raincy, or even to the Forest of Bondy, so dear to the experimental botanist. Had I not two days before me ere my compact with Hohenfels at Marly? And in two days you can go from Paris to Florence. Meantime, from the effects of famine, my ribs were sinking down upon the pelvic basin of my frame.

The walk, the open air, the sight of the fowl, whose beak now burned into my bosom's core, had sharpened my appetite beyond bearing. Yet how could I eat without some drop of cider or soft white wine to drink? Besides, slave of convention that I have grown, I no longer understand the business of eating without its concomitants—a shelter and something to sit on.

The plain became wearisome. There are two things the American-born, however long a resident abroad, never forgives the lack of in Europe. The first I miss when I am in Paris: it is the perpetual street-mending of an American town. Here the boulevards, smeared with asphaltum or bedded with c r u n c h e d macadam, attain smoothness without life: you travel on scum. But in the dear old American streets the epidermis is vital: what strength and mutual reliance in the cobbles as they stand together in serried ranks, like so many eye-teeth! How they are perpetually sinking into prodigious ruts, along which the ponderous drays are forced to dance on one wheel in a paroxysm of agony and critical equipoise! But the perpetual state of street-mending, that is the crowning interest. What would I not sometimes give to exchange the Swiss sweeping-girls, plying their long brooms desolately in the mud, for the paviors' hammers of America, which play upon the pebbles like a carillon of muffled bells? As for the other lack, it is the want of wooden bridges. Far away in my native meadows gleams the silver Charles: the tramp of horses' hoofs comes to my ear from the timbers of the bridge. *Here*, with a pelt and a scramble your bridge is crossed: nothing addresses the heart from its stony causeway. But the low, arched tubes of wood that span the streams of my native land are so many bass-viols, sending out mellow thunders with every passing wagon to blend with the rustling stream and the sighing woods. Shall I never hear them again?

A reminiscence more than ten years old came to give precision to my ramblings in the past. Beyond the rustic pathway I was now following I could perceive the hills of Trou-Vassou. Hereabouts, if memory served me, I might find a welcome, almost a home, and the clasp of cordial if humble hands. Here I might find folks who would laugh when I arrived, and would be glad to share their luncheon with me But—ten years gone by!

This computation chilled my hopes. What family remains ten years in a spot —above all, a spot on that fluctuating periphery of Paris, where the mighty

THE TWO CHICKENS.

capital, year after year, bursts belt after belt? Where might they have gone? Francine!—Francine must be twenty-two. Married, of course. Her husband, no doubt, has dragged her off to some other department. Her parents have followed. March, volunteer, and disentangle yourself from these profitless speculations!

Ten minutes farther on, in the shade of the fort at Noisy-le-Sec, I saw a red gable and the sign of a tavern. As a tourist I have a passion for a cabaret: in practice, I find Véfours to unite perhaps a greater number of advantages.

Some soldiers of the Fortieth were drinking and laughing in a corner. I took a table not far off, and drew my cold victuals out of my box of japanned tin, which they doubtless took for a new form of canteen. The red-fisted garçon, without waiting for orders, set up before me, like ten-pins, a castor in wood with two enormous bottles, and a litre of that rinsing of the vats which, under the

LOVE LEFT ALONE.

name "wine of the country," is so distressingly similar in every neighborhood. Resigned to anything, I was about drawing out my slice of ham, the chicken seeming to me just there somewhat too proud a bird and out of harmony with the local color, when my glance met two gray eyes regarding my own in the highest state of expansion. The lashes, the brows, the hair and the necklace of short beard were all very thick and quite gray. The face they garnished was that of the tavern-keeper.

"Why, it is you, after all, Father Jo-

"FOND OF CHICKEN."

liet!" I said, after a rapid inspection of his figure.

"Ah, it is Monsieur Flemming, the Américain-flamand!" cried the host, striking one hand into the other at the

THE WIFE.

imminent risk of breaking his pipe. In a trice he trundled off my bottle of rinsings, and replaced it by one of claret with an orange seal, set another glass, and posted himself in front of me.

I asked the waiter for two plates, and with a slight blush evoked the chicken from my box. The soldiers of the Fortieth opened a battery of staring and hungry eyes.

"And how came you here?" asked I of Joliet.

"It is I who am at the head of the hotel," he replied, proudly pointing out the dimensions of the place by spreading his hands. "My old establishment has sunk into the fosses of the fort: it was a transaction between the government and myself."

"And was the transaction a good one for you?"

"Not so bad, not so bad," said he, winking his honest gray eyes with a world of simple cunning. "It cannot be so very bad, since I owe nothing on the hotel, and the cellar is full, and I am selling wholesale and retail."

The vanity which a minute since had expanded his hands now got into his legs, and set them upright under his body. He stood upon them, his eyes proudly lowered upon the seal of the claret. A pang of envy actually crossed my mind. I, simple *rentier*, with my two little establishments pressing more closely upon my resources with every year's increase of house-rates, how could I look at this glorious small freeholder without comparisons?

"So, then, Father Joliet," said I, "you are rich?"

"At least I depend no longer on my horse, and that thanks to you and the government."

"To me! What do you mean?"

"Why, have you forgotten the two chickens?"

THE LONE CRUSADE.

At the allusion to the chickens we caught each other's eye, and laughed like a pair of augurs. But the myste-

TENDER CHARITY.

rious fowls shall be explained to the reader.

I need not explain that I have cast my lot with the Colonial Americans of Paris, and taken their color. It is a sweet and luxurious mode of life. The cooks send round our dinners quite hot, or we have faultless servants, recommended from one colonist to another: these capital creatures sometimes become so thoroughly translated into American that I have known them shift around from flat to flat in colonized households of the second and third stories without ever touching French soil for the best part of a lifetime. At our receptions, dancing-teas and so on we pass our time in not giving offence. Federals and Confederates, rich cotton-spinners from Rhode Island and farmers from thousand-acre granges in the West, are obliged to mingle and please each other. Naturally, we can have no more political opinions than a looking-glass. We entertain just such views as *Galignani* gives us every morning, harmonized with paste from a dozen newspapers.

NECESSITY KNOWING LAW.

Our grand national effort, I may say, the common principle that binds us together as a Colony, is to forget that we are Americans. We accordingly give our whole intellects to the task of appearing like Europeans: our women succeed in this particularly well. Miss Yuba Sequoia Smith, whose father made a fortune in water-rights, is now afraid to walk a single block without the attendance of a chambermaid in a white cap, though she came up from Cali- fornia quite alone by the old Panama route. Everybody agrees that our ladies dress well. Shall I soon forget how proud Mrs. Aquila Jones was when a gentleman of the emperor's body-guard took her for Marguerite Bellanger in the Bois? Our men, not having the culture

THE FERRY.

of costume to attend to, are perhaps a little in want of a stand-point. Still, we can play billiards in the Grand Hôtel and buy fans at the Palais Royal. We go out to Saint-Cloud on horseback, we meet at the minister's; and I contend that there was something conciliatory

JOVE'S THUNDER.

and national in a Southern colonel offering to take Bigelow to see Menken at the Gaîté, or when I saw some West Pointers and a nephew of Beauregard's lighting the pipe of peace at a handsome tobacconist's in the Rue Saint-Honoré. The consciousness that we have no longer a nationality, and that nobody respects us, adds a singular calm, an elevation, to our views. Composed as our cherished little society is of crumbs from every table under heaven, we have succeeded in forming a way of life where the crusty fortitude and integrity of patriotism is unnecessary. Our circle is like the green palace of the magpies in Musset's *Merle Blanc*, and like them we live " de plaisir, d'honneur, de bavardage, de gloire et de chiffons."

I confess that there was a period, between the fresh alacrity of a stranger's reception in the Colony and the settled habits I have now fallen into, when I was rather uneasy. A society of migrators, a system woven upon shooting particles, like a rainbow on the rain, was odd. Residents of some permanency, like myself, were constantly forming eternal friendships with people who wrote to them in a month or two from Egypt. In this way a quantity of my friendships were miserably lacerated, until I learned by practice just how much friendship to give. At this period I was much occupied with vain conciliations, concessions and the reconciling of inconsistencies. A brave American from the South, an ardent disciple of Calhoun, was a powerful advocate of State Rights, and advocated them so well that I was almost convinced; when it appeared one day that the right of States to individual action was to cease in cases where a living chattel was to escape from the South to the North. In this case the State, in violation of its own laws unrecognizant of that kind of ownership, was to account for the property and give it back, in obedience to general Congressional order and to the most advanced principles of Centralization. Before I had digested this pill another was administered to me in that small English section of our circle which gave us much pride and an occasional son-in-law. This was by no less a person than my dear old friend Berkley, now grown a ruddy sexagenarian, but still given to eating breakfast in his bath-tub. The wealthy Englishman, who had got rich by exporting chinaware, was sound on the subject of free commerce between nations. That any industry, no matter how young might be the nation practicing it, or how peculiar the difficulties of its prosecution, should ever be the subject of home protection, he stamped as a fallacy too absurd to be argued. The journals venturing such an opinion were childish drivelers, putting forth views long since exploded before the whole world. He was still loud in this opinion when his little book of epigrams, *The Raven of Zurich and Other Rhymes*, came out, and being bright and saucy was reprinted in America. The knowledge that he could not tax on a foreign soil his own ideas, the plastic pottery of his brain, was quite too much for his mental balance, and he took to inveighing against free trade in literary manufactures without the slightest perception of inconsistency, and with all the warmth, if not the eloquence, of Mr. Dickens on the same theme. The gradual accumulation of subjects like these—subjects *taboo* in gentle society—soon made it apparent that in a Colony of such diverse colors, where every man had a sore spot or a grievance, and even the Cinderellas had corns in their little slippers, harmony could only be obtained by keeping to general considerations of honor, nobility, glory, and the politics of Beloochistan; on which points we all could agree, and where Mr. Berkley's witty eloquence was a wonder.

SCHOOL.

It is to my uneasy period, when I was

ON WITH THE DANCE!

sick with private griefs and giddy with striving to reconcile incompatibilities, that the episode of the Chickens belongs. I was looking dissatisfied out of one of my windows. Hohenfels, disappointed of a promenade by an afternoon shower, was looking dissatisfied out of the other. Two or three people, waiting for four o'clock lunch, were lounging about. I had just remarked, I believe, that I was a melancholy man, for ever drinking "the sweet wormwood of my sorrows." A dark phantom, like that of Adamastor, stood up between me and the stars.

"Nonsense, you ingrate!" responded

the baron from his niche, "you are only too happy. You are now in the precise

ENDYMION.

position to define my old conception of the Lucky Dog. The Lucky Dog, you know, in my vocabulary, is he who, free from all domestic cares, saunters up and down his room in gown and slippers, drums on the window of a rainy afternoon, and, as he stirs his evening fire, snaps his fingers at the world, saying, 'I have no wife nor children, good or bad, to provide for.'"

I replied that I did not willingly give way to grief, but that the mainspring of my life was broken.

"Did you ever try," spoke up a buxom lady from a sofa—it was the Frau Kranich, widow of the Frankfort banker, the same who used to give balls while her husband was drugged to sleep with opium, and now for a long time in Paris for some interminable settlement with Nathan Rothschild—"Did you ever try the tonic of a good action? *I* never did, but they actually say it rejuvenates one considerably."

I avowed that I had more faith in the study of Geography. Nevertheless, to oblige her, I would follow any suggestion.

HOW THE MODERN DOG TREATS LAZARUS.

"Benefit the next person who applies to you."

"Madame, I will obey."

At this moment a wagon of singular appearance drew up before my windows. I knew it well enough: it was the vehicle of a handy, convenient man who came along every other morning to pick up odd jobs from me and my neighbors. He could tinker, carpenter, mend harness: his wife, seated in the wagon by his side, was good at a button, or could descend and help Josephine with her ironing. A visit at this hour, however, was unprecedented.

As Charles was beginning a conversation under the hood of the wagon, I opened the window. "Come into the room," I said.

Hohenfels maliciously opened his. "Come in," he added—"Monsieur Flemming is especially anxious to do you a benefit."

The man, uncovering, was now standing in the little garden before the house —a man with a face at once intelligent and candid, which is unfortunately rare among the poor rascals of his grade. Although still young, he was growing gray: his blouse, patched and re-sewed at all the seams, was clean and whole. Poverty had tested him, but had as yet picked no flaws in him. By this time my windows were alive with faces.

The man, humble but not awkward, made two or three respectful bows. "Monsieur," he said to me, "I hope you are fond of chickens. I am desirous to sell you a fine pair."

Chickens for me! and what was it supposed I should do with them? At

THE LAUGHING LACKEY.

this point the voice of the Frau Kranich was heard, clear and malicious: "It is a bargain: bring them in."

At the same time the canvas cover of the wagon puffed outward, giving issue to a heavy sigh.

The man went to a sort of great cage in lattice-work occupying the back of the vehicle. Then he backed his wagon up to the sidewalk, and we saw, sitting on the cage and framed by the oval of the wagon-cover, a young woman of excellent features, but sadly pale. She now held the two chickens in her lap, caressing them, laying their heads against her cheek, and enwreathing them in the folds of her great shawl. I could only close the bargain with the utmost speed, to be safe from ridicule.

"Your price?" I asked.

"Fix it yourself, sir," said the man, determined to confuse me. "You are doubtless thoroughly acquainted with poultry."

"The nankeen-colored one," spoke up again the bell-like and inexorable voice from the other window, "is a yellow Crèvecœur, very well formed and lively-looking: the slate-colored one is a Cochin-China, with only a few of the white feathers lacking from the head. They are chef-d'œuvres, and are worth fully forty francs apiece."

"Only look, sir, at their claws and bills, see their tongues, and observe under their wings: they are young, wholesome and of fine strain—"

He was running on when I stopped him: "Here are a hundred francs for you, brave man."

The patchwork blouse cut a caper, a look of lively joy shot from the man's eyes, where a tear was gathering, and the wagon, from its bursting cover, gave utterance to a sob.

"Why sell them," I asked, touched in spite of myself, "if you are so attached to them? Is the money indispensable to you? I might possibly make an advance."

"Ah, you are a real Christian—you are now," said the honest Joliet, polishing his eyeball with his coat-cuff. "The good woman holds by them, it is true. Holy Virgin! it's she that has raised them, and I may say brooded over them in the coop. The eggs were for our

THE PRESENT.

salad when we had nothing better than nettles and sorrel. But, day in and night in, we have no other lodging than our wagon, and the wife is promising to give me a dolly; and if we don't take out the cage, where will the cradle go, sir?"

The calculation appeared reasonable. I received the birds, and they were the heroes, in their boudoir under the piano, of that night's conversazione.

How hard it is for a life cast upon the crowded shores of the Old World to regain the place once lost is shown by the history of my honest friend Joliet. Born in 1812, of an excellent family living twenty miles from Versailles, the little fellow lost his mother before he could talk to her. When he was ten years old, his father, who had failed after some land speculations, and had turned all he had into money, tossed him up to the lintel of the doorway, kissed him, put

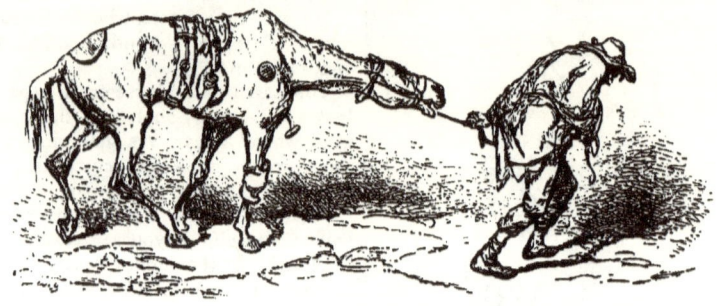

THE CONVALESCENT.

a twenty-franc gold-piece into his little pocket, and went away to seek his fortune in Louisiana: the son never heard of him more. The lady-president of a charitable society, Mademoiselle Marx, took pity on the abandoned child: she fed him on bones and occasionally beat him. She was an ingenious and inventive creature, and made her own cat-o'-nine-tails: an inventor is for ever demonstrating the merits of his implement. Soon, discovering that he was thankless and unteachable, she made him enter, as youngest clerk, the law-office of her admirer and attorney, Constabule. This gentleman, not finding enough engrossing-work to keep the lad out of mischief, allowed him to sweep his rooms and blacken his boots. Little Joliet, after giving a volatile air to a great many of his employer's briefs by making paper chickens of them, showed his imperfect sense of the favors done him by absconding. In fact, proud and independent, he was brooding over boyish schemes of an honorable living and a hasty fortune. He soon found that every profession required an apprenticeship, and that an apprenticeship could only be bought for money. He was obliged, then, to seek his grand fortune through somewhat obscure avenues. If I were to follow my poor Joliet through all his transmigrations and metempsychoses, as I have learned them by his hints, allusions and confessions, I should show him by turns working a rope ferry, where the stupid and indolent cattle, whose business it is to draw men, were drawn by him; then letter-carrier; supernumerary and call-boy in a village theatre; road-mender on a vicinal route; then a beadle, a bell-ringer, and a sub-teacher in an infant school, where he distributed his own ignorance impartially amongst his little patrons at the end of a stick; after this, big drum in the New Year's festivals,

THE DIVIDED BURDEN.

and ready at a moment's opportunity to throw down the drumstick and plunge among the dancers, for Joliet was a well-hinged lad, and the blood of nineteen years was tingling in his heels. After fluttering thus from branch to branch, like the poor birdling that cannot take its flight, discouraged by his wretched attempts at life, he plunged straight before him, hoping for nothing but a turn of luck, driving over the roads and fields, lending a hand to the farmers, sleeping in stables and garrets, or oftener in the open air; sometimes charitably sheltered in a kind man's barn, and perhaps—oh bliss!—honestly employed with him for a week or two; at others rudely repulsed

SHARE MY CUP.

as a good-for-nothing and vagabond. Vagabond! That truly was his profession now. He forgot the charms of a fixed abode. He came to like his gypsy freedom, the open air and complete independence. He laughed at his misery, provided it shifted its place occasionally.

One day, when Hazard, his ungener-

BREAKING STONES.

ous guardian, seemed to have quite forgotten him, he walked — on an empty stomach, as the doctors say — past the lofty walls of a château. A card was placed at the gate calling for additional hands at a job of digging. Each workman, it was promised, had a right to a plate of soup before beginning. This article tempted him. At the gate a lackey, laughing in his face, told him the notice had been posted there six months: workmen were no longer wanted. "Wait, though," said the servant, and in another minute gave the applicant a horse!—a real, live horse in blood and bones, but in bones especially.

SICKNESS AND COURTSHIP.

"There," said the domestic, "set a beggar on horseback and see him ride to the devil!" And, laughing with that unalloyed enjoyment which one's own wit alone produces, he retired behind his wicket.

The horse thus vicariously fulfilling the functions of a plate of soup was a wretched glandered beast—not old, but shunned on account of the contagious nature of his disease. Having received the order to take him to be killed at the abattoir, monsieur the valet, having better things to do, gave the commission to Joliet, with all its perquisites.

Joliet did not kill the steed: he cured it. He tended it, he drenched it, he saved it. By what remedy? I cannot tell. I have never been a farrier, though Joliet himself made me perforce a poulterer. Many a bit of knowledge is picked up by those who travel the great roads. The sharp Bohemian, by playing at all trades, brushing against gentry

THE WAGON.

of all sorts and scouring all neighborhoods, becomes at length a living cyclopædia.

Joliet, like Democritus and Plato, saw everything with his own eyes, learned everything at first hand. He was a keen observer, and in our interviews subsequent to the affair of the chickens I was more than once surprised by the extent of his information and the subtlety of his insight. His wits were tacked on to a number of remote supports. In our day, when each science has become so complicated, so obese, that a man's lifetime may be spent in exercising round one of them, there are hardly any generalizers or observers fit to estimate their relativity, except among the two classes called by the world idlers and ignorants —the poets and the Bohemians.

Joliet, now having joined the ranks of the cavalry, found his account in his new dignity. He became an orderly, a messenger. He carried parcels, he transported straw and hay. If the burden was too heavy for the poor convalescent, the man took his own portion with a good grace, and the two mutually aided each other on the errand. Thanks to his horse, the void left by his failure to learn a trade was filled up by a daily and regular task: what was better, an affection had crept into his heart. He loved his charge, and his charge loved him.

This great hotel, the world, seemed to be promising entertainment then for both man and beast, when an epoch of disaster came along—a season of cholera. In the villages where Joliet's business lay the doors just beginning to be hospitable were promptly shut against him. Where the good townsmen had recognized Assistance in his person, they now saw Contagion.

DINNER-TIME!

If he had been a single man, he could have lain back and waited for better times. But he now had two mouths to feed. He kissed his horse and took a resolution.

He had never been a mendicant. "Beggars don't go as hungry as I have gone," said he. "But what will you have? Nobility obliges. My father was a gentleman. I have broken stones, but never the *devoirs* of my order."

He left the groups of villages among which his new industry had lain. The cholera was behind him: trouble, beggary perhaps, was before him. As night was coming on, Joliet, listlessly leading his horse, which he was too considerate to ride, saw upon the road a woman whom he took in the obscurity for a farmer's wife of the better class or a decent villager. For an introduction the opportunity was favorable enough. On her side, the *quasi* farmer's wife, seeing in the dusk an honest fellow dragging a horse, took him for a "gentleman's gentleman" at the least, and the two accosted each other with that easy facility of which the French people have the secret. Each presented the other with a hand and a frank smile.

Joliet, whom I have erred perhaps in comparing to Democritus, was nevertheless a laugher and a philosopher. But his grand ha-ha! usually infectious, was not shared on this occasion. The wanderer could not show much merriment. A sewing-woman with a capacity for embroidery, her needle had given

FIDELITY.

3

her support, but now a sudden warning of paralysis, and symptoms of cholera added to that, had driven her almost to

A LITTLE VISITOR.

despair. She was without home, friend or profession.

Joliet set her incontinently on horseback, and walked by her side to a good village curé's two miles off—the same who had assisted him to his first communion, and for whom he subsequently became a beadle. The kind priest opened his arms to the man, his heart to the woman, his stable to the horse. For his second patient my Bohemian set in motion all his stock of curative ideas. In a month she was well, and the curé no longer had three pensioners, for of two of them he made one.

Two poverties added may make a competence. Monsieur and Madame Joliet were good and willing. The man began to wear a strange not unbecoming air of solidity and good morals. The girls now saluted him respectfully when he passed through a village.

One thing, however, in the midst of his proud honeymoon perplexed him much. Hardly married, and over head and ears in love, he knew not how to invite his bride to some wretched garret, himself deserting her to resume his former life in the open air. To give up the latter seemed like losing existence itself.

One morning, as he asked himself the difficult question, a pair of old wheels at the door of a cartwright seemed of their own accord to resolve his perplexity. He bought them, the payment to be made in labor: for a week he blew the wheelwright's bellows. The wheels were his own: to make a wagon was now the affair of a few old boards and a gypsy's inventiveness.

Thus was conceived that famous establishment where, for several years, lived the independent monarch and his spouse, rolling over the roads, circulating through the whole belt of villages around Paris, and carrying in their ambulant home, like the Cossacks, their utensils, their bed, their oven, their all.

From town to town they carried packages, boxes and articles of barter. At dinner-time the van was rolled under a tree. The lady of the house kindled a fire in the portable stove behind a hedge or in a ditch. The hen-coop was opened, and the sage seraglio with their sultan

FRANCINE.

prudently pecked about for food. At the first appeal they re-entered their cage.

At the same appeal came flying up the dog of the establishment, a most piteous-looking griffin, disheveled, moulted, staring out of one eye, lame and wild. For devotion and good sense his match could be found nowhere. Like his horse, his wife, his house and the pins in his sleeve, Joliet had picked the collie up on the road.

The arrival of a tiny visitor to the Bohemian's address made a change necessary. Little Francine's dowry was provided by my humorous acquisition of the yellow and slate-colored chickens. With his savings and my banknote Joliet determined to have a fixed residence. He succeeded of course. The walls, the windows, the doors, every-

"DON'T WRING MY HEART!"

thing but the garden-patch, he picked up along the roads.

Buried in eglantine and honeysuckle, soon no one would suspect the home-made character of Joliet's château. It became the centre of my botanizing excursions. Francine grew into a fair, slim girl, like the sweetest and most innocent of Gavarni's sketches, and sold flowers to the passers-by.

Such were the souvenirs I had of this brave tavern-keeper in his old capacity of roadster and tramp. Now, after an hiatus of years, I found him before me in a different character at the beginning of my roundabout trips to Marly.

But what had become of my favorite little rose-merchant?

"Francine?" asked Joliet briskly, as if he was wondering whom I could mean by such a name. "You mean my wife? Poor thing! She is dead."

"I am speaking of your daughter, Father Joliet."

"Oh, my daughter, my girl Francine? She went to live with her godmother. It was ten years ago."

"And you have not seen her since?"

"Yes—yes—two years back. She has gone again."

"To her godmother?"

"No."

"Why so?"

"Her godmother would not receive her. Don't wring my heart so, sir!"

PART III.

THE FEAST OF SAINT ATHANASIUS.

THE PAULISTS.

A S I parted from my stout old friend Joliet, I saw him turn to empty the last half of our bottle into the glasses of a couple of tired soldiers who were sucking their pipes on a bench. And again the old proverb of Aretino came into my head: "Truly all courtesy and good manners come from taverns." I grasped my botany-box and pursued my promenade toward Noisy.

The village of Noisy has made (without a pun) some noise in history. One of its ancient lords, Enguerrand de Marigny, was the inventor of the famous gibbet of Montfauçon, and in the poetic justice which should ever govern such cases he came to be hung on his own gallows. He was convicted of manifold extortions, and launched by the common executioner into that eternity whither he could carry none of his ill-gotten gains with him. Here, at least, we succeed in meeting a guillotine which catches its maker. By a singular coincidence another lord of Noisy, Cardinal Balue, underwent a long detention in an iron-barred cage—one of those famous cages, so much favored by Louis XI., of which the cardinal, as we learn from the records of the time, had the patent-right for invention, or at least improvement. Once firmly engaged in his own torture —while his friend Haraucourt, bishop of Verdun, experienced a like penalty in a similar box, and the foxy old king paced his narrow oratory in the Bastile tower overhead — we may be sure that Balue gave his inventive mind no more

THE REWARD OF AN INVENTOR.

to the task of fortifying his cages, but rather to that of opening them.

These ugly reminiscences were not so much the cause of a prejudice I took against Noisy, as caused by it. At Noisy I was in the full domain of my ancient foe the railway, where two lines of the Eastern road separate — the Ligne de Meaux and the Ligne de Mulhouse. The sight of the unhappy second-class passengers powdered with dust, and of the frantic nurses who had mistaken

CARDINAL BALUE.

their line, and who madly endeavored to leap across to the other train, stirred all my bile. It was on this current of thought that the nobleman who had been hung and the cardinal who had pined in a cage were borne upon my memory. "Small choice," said I, "whether the bars are perpendicular or horizontal. You lose your independence about equally by either monopoly."

I crossed the Canal de l'Ourcq, and watched it stretching like a steel tape to meet the Canal Saint-Denis and the Canal Saint-Martin in the great basin at La Villette — a construction which, finished in 1809, was the making of La Villette as a commercial and industrial entrepôt. I meant to walk to Bondy, and after a botanic stroll in its beautiful forest to retrace my steps, gaining Marly next day by Baubigny, Aubervilliers and Nanterre. "The Aladdins

AN UNCIVIL ENGINEER.

of our time," I said as I leaned over the soft gray water, "are the engineers. They rub their theodolites, and there springs up, not a palace, but a town."

"Who speaks of engineers?" said a strong baritone voice as a weighty hand fell on my shoulder. "Are you here to take the train at Noisy?"

"Let the train go to Jericho! I am trying, on the contrary, to get away from it."

"Do you mean, then, to go on foot to Épernay?"

"What do you mean, Épernay?"

"Why, have you forgotten the feast of Saint Athanasius?"

"What do you mean, Athanasius?"

The baritone belonged to one of my

friends, an engineer from Boston. He had an American commission to inspect the canals of Europe on the part of a company formed to buy out the Sound line of steamers and dig a ship-canal from Boston to Providence. The engineer had made his inspection the excuse for a few years of not disagreeable travel, during which time the company had exploded, its chief financier having cut his throat when his peculations came out to the public.

LOCOMONIAC POSSESSION.

"Are you trying, then, to escape from one of your greatest possible duties and one of your greatest possible pleasures? You have the remarkable fortune to possess a friend named Athanasius; you have in addition, the strange fate to be his godfather by secondary baptism; and you would, after these unparalleled chances, be the sole renegade from the vow which you have extracted from the others."

The words were uncivil and rude, the hand was on my shoulder like a vise; but there floated into my head a recollection of one of the pleasantest evenings I have ever enjoyed.

We were dining with James Grandstone, one of my young friends. I have some friends of whom I might be the father, and doubt not I could find a support for my practice in Sir Thomas Browne or Jeremy Taylor if I had time to look up the quotation. We dined in the little restaurant Ober, near the Odéon, with a small party of medical students, to which order Grandstone's friends mostly belonged. We were all young that night; and truly I hold that the affectionate confusion of two or three different generations adds a charm to friendship.

At dessert the conversation happened

LE RAINCY: THE CHATEAU.

to strike upon Christian names. I attacked the cognomens in ordinary use, maintaining that their historic significance was lost, their religious sentiment forgotten, their euphony mostly questionable. Alfred, Henry and William no longer carried the thoughts back to the English kings—Joseph and Reuben were powerless to remind us of the mighty family of Israel.

"I have no complaint to make of my own name," I protested, "which has been praised by Dannecker the sculptor. That was at Würtemberg, gentlemen. 'You are from America,' the old man said to

CATHEDRAL OF MEAUX.

me, 'but you have a German name: Paul Flemming was one of our old poets.' The thought has been a pleasant one to me, though I have not the faintest idea what my ancient godparent wrote. But in the matter of originality my Christian name of Paul certainly leaves much to desire."

I was gay enough that evening, and in the vein for a paradox. I set up the various Pauls of our acquaintance, and maintained that in any company of fifty persons, if a feminine voice were to call out "Paul!" through the doorway, six husbands at least would start and say, "Coming, dear!" I computed the Pauls belonging to one of the grand nations, and proved that an army recruited from them would be large enough to carry on a war against a power of the second order.

"If the Jameses were to reinforce the Pauls," I declared, looking toward my young host, "Russia itself would tremble. —Are you to make your start in life with no better name?" I asked him maliciously. "Must you be for ever kept in mediocrity by an address that is not the designation of an individual, but of a whole nation? Could you not have been called by something rather less œcumenical?"

"You may style me by what title you please, Mr. Flemming," said Grandstone nonchalantly. "I am to enter a great New York wine-house after a little examination of the grape-country here. Doubtless a Grandstone will have, by any other name, a bouquet as sweet."

The idea took. An almanac of saints' days, which is often printed in combination with the *ménu* of a restaurant, was lying on the table. Beginning at the letter A, the name of Ambrose was within an ace of being chosen, but Grandstone protested against it as too short, and Athanasius was the first of five syllables that presented. Our engineering friend, who was present, had in his pocket a vial of water from the Dardanelles, which fouls ships' bottoms; and with that classic liquid the baptism was effected by myself, the bottle being broken on poor Grandstone's crown as on the prow of a ship.

"You are no longer James to us, but Athanasius," I said. "If you remain moderately virtuous, we will canonize you. Meantime, let us vow to meet on the next canonical day of Saint Athanasius and hold a love-feast."

We drank his health, and glorified him, and laughed, and the next day I forgot whether Grandstone was called Athanasius or Epaminondas. And my confusion on the subject had not clarified in the least up to the rude reminder given by my engineer.

"I had quite forgotten my engagement," I confessed. "Besides, Grandstone is living now, as you remind me, at Épernay — that is to say, at seventy or eighty miles' distance."

"Say three hours," he retorted: "on a railway line we don't count by miles. But are you really not here at Noisy to satisfy your promise and report yourself for the feast of Saint Athanasius? If you are not bound for Épernay, where *are* you bound?"

"I am off for Marly."

"You are going in just the contrary direction, old fellow. You can be at Épernay sooner."

"And Hohenfels joins me at Marly to-morrow," I continued, rather helplessly; "and Josephine my cook is there this afternoon boiling the mutton-hams."

"Fine arguments, truly! You shall sleep to-night in Paris, or even at Marly, if you see fit. I have often heard you argue against railroads—a fine argument for a geographer to uphold against an engineer! Now is the instant to bury

BOURSAULT, THE RESIDENCE OF CLIQUOT.

your prejudice. Do you see that soft ringlet of smoke off yonder? It is the message of the locomotive, offering to reconcile your engagements with Grandstone and Hohenfels. Come, get your ticket!"

And his hand ceased squeezing my shoulder like a pincer to beat it like a mallet. A rapid sketch of the situation was mapped out in my head. I could reach Épernay by five o'clock, returning at eight, and, notwithstanding this little lasso flung over the champagne-country, I could resume my promenade and modify in no respect my original plan; and I could say to Hohenfels, "My boy, I have popped a few corks with the widow Cliquot."

Such was my vision. The gnomes of the railway, having once got me in their grasp, disposed of me as they liked, and quite unexpectedly.

From the car-window, as in a panorama of Banvard's, the landscape spun out before my eyes. Le Raincy, which I had intended to visit at all events on the same day, but afoot, offered me the roofs of its ancient château, a pile built in the most pompous spirit of the Renaissance, and whose alternately round and square pavilions, tipped with steep mansards, I was fain to people with throngs of gay visitors in the costume of the *grand siècle*. Then came the cathedral of Meaux, before which I reverently took off my cap to salute the great Bossuet—"Eagle of Meaux," as they justly called him, and on the whole a noble bird, notwithstanding that he sang his Te Deum over some exceedingly questionable battle-grounds. Then there presented itself a monument at which my engineering friend clapped his hands. It was a crown of buildings with extin-

CHURCH-DOOR, ÉPERNAY.

guisher roofs encircling the brow of a hill, and presenting the antique appearance of some chastel of the Middle Ages.

"Do you see those round, pot-bellied towers, like tuns of wine stood upon end?" he said—"those donjons at the corners, tapering at the top, and presenting the very image of noble bottles? There needs nothing but that palace to convince you that you have arrived in the champagne region."

"I do not know the building," I confessed.

"Can you not guess? Ah, but you should see it in a summer storm, when the rain foams and spirts down those huge bottles of mason-work, and the thunder pops among the roofs like the corks of a whole basket of champagne! That fine castle, Flemming, is the château of Boursault, apparently built in the era of the Crusades, but really a marvel of yesterday. It rose into being, not to the sound of a lyre, like the towers of Troy, but at the bursting of innumerable bottles, causing to resound all

over the world the name of the widow Cliquot."

At length we entered the station of Épernay. There I received my first shock in learning that the only return-train stopping at Noisy was one which left at midnight, and would land me in the extreme suburbs of Paris at three o'clock in the morning.

Our friend Grandstone, whom we found amazing the streets of Épernay with a light American buggy drawn by a colossal Norman horse, received us with still more surprise than delight. He had relapsed into plain James, and had never dreamed that his second baptism would bear fruit. Besides, he proved to us that we were in error as to the date. The feast of Saint Athanasius, as he showed from a calendar shoved beneath a quantity of vintners' cards on his study-table, fell on the second of May, and could not be celebrated before the evening of the first. It was now the thirtieth of April. He invited us, then, for the next day at dinner, warning us at the same time that the evening of that same morrow would see him on his way to the Falls of Schaffhausen. This idea of dining with an absentee puzzled me.

THE BEGGAR WHO DRANK CHAMPAGNE.

We both laughed heartily at the engineer's mistake of twenty-four hours, and he for his part made me his excuses.

Athanasius—whose name I obstinately keep, because it gives him, as I main-

tain, a more distinct individuality,—
Athanasius happened to be driving out
for the purpose of collecting some friends
whom he was about to accompany to
Schaffhausen, and whom he had invited
to dinner. He contrived to stow away
two in his buggy, and the rest assembled
in his chambers. We dined gayly and
voraciously, and I hardly regretted even
that old hotel-dinner at Interlaken, when
the landlord waited on us in his green
coat, and when Mary Ashburton was by
my side, and when I praised hotel-din-
ners because one can say so much there
without being overheard.

Dinner over, we went out for a stroll
through the town. The city of Épernay
offers little remarkable except its Rue du
Commerce, flanked with enormous buildings, and its church, conspicuous only
for a flourishing portal in the style of
Louis XIV., in perfect contradiction to
the general architecture of the old sanc-
tuary. The environs were little noteworthy at the season, for a vineyard-land has this peculiarity—its veritable spring, its pride of May, arrives in the autumn.

ADMIRATION.

One very vinous trait we found, however, in the person of a beggar. He
was sitting on Grandstone's steps as we
emerged. Aged hardly fourteen, he had
turned his young nose toward the rich
fumes coming up from the kitchen with
a look of sensuality and indulgence that
amused me. The maid, on a hint of
mine, gave him a biscuit and the re-
mainders of our bottles emptied into a
bowl. A smile of extreme breadth and
intelligence spread over his face. Opening his bag, he laid by the biscuit, and
extracted a morsel of iced cake: at the
same time he produced an old-fashioned,
long-waisted champagne-glass, nicked
at the rim and quite without a stand.
Filling this from his bowl, he drank to
the health of the waitress with the easiest
politeness it was ever my lot to see.
Ragged as a beggar of Murillo's, cour-

teous as a hidalgo by Velasquez, he
added a grace and an epicurism completely French. I thought him the best
possible figure-head for that opulent

MAC MEURTRIER.

spot, cradle of the hilarity of the world.
I gave him five francs.

We proceeded to admire the town.
The great curiosities of Épernay, its
glory and pomp, are not permitted to
see the daylight. They are subterranean
and introverted. They are the cellars.

THE BLACK DOMINO.

Those rich colonnades of Commerce
street, all those porticoes surmounted
with Greek or Roman triangles in the
nature of pediments, of what antique

religion are they the representations? They are cellar-doors.

It was impossible to quit the city without visiting its cellars, said Grandstone, and we betook ourselves under his guidance to one of the most renowned.

TAM O'SHANTER'S RIDE.

I only thought of seeing a battle-field of bottles, but I found the Eleusinian mysteries.

In the temple-porch of Eleusis was fixed a large pale face, in the middle parts of which a red nose was glowing like a fuse. Several other personages, in company with this visage, received us on our approach with a world of solemn and terrifying signals.

Directly a man in a cloak and slouched hat, and holding in his hands a wire fencing-mask, extinguished with it the red nose. The latter met his fate with stolid fortitude. All were perfectly still, but the twitching cheeks of most of the spectators betrayed a laugh retained with difficulty. The cloak then advanced, like a less beautiful Norma, to a bell in the portico, and struck three tragical strokes. A strong, pealing deep voice came from the interior: "Who dares knock at this door?"

"A night-bird," said the man in the cloak, who took the part of spokesman.

"What has the night-bird to do with the eagle?" replied the strong voice.

"What can there be in common between the heathen in his blindness and the Ancient of the Mountain throned in power and splendor?"

"Grand Master, it is in that splendor the new-comer wishes to plunge."

After this imitation of some Masonic mystery the red-nosed man was quickly taken by the shoulders and hurtled in at the door, where a flare of red theatrical fire illuminated his sudden plunge.

"What nonsense is this?" I said to Athanasius.

"The man in the iron mask," he explained, "is in that respect what we shall all be in a minute. Without such a protector, in passing amongst the first year's bottles we might receive a few hits in the face."

"And do you know the new apprentice?"

"No: some stranger, evidently."

"It is not hard to guess his extrac-

THE CROOKED MAN.

tion," said one of our dinner-party. "In the East there are sorcerers with two pupils in each eye. For his part, he seems to be braced with two pans in each knee. He is long in the stilts like a heron, square-headed and square-shouldered: I give you my word he is a Scotchman. For certain," he added, "I have seen his likeness somewhere— Ah yes, in an engraving of Hogarth's!"

The author of this charitable criticism was a little crooked gentleman, at whose side I had dined—a man of sharpness and wit, for which his hunch gave him

THE GRAVITY ROAD.

the authority. As we penetrated finally into the immense crypt, long like a street, provided with iron railways for handling the stores, and threaded now and then by heavy wagons and Normandy horses, my interest in the surrounding wonders was distracted by apprehensions of the fate awaiting the unfortunate red nose.

The gallop of a steed was heard at length, then a dreadful exploding noise. I should have thought that a hundred drummers were marching through the catacombs.

Relieved of his mask, fixed like a dry forked stick, wrong side foremost, on a frightened steed which galloped down the avenue, and pursued by the racket of empty bottles beaten against the wine-frames, came the Scotchman, like an unwilling Tam O'Shanter. At a new outburst of resonant noises, which we could not help offering to the general confusion, the horse stopped, and assumed twice or thrice the attitude of a gymnast who walks on his hands. The figure of the man, still rigid, flew up into the air like a stick that pops out of the water. The Terrible Brothers received him in their arms.

Hardly restored to equilibrium, the patient was quickly replaced in the saddle, but the saddle was this time girded upon a barrel, and the barrel placed upon a truck, and the truck upon an inclined tramway. His impassive countenance might be seen to kindle with indignation and horror, as the hat which had been jammed over his eyes flew off, and he found himself gliding over an iron road at a rate of speed continually increasing.

He was fated to other tests, but at this point a little discussion arose among ourselves. Grandstone, his fluffy young whiskers quite disheveled with laughter, said, "Fellows, we had better stop somewhere. There will be more of this, and it will be tedious to see in the rôle of uninvited spectators, and it is not certain we are wanted. I always knew there was a Society of Pure Illumination at Épernay. It is not a Masonic order, but it has its signs, its passes, its grips, and in a word its secret. I have recognized among these gentlemen some active members of the order—among others, notwithstanding his disguise, a jolly good fellow we have here, Fortnoye."

"You cannot have seen Fortnoye," said one of the party: "he is at Paris."

"And who is your Fortnoye, pray?" I asked.

"The best tenor voice in Épernay; but his presence here does not give *me* an invitation, you see. The Society of Pure Illumination has its rites and mysteries more important than everybody supposes, and probably complicated with board-of-trade secrets among the wine-merchants. We have hit upon a bad time. Let us go and visit another cellar."

There was opposition to this measure: different opinions were expressed, and I was chosen for moderator.

"My dear boys," I said, "as the grayest among you I may be presumed to be the wisest. But I do not feel myself to be myself. I have received to-day a succession of unaccustomed influences I have been dragged about by an impertinent locomotive; I have been induced to dine heavily; I have absorbed

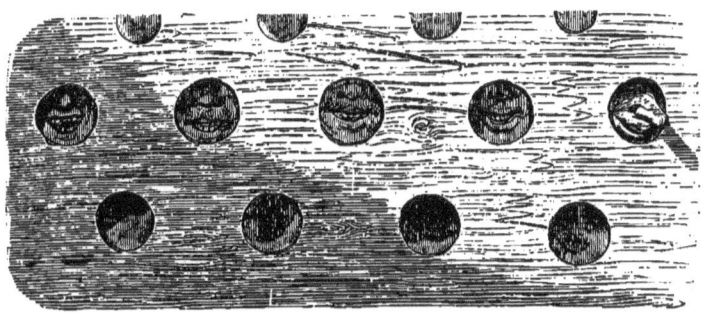

THE ANIMATED CELLS.

champagne, perhaps to the limit of my measure. These are not my ordinary ways: I am naturally thoughtful, studious and pensive. The Past, gentlemen, is for me an unfaded morning-glory, whose closed cup I can coax open at pleasure, and read within its tube legends written in dusted gold. But the Present to the true philosopher is also— In fact, I never was so much amused in my life. I am dying to see what they will do with that Scotchman."

Athanasius submitted. At the end of one of the cross galleries we could already see a flickering glimmer of torches. There, evidently, was held the council. We stole on tiptoe in that direction, and ensconced ourselves behind a long file of empty bottle-shelves, worn out after long service and leaning against a wall.

Through the holes which had fixed the bottles in position we could see everything without being discovered. The grand dignitaries, sitting in a semicircle, were about to proceed from physical to moral tests. Before them, his red nose hanging like a cameo from the white bandage which covered his eyes, and relieved upon his face, still perfectly white and calm, stood the Scot. The Grand Master arose—I should have said the Reverend—his head nodding with senility, his beard white as a waterfall: he appeared to be eighty years of age at least. He was truly venerable to look at, and reminded me of Thor. He wore a sort of dalmatica embroidered with gold. Calmness and goodness were so plainly marked on the aspect of this worthy that I felt ashamed of playing the spy, and felt inclined to return humbly to the good counsel of Athanasius, when the latter, pushing my elbow behind the shelves, said, referring to the

Ancient of the Mountain, "That's Fortnoye: I knew I couldn't be mistaken."

I was greatly mystified at discovering the first tenor voice of Épernay in an aged man; but the catechism now commencing, I thought only of listening.

"The barleycorns of your native North having been partially cleaned out of your hair by contact with the two enchanted steeds—the steed you bridled without a head, and the steed that ran away with you without legs," said the Ancient—"we have brought you hither for examination. We might have gone much farther with the physical tests: we might have forced you, at the present session, to relieve yourself of those envelopes considered indispensable by all Europeans beneath your own latitude, and in our presence perform the sword-dance."

"So be it," said the disciple, executing a galvanic figure with his legs, his countenance still like marble.

"If we demanded the head of your best friend, would you bring it in?"

"I am the countryman of Lady Macbeth," replied the red nose. "Give me the daggers."

"We would fain dispense with that proof, necessarily painful to a man of such evident sensibility as yours." The red nose bowed. "What is your name?"

He pronounced it—apparently MacMurtagh.

"In future, among us, you are named Meurtrier."

"MacMeurtrier," muttered the Scotchman in a tone of abstraction.

"No! Meurtrier unadulterated. Your business?"

"I am a homœopathic doctor."

"Are you a believer in homœopathy? Be careful: remember that the Ancient of the Mountain hears what you say."

The Scot held up his hand: "I believe in the learned Hahnemann, and in Mrs. Hahnemann, no less learned than himself; but," he added, "homœopathy is a science still in its baby-clothes. I have invented a system perfectly novel. In mingling homœopathy with vegetable magnetism the most encouraging results are obtained, as may be observed daily in the villa of Dr. Mac Murtagh, near Edinburgh—"

"Enough!" cried the Ancient: "circulars are not allowed here. Forget nothing, Meurtrier! And how were you inspired with the pious ambition of becoming our brother?"

"At the hotel table: it was the young clerks from the wine-houses. I mentioned that I wished to be a Free Mason, and the lodge of Épernay—"

"Silence! The words you use, *lodge* and *Free Mason*, are most improper in this temple, which is that of the Pure Illumination, and nothing less. Will you remember, Meurtrier?"

"MacMeurtrier," muttered the novice again. The last proofs were now tried upon him, called the "five senses." For that of hearing he was made to listen to

THE TRAVELER'S REST.

a jewsharp, which he calmly proclaimed to be the bagpipe; for that of touch, he was made to feel by turns a live fish, a hot iron and a little stuffed hedgehog. The last he took for a pack of toothpicks, and announced gravely, "It sticks me." The laughs broke out from all sides, even from behind the bottle-shelves. Alas! on this occasion the laugh was not altogether on my side of that fatal honeycomb!

They had made him swallow, in a glass, some fearful mixture or other, and he had imperturbably declared that it was in his opinion the wine of Moët: after this evidence of taste the proof of sight was to follow, and the semicircle of purple faces was quite blackening with bottled laughter, when Grandstone touched me on the shoulder. My hour for departure was come, and I had not a minute to spare. Apparently, the last test of the red

PALACE AT STRASBURG.

nose resulted in a triumph: as we were effecting our covert and hasty retreat we heard all the voices exclaim in concert, "It is the Pure Illumination!"

Gay as we were on entering the great wine-cellar, we were perfectly Olympian when we came out. The crypts of these vast establishments, where a soft inspiration perpetually floats upward from the wine in store, often receive a visitor as a Diogenes and dismiss him as an Anacreon.

Our consumption of wine at dinner had been, like Mr. Poe's conversation with his soul, "serious and sober." In the cellar no drop had passed our mouths. I was alert as a lark when I entered: I came out in a species of voluptuous dream.

All the band conducted me to the railway-station, and I was very much touched with the attention. It was who should carry my botany-box, who should set my cap straight, who should give me the most precise and statistical information about the train which returned to Paris, with a stop at Noisy; the while, Ophelia-like, I chanted snatches of old songs, and mingled together in a tender reverie my recollections of Mary Ashburton, my coming Book and my theories of Progressive Geography.

"Take this shawl: the night will be chilly before you get to the city."

"Don't let them carry you beyond Noisy."

"Come back to Épernay every Mayday: never forget the feast of Saint Athanasius."

"Be sure you get into the right train: here is the car. Come, man, bundle up! they are closing the barrier."

I was perfectly melted by so much sympathy. "Adieu," I said, "my dear champanions—"

I turned into an excellent car, first class, and fell asleep directly.

Next day I awoke—at Strasburg! The convivials of the evening before, making for the Falls of Schaffhausen on the Rhine, had traveled beside me in the adjoining car.

My friends, uncertain how their practical joke would be received, clustered around me.

"Ah, boys," I said, "I have too many griefs imprisoned in this aching bosom to be much put out by the ordinary 'Horrid Hoax.' But you have compromised my reputation. I promised to meet Hohenfels at Marly: children, bankruptcy stares me in the face."

Grandstone had the grace to be a little embarrassed: "You wished to dine with me at the Feast of Saint Athanasius, but you mistook the day. Your engineer is the true culprit, for he voluntarily deceived you. The fact is, my dear Flemming, we have concocted a little conspiracy. You are a good fellow, a joyful spirit in fact, when you are not in your *lubies* about the Past and the Future. We wanted you, we conspired; and, Catiline having stolen you at Noisy, Cethegus tucked you into a car with the intention of making use of you at Schaffhausen."

"Never! I have the strongest vows that ever man uttered not to revisit the Rhine. It is an affair of early youth, a solemn promise, a consecration. You have got me at Strasburg, but you will not carry me to Schaffhausen."

He was so contrite that I had to console him. Letting him know that no great harm was done, I saw him depart with his friends for Bâle. For my part, I remained with the engineer, whose professional duties, such as they were, kept him for a short time in the capital of Alsace. In his turn, however, the latter took leave of me: we were to meet each other shortly.

It was seven in the morning. This time, to be sure of my enemy the railroad, I procured a printed Guide. But the Guide was a sorry counselor for my impatience. The first train, an express, had left: the next, an accommodation, would start at a quarter to one. I had five hours and three-quarters to spare.

One of the greatest pleasures in life, according to my poor opinion, is to have a recreation forced on one. Some cherub, perhaps, cleared the cobwebs away from my brain that morning; but, however it might be, I was glad of everything. I was glad the "champanions" were departed, glad I had a stolen morning in Strasburg, glad that Hohenfels and my domestics would be uneasy for me at Marly.

In such a mood I applied myself to extract the profit out of my detention in the city.

PART IV.

A DAY IN STRASBURG.

TEARING UP THE PONTOON BRIDGE.

BEHOLD me, then, with five hours around my neck, like so many millstones, in Strasburg, on the abjured Rhine! Had I not vowed never to visit that bewitched current again? Was it not by Rhine-bank that I learned to quote the minnesingers and to unctuate my hair? From her owl-tower did not old Frau Himmelauen use to observe me, my cane, and my curls, and my gloves? Did not her gossips compare me to Wilhelm Meister? And so, when he thought he was ripe, the innocent Paul Flemming must needs proceed to pour his curls, his songs and his love into the lap of Mary Ashburton; and the discreet siren responded, "You had better go back to Heidelberg and grow: you are not the Magician."

Yet before that little disaster of my calf period I sighed for the Rhine: I used its wines more freely than was perhaps good for me, and when the smoke-colored goblet was empty would declare that if I were a German I should be proud of the grape-wreathed river too. At Bingen I once sat up to behold the bold outline of the banks crested with ruins, which in the morning proved to be a slated roof and chimneys. And when at Heidelberg I saw the Neckar open upon the broad Rhine plain like the mouth of a trumpet, I felt inspired, and built every evening on my table a perfect cathedral of slim, spire-shaped bottles — sunny pinnacles of Johannisberger.

And now, decoyed to the Rhine by a puerile conspiracy, how could I best get the small change for my five hours?

STRASBURG CATHEDRAL IN FLAMES.

Should I sulk like a bear in the parlor of the Maison Rouge until the departure of the Paris train, or should I explore the city? Some wave from my fond, foolish past flowed over me and filled me with desire. I felt that I loved the Rhine and the Rhine cities once more. And where could I better retie myself to those old pilgrim habits than in this citadel of heroism, a place sanctified by recent woes, a city proved by its endurance through a siege which even that of Paris hardly surpassed? One draught, then, from the epic Rhine! To-morrow, at Marly, I could laugh over it all with Hohenfels.

The Münster was before me — the highest tower in Europe, if we except the hideous cast-iron abortion at Rouen. I recollected that in my younger days I had been defrauded of my fair share of tower-climbing. Hohenfels had a saying that most travelers are a sort of children, who need to touch all they see, and who will climb to every broken tooth of a castle they find on their way, getting a tiresome ascent and hot sunshine for their pains. "I trust we are wiser," he would observe, so unanswerably that I passed with him up the Rhine quite, as I may express it, on the ground floor.

I marched to the cathedral, determined to ascend, and when I saw the look of it changed my mind.

The sacristan, in fact, advised me not to go up after he had taken my fee and obtained a view of my proportions over the tube of his key, which he pretended to whistle into. We sat down together as I recovered my breath, after which I wandered through the nave with my guide, admiring the statue of the original architect, who stands looking at the interior — a kind of Wren "circumspecting" his own monument. At high noon the twelve apostles come out from the famous horologe and take up their march, and chanticleer, on one of the summits of the clock-case, opens his brazen throat and crows loud enough to fill the farthest recesses of the church with his harsh alarum.

A portly citizen was talking to the sacristan. "I hear many objections to that bird, sir," he remarked to me, "from fastidious tourists: one thinks that a peacock, spreading its jewels by mechanism, would have a richer effect. Another says that a swan, perpetually wrestling with its dying song, would be more poetical. Others, in the light of late events, would prefer a phœnix."

The dress of the stout citizen announced a sedentary man rather than a cosmopolitan. He had a shirt-front much hardened with starch; a white waistcoat, like an alabaster carving, which pushed his shirt away up round his ears; and a superb bluebottle-colored coat, with metal buttons. It was the costume of a stay-at-home, and I learned afterward that he was a local professor of geography and political science—the first by day, the last at night only in beer-gardens and places of resort.

THE HIGHEST SPIRE IN EUROPE.

"Nay," I said, "the barnyard bird is of all others the fittest for a timepiece: he chants the hours for the whole country-side, and an old master of English song has called him Nature's 'crested clock.'"

"With all deference," said the bourgeois, "I would still have a substitute provided for yonder cock. I would set up the Strasburg goose. Is he not our emblem, and is not our commerce swollen by the inflation of the *foie gras*? In one compartment I would show him fed with sulphur-water to increase his biliary secretion; another might represent his cage, so narrow that the pampered creature cannot even turn round on his stomach for exercise; another division might be anatomical, and present the martyr opening his breast, like some tortured saint, to display his liver, enlarged to the weight of three pounds; while the apex might be occupied by the glorified gander in person, extending his neck and commenting on the sins of the Strasburg pastry-cooks with a cutting and sardonic hiss."

You have not forgotten, reader, the legend of the old clock?

Many years ago there lived here an aged and experienced mechanic. Buried in his arts, he forgot the ways of the world, and promised his daughter to his gallant young apprentice, instead of to the hideous old magistrate who approached the maiden with offers of gold and dignity. One day the youth and damsel found the unworldly artist weeping for joy before his completed clock, the wonder of the earth. Everybody came to see it, and the corporation bought it for the cathedral. The city of Bâle bespoke another just like it. This order aroused the jealousy of the authorities, who tried to make the mechanic promise that he would never repeat his masterpiece for another town. "Heaven gave me not my talents to feed your vain ambition," said the man of craft: "the men of Bâle were quicker to recognize my skill than you were. I will make no such promise." Upon that the rejected suitor, who was among the magistrates, persuaded his colleagues to put out the artist's eyes. The old man heard his fate with lofty fortitude, and only asked that he might suffer the sentence in the presence of his darling work, to which he wished to give a few final strokes. His request was granted, and he gazed long at the splendid clock, setting its wonders in motion to count off the last remaining moments of his sight. "Come, laggard," said the persecuting magistrate, who had brought a crowd of spectators, "you are taxing the patience of this kind audience." "But one touch remains," said the old mechanic, "to complete my work;" and he busied himself a moment among the wheels. While he suffered the agonies of his torture a fearful whir was heard from the clock: the weights tumbled crashing to the floor as his eyes fell from their sockets. He had removed the master-spring, and his revenge was complete. The lovers devoted their lives to the comfort of the blind clockmaker, and the wicked magistrate was hooted from society. The clock remained a ruin until 1842, when parts of it were used in the new one constructed by Schwilgué.

I found my bluebottle professor to be a Swiss, thirty years resident in the city, very accessible and talkative, and, like every citizen by adoption, more patriotic than even the native-born.

"It was a cheerless time for me, sir," said he as we contemplated together the façade of the church, "when I saw that spire printed in black against the flames of the town."

I begged frankly for his reminiscences.

"The bombardment of 1870," said the professor, "was begun purposely, in contempt of the Bonapartist tradition, on the 15th of August, the birthday of Napoleon. At half-past eleven at night, just as the fireworks are usually set off on that evening, a shell came hissing over the city and fell upon the Bank of France, crushing through the skylight and shivering the whole staircase within: the bombardment that time lasted only half an hour, but it found means, after much killing and ruining among the private houses, to reach the buildings of the Lyceum, where we had placed the wounded from the army of Woerth. While the

THE GREAT CLOCK.

city was being touched off in every direction, like a vast brush-heap, we had to take these poor victims down into the cellars."

"Do you think the bombs were purposely so directed?" I asked.

"Don't talk to me of stray shots!" said the burgher, hotly enough. "The enemy was better acquainted with the city than we were ourselves, and his fire was of a precision that extorted our admiration more than once. Cannons planted in Kehl sent their shells high over the citadel, like blows from a friend. An artillery that, after the third shot, found the proper curve and bent the cross on the cathedral, cannot plead extenuating circumstances and stray shots."

"Was the greatest damage done on that first night?"

"Ah no! The bombardment was addressed to us as an argument, proceeding by degrees, and always in a *crescendo*: after the 15th there was silence until the 18th; after the 18th, silence up to the 23d. The grand victim of the 23d, you know, was the city library, where lay the accumulations of centuries of patient learning—the mediæval manu-

CHURCH OF SAINT THOMAS.

scripts, the *Hortus deliciarum* of Herrade of Landsberg, the monuments of early printing, the collections of Sturm. Ah! when we gathered around our precious reliquary the next day and saw its contents in ashes, amid a scene of silence, of people hurrying away with infants and valuable objects, of firemen hopelessly playing on the burned masterpieces, there was one thought that came into every mind—one parallel! It was Omar the caliph and the library of Alexandria."

"And you imagine that this offence to civilization was quite voluntary?" I argued with some doubt.

"It is said that General Werder acted under superior orders. But, sir, you must perceive that in these discretionary situations there is no such dangerous man as the innocent executant, the martinet, the person of routine, the soldier stifled in his uniform. I saw Werder after the capitulation. A little man, lean and bilious. Such was the opponent who reversed for us successively, like the premises of an argument, the bank, the library, the art-museum, the theatre, the prefecture, the arsenal, the palace of justice, not to speak of our churches. A man like that was quite capable of replying, as he did, to a request that he would allow a safe-conduct for non-combatants, that 'the presence of women and children was an element of weakness to the fortress of which he did not intend to deprive it.' The night illuminated by our burning manuscripts was followed by the day which witnessed the conflagration of the cathedral. Look at that noble front, sir, contemplating us with the hoary firmness of six hundred years! You would think it a sad experience to see it, as I have seen it, crowned with flames which leaped up and licked the spire, while the copper on the roof curled up like paper in the heat; and to hear, as I heard, the poor beadles and guards, from the height of yonder platform, calling the city to the aid of its cathedral. The next day the mighty church, now so imperfectly restored, was a piteous sight. The flames had gone out for want of fuel. We could see the sky through holes in the roof. The organ-front was leaning over, pierced with strange gaps; the clock escaped as by miracle; and the mighty saints, who had been praying for centuries in the stained windows, were scat-

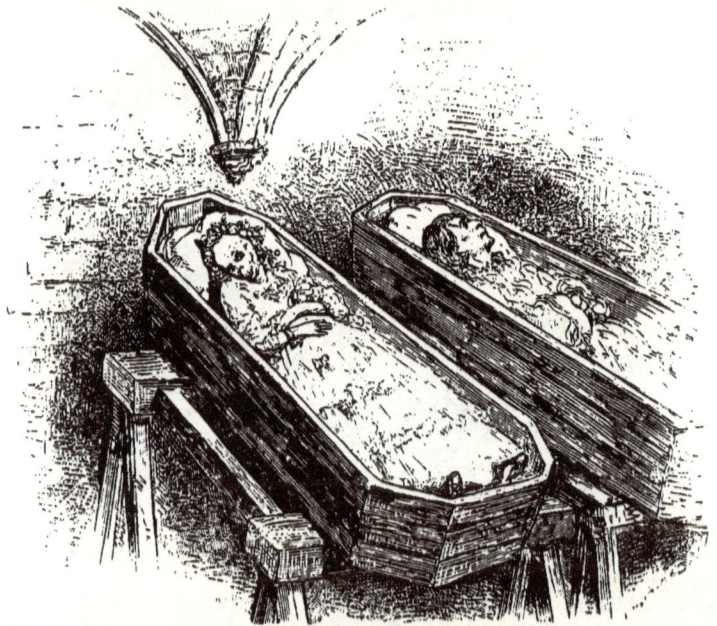

BEAUTY'S QUINTESSENCE.

tered upon the floor. On the 25th the systematic firing of the faubourgs began, and the city was filled with the choking smell of burning goods: on the 28th the citadel was kindled."

"And what opposition," I naturally demanded, "were you able to make to all this? I believe your forces were greatly shortened?'

"We were as short as you can think, sir. Most of the garrison had been withdrawn by MacMahon. The soldiers still among us were miserably demoralized by the entrance of the fugitives from Woerth. Our defence was the strangest of mixtures. The custom-house officers were armed and mobilized: the naval captain Dupetit-Thouars happened to be in the walls, with some of the idle marine. Colonel Fiévée, with his pontoneers, hurriedly tore up the bridge of boats leading over to Kehl, and united himself with the garrison. From the outbreak of the war we civilians had been invited to form a garde nationale, but never was there a greater farce. We were asked to choose our own grades, and when I begged to be made colonel, they inquired if I would not prefer to be lieutenant or adjutant. Most of us, those at least who had voted against the imperial candidates, never received a gun. Our artillery, worthy of the times of Louis XIV., scolded in vain from the ramparts against the finest cannons in the world, and we were obliged to watch the Prussian trenches pushing toward the town, and to hear the bullets beginning to fall where at first were only bombs."

"The capitulation was then imminent." "There were a few incidents in the mean time. The deputation from Switzerland, of ever-blessed memory, entered the city on the eleventh of September. Angels from heaven could not have been more welcome. You know that a thousand of our inhabitants passed over into Switzerland under conduct of the delegate from Berne, Colonel Büren, and that they were received like brothers. From Colonel Büren also we learned for the first time about Sedan, the disasters of Bazaine and MacMahon, and the hopelessness of the national cause. We learned that, while they were crowning with flowers the statue of our city in Paris, they had no assistance but handsome words to send us. Finally, we learned the proclamation of the French republic—a republic engendered in desolation, and so powerless to support its distant provinces! We too had our little republican demonstration, and on the 20th of September the prefect they had sent us from Paris, M. Valentin, came dashing in like a harlequin, after running the gauntlet of a thousand dangers, and ripped out of his sleeve his official voucher from Gambetta. Alas! we were a republic for only a week, but that week of fettered freedom still dwells like an elixir in some of our hearts. For eight days I, a born Switzer, saw the Rhine a republican river."

"Give me your hand, sir!" I cried, greatly moved. "You are talking to a republican. I am, or used to be, a citizen of free America!"

"I am happy to embrace you," said the burgher; and I believe he was on the point of doing it, literally as well as figuratively. "I, for my part, whatever they make of me, am at least an Alsatian. But I am half ashamed to talk to an American. On the 29th I went to see our troops evacuate the city by the Faubourg National. I found myself elbow to elbow in the throng with the consul from the United States: never in my life shall I forget the indignant surprise of your compatriot."

"Why should our consul be indignant at disaster?" I demanded.

"Why, sir, the throng that rolled toward the grave Prussian troops was composed of desperadoes inflamed with wine, flourishing broken guns and stumps of sabres, and insulting equally, with many a drunken oath, the conquerors and our own loyal general Uhrich. The American consul, blushing with shame for our common humanity, said, 'This is the second time I have watched the capitulation of an army. The first time it was the soldiers of General Lee, who yielded to the Northern troops. Those brave Confederates came toward us silent and dignified, bearing arms reversed, as at a funeral. We respected them as heroes, while here—' But I cannot repeat to you, sir, what your representative proceeded to add. That revolting sight," continued my informant, "was the last glimpse we had of France our protector. When we returned to the city a Prussian band played German airs to us

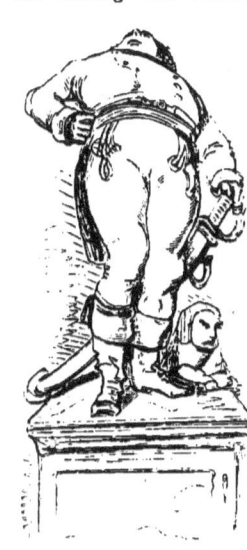

"VOICI LE SABRE!"

at the foot of Kleber's statue. We are Teutonized now. At least," concluded the burgher, taking me by the shoulders to hiss the words through my ears in a safe corner, "we are Germans officially. But I, for my part, am Alsatian for ever and for ever!"

Greatly delighted to have encountered so near a witness and so minute a chronicler of the disasters of the town, I invited the professor to accompany me in exploring it, my interest having vastly increased during his recital; but he pleaded business, and, shaking both my hands and smiling upon me out of a sort of moulding formed around his face by his shirt-collars, dismissed me. So, then, once more, with a hitch to my tin box, I became a lonely lounger. I viewed the church of Saint Thomas, the public place named after Kleber, who was born here, some of the markets and a beer establishment. In the church of Saint Thomas I examined the monument to Marshal Saxe, by Pigalle. I should have expected to see a simple statue of the hero in the act of breaking a horseshoe or rolling up a silver plate into a bouquet-holder, according to the Guy-Livingstone habits in which he appears to have passed his life, and was more surprised than edified at sight of the large allegorical family with which the sculptor has endowed him. In the same church I had the misfortune to see in the boxes a pair of horrible mummies, decked off with robes and ornaments—a count of Nassau-Saarwerden and his daughter, according to the custodian—an unhappy pair who, having escaped our common doom of corruption by some physical aridity or meagreness, have been compelled to leave their tombs and attitudinize as works of art. In Kleber's square I saw the conqueror of Heliopolis, excessively pigeon-breasted, dangling his sabre over a cowering little figure of Egypt, and looking around in amazement at the neighboring windows: in fact, Kleber began his career as an architect, and there were solecisms in the surrounding structure to have turned a better balanced head than his. In the markets I saw peasants with red waistcoats and flat faces shaded with triangles of felt, and peasant-girls bareheaded, with a gilded arrow apparently shot through their brains. I traversed the Street of the Great Arcades, and saw the statue of Gutenberg, of whom, as well as of Peter Schöffer, the natives seem to be proud, though they were but type-setters. Finally, in the Beer-hall, that of the dauphin, I tasted a thimbleful of inimitable beer, the veritable beer of Strasburg. Already, at half-past eight on that fine May morning, I persuaded myself that I had seen everything, so painful had my feet become by pounding over the pavements.

STREET OF THE GREAT ARCADES.

My friend the engineer had agreed to breakfast with me at the hotel. When

I entered the dining-room with the intention of waiting for him, I found two individuals sitting at table. One was no other than the red-nosed Scotchman, the Eleusinian victim whom I had watched through the bottle-rack at Épernay. Of the second I recognized the architectural back, the handsomely rolled and faced blue coat and the marble volutes of his Ionic shirt-collar: it was my good friend of the cathedral. Every trace of his civic grief had disappeared, and he wore a beaming banquet-room air, though the tear of patriotism was hardly dry upon his cheek.

As I paused to dispose of my accoutrements the red nose was saying, "Yes, my dear sir, since yesterday I am a Mason. I have the honor," he pursued, "to be First Attendant Past Grand. It will be a great thing for me at Edinburgh. Burns, I believe, was only Third Assistant, Exterior Lodge: the Rank, however, in his opinion, was but the guinea's stamp. But the advantages of Masonry are met with everywhere. Already in the train last night I struck the acquaintance of a fine fellow, a Mason like myself."

"Allow me to ask," said the cheerful bluebottle, "how you knew him for a Mason like yourself?"

"I'll tell you. I was unable to sleep, because, you see, I had to drink Moët for my initiation: as I am unaccustomed to anything livelier than whisky, it unnerved me. To pass the time I went softly over the signals."

"What signals, if I may be so indiscreet?"

"Number one, you scratch the nose, as if to chase a fly; number two, you put your thumb in your mouth; number three—"

"H'm!" said the professor doubtfully,

BEER-GARDEN OF THE DAUPHIN.

"those are singular instructions, scratching the nose and sucking the thumb. It strikes me they have been teaching you nursery signals rather than Masonry signals."

"My good friend," said the Scot with extreme politeness, yet not without dignity, "you cannot understand it, because you were not present. I received a Light which burned my eyelashes. The sage always examines a mystery before he decides upon it. My Masonic friend will be here at breakfast to-day: he promised me. Only wait for him. He can explain these things better than I, you will see. The little experiments with our noses and thumbs, you understand, are symbols — Thummim and Urim, or something of that kind."

"Or else nonsense. You have been quizzed, I fear."

The North Briton bridled his head, knitted his brows and pushed back his chair; then, after a moment of pregnant and stormy silence, he turned suddenly around to me, who was enjoying the comedy—"Hand me the cheese."

To be taken for a waiter amused me. Never in the world would a domestic have dared to present himself in a hotel habited as I was. I was in the same clothes with which I had left Passy the morning previous: my coat was peppered with dust, my linen bruised and dingy, my tie was nodding doubtfully over my right shoulder. A waiter in my condition would have been kicked out without arrears of wages.

The professor, looking quickly around, recognized me with a ludicrous endeavor to relapse into the fiery and outraged patriot. He expended his temper on the red nose. "Take care whom you speak to," he cried in a high, portly voice, and pointing to my japanned box, which I had slung upon a curtain-hook.

SUCKLED IN A CREED OUTWORN.

"Monsieur is not an attaché of the house. Monsieur is doubtless an herb-doctor."

There are charlatans who pervade the provincial parts of France, stopping a month at a time in the taverns, and curing the ignorant with simples according to the old system of *signaturis*—prescribing hepatica for liver, lentils for the eyes and green walnuts for vapors, on account of their supposed correspondence to the different organs. I settled my cravat at the mirror to contradict my resemblance to a waiter, threw my box into a wine-cooler to dispose of my identity with the equally uncongenial herbalist, and took a seat. Nodding paternally to the coat of Prussian blue, I proceeded to order Bordeaux-Léoville, capon with Tarragon sauce, compôte of nectarines in Madeira jelly—all superfluous, for I was brutally hungry, and wanted chops and coffee; but what will not an unsupported candidate for respectability do when he desires to assert his caste? I was proceeding to ruin myself in playing the eccentric millionaire when the door opened, giving entrance to a group of breakfasters.

"There he is—that's the man!" said the homœopathist, much excited, and indicating to the blue coat a brisk, capable-looking gentleman of thirty-two in a neat silver-gray overcoat. The latter, after slightly touching his nose, nodded to the Sotchman, who in return drew himself up to his full height and formally wiped his mouth with a napkin, as if preparing himself for an oration. Happily, he contented himself with rubbing his own nose with each hand in turn, and bowing so profoundly that he appeared ready to break at the knees.

"*Kellner!*" said the silver-gray, making a grand rattle among the plates and glasses, "some wine! some water! some ink! an omelette! a writing-pad! a *filet à la Chabrillant!*"

The last-named dish is one which sciolists are perpetually calling *filet à la Chateaubriand*, saddling the poetic defender of Christianity with an invention in cookery of which he was never capable. I approved the new-comer, who was writing half a dozen notes with his mouth full, for his nicety in nomenclature: to get the right term, even in kitchen affairs, shows a reflective mind and tenderness of conscience. My friend the engineer arrived, and placed himself in the chair I had turned up beside my own. I was ashamed of the rate at which I advanced through my capon, but I recollected that Anne Boleyn, when she was a maid of honor, used to breakfast off a gallon of ale and a chine of beef.

My canal-maker interrupted me with a sudden appeal. "Listen—listen yonder," he said, jogging my knee, "it is very amusing. He is in a high vein to-day."

The gray coat, who had already directed four or five letters, and was cleaning his middle finger with a lemon over the glass bowl, had just opened a lofty geographical discussion with the bluebottle. I cannot express how eagerly I, as a theorist of some pretension in Comparative Geography, awoke to a discussion in which my dearest opinions were concerned.

"Geography," the active gentleman was saying as he dipped his finger in water to attach the flaps of his envelopes —"geography, my dear professor, is the most neglected of modern sciences. Excuse me if I take from under you, for a moment, your doctoral chair, and land you on one of the forms of the primary department. I would ask a simple elementary question: How many parts of the globe are there?"

"Before the loss of Alsace and Lorraine," said the professor with plaintive humor, "I always reckoned six."

"Very well: on this point we agree."

"Six!" said the Scotchman in great surprise. "You are liberal: I make but five."

"Not one less than six," said the patriot, vastly encouraged with the support he got: "am I not right, sir? We have, first, Europe—"

"Ah, professor," said the silver-gray, interrupting him, "how is this? You, such a distinguished scholar — you still believe in Europe? Why, my dear sir, Europe no longer exists—certainly not as a quarter of the globe. It is simply, as Humboldt very truly remarks in his *Cosmos*, the septentrional point of Asia."

The surprise seemed to pass, at this point, from the face of the Scot to that of the Strasburger. After reflecting a moment, "Really," murmured he, "I recollect, in *Cosmos*— But how, then, do you reach six parts of the globe?"

"Only count, professor: Asia, one; Africa, two; Australia, three; Oceanica, four; North America, five; and South America, six."

"You cut America in two?"

"Nature has taken that responsibility. Each part of the world being necessarily an insulated continent, an enormous island, it is too much to ask me to confound the northern and southern continents of America, hung together by a thread — a thread which messieurs the engineers"—he bowed airily to my companion —"have very probably severed by this time."

The honest professor passed his hand over his forehead. "The deuce!" he said. "That is logic perhaps. Still, sir, I think it is rather hardy in you to double America and annihilate Europe, when Europe discovered America."

"The Europeans did not discover America," replied the young philosopher. "The Americans discovered Europe."

The professor of geography remained stunned: the homœopathist gave utterance to a cry—one of admiration, doubtless.

"An American colony was settled in Norway long before the arrival of Columbus in Santo Domingo: who will contradict me when Humboldt says so? Only read your *Cosmos!*"

"The dickens! prodigious! prodigious!" repeated the man of blue.

THE BLESSING OF THE BÂB.

The young silver coat went on: "I have been three times around the world, professor. The terrestrial globe was my only chart. I have studied in their places its divisions, continents, capes and oceans; also the customs, politics and philosophies of its inhabitants. I have a weakness for learning; I have caused myself to be initiated in all secret and philosophical societies; I have taken a degree from the Brahmans of Benares; I have received the accolade from the emir of the Druses; I have been instructed by the priests of the Grand Lama, and have joined the Society of Pure Illumination, the sole possessors of the Future Light. I have just returned from Persia, where I received the blessing of the great Bâb; and, like Solomon, I can say, *Vanitas vanitatum!*"

The red nose was by this time quite inflated and inflamed with disinterested pride. The blue was crushed, but he made a final effort, as the silver-gray made his preparations to depart and adjusted his breakfast-bill. "Pardon me, sir," he said, with a little infusion of provincial pride. "I am not a cosmopolitan, a Constantinopolitan or a Bâbist. But I enjoy your conversation, and am not entirely without the ability to sympathize in your geographical calculations. I am preparing at the present moment a small treatise on Submarine Geography; I am conducting, if that gives me any right to be heard, the geographical department in the chief gym-

THE BOTANIST.

nasium here: in addition, my youngest sister lost her ulnar bone by the explosion of an obus in the seminary on the night of August 18th, when six innocent infants were killed or maimed by the Prussians, who put a bomb in their little beds like a warming-pan."

"Never mind the warming-pan," said the traveler kindly, seeing that the professor was making himself cry, and unconsciously quoting Pickwick.

"I will not dilate on my title to trouble you for a few words more. I perceive that I shall have a good deal to modify in my modest treatise. I beg you to give us your views on some of the modifications now going on in the East, especially the Turkish question and the civilization of China."

"My dear professor," said the youthful Crichton sententiously, "do not disturb yourself with those problems, which are already disposed of. In twenty years the sultan will become a monk, to get rid of the chief sultana, who has pestered his life out with her notions of woman's rights, and who wore the Bloomer costume before the Crimean war. As for the question about China, it is better to let sleeping dogs lie: it has been a great mistake to arouse China, for it is a dog that drags after it three hundred millions of pups. Only see the effect already in Lima and San Francisco! Before a century has elapsed all Asia, with Alaska and the Pacific part of America, to say nothing of that petty extremity you persist in calling Europe, will be in the power of China. Your little girls, professor, will be more liable to lose their feet than their arms, for it is a hundred chances to one but your great-grand-nieces grow up Chinawomen."

"Astonishing!" murmured the professor of geography.

"Admirable!" cried the doctor.

I had hitherto said nothing, though I was capitally entertained. At length I ventured to take up my own parable, and, addressing the pretended disciple of the Brahmans, I asked, "Can you enlighten us, sir, on the true reason of the revolt of the slave States in America?"

The cosmopolitan, by this time standing, turned to me with a courteous motion of acquiescence; and, after having given me to understand by an agreeable smile that he did not confound me with his pair of victims, he said pompously, "The true cause was that each Northern freeholder demanded the use of two planters, now mostly octoroons, for body-servants."

"You don't say so?" said the schoolteacher, profoundly impressed.

The Scotchman looked like him who digesteth a pill. I decided quickly on my own rôle, and briskly joined the conversation. Fishing up my botany-box and extracting the little flower, "Nothing is more likely when you know the country," I observed. "I have lived in Florida, gentlemen, where I undertook, as Comparative Geographer and as amateur botanist" (I looked searchingly at the professor, who had called me an herb-doctor), "to fix the location of Ponce de Leon's fountain and observe the medicinal plants to which it owes its virtue. America, I must explain to you, is a country where proportions are greatly changed. The pineapple tree there grows so very tall that it is impossible from the ground to reach the fruit. This little flower now in my hand becomes in that climate a towering and sturdy plant, the tobacco plant. The wild justice of those lawless savannahs uses it as a gibbet for the execution of criminals, whence the term 'Lynchburg tobacco.' You cannot readily imagine the scale on which life expands. It was formerly not necessary to be a great man there to have a hundred slaves. For my part, sixty domestics sufficed me" (I regarded sternly the homœopathist, who had taken me for a waiter): "it was but a scant allowance, since my pipe alone took the whole time of four."

"Oh," said the Scotchman, "allow me to doubt. I understand the distribution of blood among the planters, because I am a homœopathist; but what could your pipe gain by being diluted among four men?"

"The first filled it, the second lighted it, the third handed it and the fourth smoked it. I hate tobacco."

The witticism appeared generally agreeable, and I laughed with the rest. The cheerful philosopher in the gray coat passed out: as he left the room, followed subserviently by his interlocutors, he bowed very pleasantly to me and shook hands with my guardian the engineer.

"You know him?" I said to the latter.

"Just as well as you," he replied: "is it possible you don't recognize him? It is Fortnoye."

"What! Fortnoye—the Ancient of the wine-cellar at Épernay?"

"Certainly."

"In truth it is the same jolly voice. Then his white beard was a disguise?"

"What would you have?"

"I am glad he is the same: I began to think the mystifiers here were as dangerous as those of the champagne country. At any rate, he is a bright fellow."

"He is not always bright. A man with so good a heart as his must be saddened sometimes, at least with others' woes, and he does not always escape woes of his own."

This sentiment affected me, and irritated me a little besides, for I felt that it was in my own vein, and that it was I who had a right to the observation. I immediately quoted an extract from an Icelandic Saga to the effect that dead bees give a stinging quality to the very metheglin of the gods. We exchanged these remarks in crossing the vestibule of the hotel: a carriage was standing there for my friend.

"I am sorry to leave you. I have a meeting with a Prussian engineer about bridges and canals and the waterworks of Vauban, and everything that would least interest you. I must cross immediately to Kehl. I leave you to finish the geography of Strasburg."

"I know Strasburg by heart, and am burning to get out of it. I want to cross the Rhine, for the sake of boasting that I have set foot in the Baden territory. By the by, how have I managed to come so far without a passport?"

"*This* did it," said my engineer, tapping the tin box, which a waiter had restored to me in a wonderful state of polish. "I put a plan or two in it, with some tracing muslin, and allowed a spirit-level to stick out. You were asleep. I know all the officials on this route. I had only to tap the box and nod. You passed as my assistant. Nobody could have put you through but I."

"You are a vile conspirator," said I affectionately, "and have all the lower traits of the Yankee character. But I will use you to carry me to Kehl, as Faust used Mephistopheles. By the by, your carriage is a comfortable one and saves my time. I have two hours before I need return to the train."

"It is double the time you will need."

PART V.

IN PURSUIT OF A PASSPORT.

THE SIGN OF THE "STORK."

"THE Strasburgers have a legend—" We were rolling along very comfortably in the engineer's coach. From pavement to bridge, and from bridge to pavement, we effected the long step which bestrides the Rhine.

"I knew you would prick your ears up at the word. Well, I have found a legend among the people here about the original acquisition of Strasburg by the French. You know Louis XIV. bagged the city quite unwarrantably in 1681, in a time of peace."

I was much delighted with this beginning, and told my friend that to cross the storied Rhine and simultaneously listen to a legend made me feel as if I were Frithiof the Viking entertained on his voyage by a Skald.

"The Alsatians will have it," said my

canal-digger, "that the Grand Monarch was a bit of a magician. The depth of what I may call his High-Church sentiment, which at last proved so edifying to the Maintenon, has never convinced them that he wasn't a trifle in league with the devil. At the foot of his praying-chair was always chained a small casket of ebony, bound with iron. In this he imprisoned a little yellow man, a demon of the most concentrated structure, hardly a foot long. This goblin ran through the air, on an errand or with a letter, about as fast as a stroke of lightning, and admirably filled the place of the modern telegraph. For each meal he took three seeds of hemp, which he loved to receive from the king's hand. By and by the little yellow man became more of a gourmand. He demanded seed-pearls, and the king was obliged to rob the queen's jewel-boxes. Then the yellow dwarf's appetite changed, and he required stars, orders and garters: one by one the obedient monarch gave him the decorations of count, marquis, duke. The demon's name was Chamillo.

"One day the small devil-duke of a Chamillo hovered over the imperial free city of Strasburg. Entering by keyholes and doors ajar, he stole into the presence of the principal magistrates, and shortly after the impregnable capital of Alsace opened its gates at a show of French investment.

"For this important service Louis XIV. fancied that Chamillo would require the letters patent constituting him a prince. Not at all. Chamillo was tired of secular honors: he had seen the bishop of Strasburg officiating in scarlet, and he insisted on being made cardinal. The king could not make cardinals, and he doubted whether he could induce the pope to receive a devil among the upper clergy. He refused absolutely. Chamillo left him in dudgeon and went over to Prussia. Apparently he has remained there. At any rate, the French king's fortunes commenced at that epoch to decline, and the Peace of Ryswick almost deprived him of Strasburg, which the little yellow man wanted to get back for Germany."

We had quitted Strasburg by the gate of Austerlitz. While listening to my friend I kept an eye open, and examined the present state of the fortress, the incidents of the road to Kehl, and that fairy Ile des Épis, a perfect little Eden in the Rhine, where the tall trees and nod-

A GRAND MONARCH AND A LITTLE YELLOW IMP.

ding flowers bury the tomb of Dessaix, with its inscription, "À Dessaix, l'Armée du Rhin, 1800." This bright morning-ride enchanted me, seasoned as it was with a goblin-story.

"Behind this tale, now, there must be

ILE DES ÉPIS.

a fact," I said. "There is some bit of history concealed there. The common people never invent: they distort."

"It is possible," he answered. "I tell you the story as it was told me by one of my theodolite-bearers. You may find out the rest: it is in your line."

Kehl has been bombarded or razed a dozen times by French armies crossing the Rhine. The last occasion when the

French ruined it, however, was not in vain-glory, but in impotent malice. They fired it on August 19, 1870, during the horrors of the Strasburg bombardment.

It is a town formed of a single street— But I will enter no further into topographic details.

I entered this town or street in haste,

BEGGARS AT BÂLE.

leaving my engineering acquaintance talking to a Prussian general. The idea had seized me of writing a line to Hohenfels at Marly, actually dated from the grand duchy of Baden. Undoubtedly I should reach Marly before my letter, but the postal mark would be a good proof of the actuality of my wanderings. Clinging, then, to my childishness, as we

HOW THINGS FELL OUT.

do to most of our follies, with a fidelity which it would be well to imitate in our grave affairs, and feeling pressed for time, I looked eagerly around for a resting-place where I could procure ink and

paper, and entered at the sign of the "Stork." I found a smoky crowd, peasants and military, sucking German pipes and drinking from a variety of glasses, pots, syphons and jugs. I had taken up my pen when an individual by my side, at the next table, said to his opposite neighbor, "The French will hardly take Strasburg again by surprise, as they did two centuries ago."

"It was not the French who took Strasburg," replied the *vis-à-vis*, evidently a native: "it was *the little urchin in yellow*."

The expression, joined to what I had just heard in the carriage, was sufficient to attract my attention. My neighbor, a Belgian by his accent, opened his eyes. The man opposite, perceiving that he had more than one auditor, narrated at length, in substance and detail, not the fairy legend of the Alsatians, but accurately, and to my amusement, the historical anecdote which I had imagined to be wrapped up in that tale. So then, while he spoke, I wrote—no longer to Hohenfels, but to my own consciousness and memory—these little notes on Chamillo, or rather Chamilly, and obtained a trifling contribution to the back-stairs history of the Grand Nation.

"The marquis of Chamilly, afterward marshal of France, was often promised a good place for a young nephew he had by the powerful Minister de Louvois. Each time, however, that the youth pre-

THE LITTLE IMP IN YELLOW

sented himself the experienced minister said, 'Bide your time, young man : I see nothing yet on the horizon worthy of you.' The boy sulked in the tortures of hope deferred. One day in September, 1681, Louvois said, 'Young man, post yourself at Bâle on the 18th day of this month, from noon to four o'clock : stand on the bridge; take a note of all you see, without the least omission; come back and report to me; and as you acquit yourself so your future shall be.' The young chevalier found himself on the bridge at Bâle at high noon. He expected to meet some deputation from the Swiss cantons, with the great landamman at the head. What he really saw were carts, villagers, flocks of sheep, children who chased each other, mendicants who, with Swiss independence, demanded alms rather than begged it. He gave to each, imagining in each a mysterious agent. An old woman crossing the bridge on a bucking donkey, who threw her, he picked up obsequiously, not knowing but this fall might be a manœuvre of state, and the precipitate take the form of the landamman in disguise: he had even the idea of running after the donkey, but the animal was already galloping with great relish outside the assigned limits to his diplomacy. When tired of the sun, the dust and the triviality of the panorama, Chamilly prepared to go. It was nearing the hour fixed for his departure, and the absence of all significant events vexed him. As if to put a crown on his discomfiture, toward the close of the last hour an odd little urchin, grotesquely dressed in a yellow coat, came to beat old blankets over the parapet, and flirted the dirt and fluff into the young man's eyes. Already angered, he was about to hang the young imp for a minute or two over the bridge, when four o'clock sounded, his duty came to his mind, and he departed.

"In the middle of the third night, tired and humiliated, he reappeared before the minister and recounted his failure. When he came to the little page in yellow, Louvois fell on his neck and kissed him. Chamilly was dragged incontinently before the king. Louis XIV., who was snoring with his royal nose in the air, was waked for the purpose, and heard with attention the story

"THE TRAIN IS STARTING."

of the beggars, the donkey and the little monkey in yellow livery. At the apparition of the Yellow Jacket, Louis XIV. leaped over the *ruelle* and danced a saraband in his night-gown. Chamilly might perhaps have considered himself sufficiently rewarded in being the only man who ever saw the superb king dancing with bare legs in a wig hastily put on crosswise. But to this recompense others were added. The monarch named him chevalier of his orders, count and counselor of state, to the grand stupefaction of the young man, who understood nothing about it.

"The little yellow urchin, shaking his blankets, announced to the king's envoy, on the part of the perjured Strasburg magistrates, that the city was betrayed." I had now that rare complementing pair, a legend and its historical foundation. I had been obliged to cross the Rhine to obtain my prize, but I did not regret the journey. How far I was from fancying the ill-natured turn that the little yellow man was playing me!

While my neighbor of the Stork was talking, and I was taking down his words with my utmost rapidity, Time took advantage of me, and put double the accustomed length into each of his steps. On recrossing into Strasburg I had before me barely the moments necessary to regain the railway station. The gate at the first-class passenger-exit was about closing, fifteen minutes in advance of the start, according to the European custom. I pushed in rather roughly.

The railway-officer or porter was at the gate, barring my passage until I could exhibit a ticket. I had not taken time to purchase one: the train was

"JUSTICE AND VENGEANCE PURSUING CRIME."

fuming and threatening the belated passengers with a series of false starts. Surprised into rudeness, and quite forgetting that my appearance warranted no airs of autocracy, I made some contemptuous remark.

"Der Herr is much too hasty. Der Herr is doubtless provided with the necessary papers which will enable him to pass the French frontier."

It was not the porter who spoke now: it was some kind of official relic or shadow or mouchard left from the old custom-house, and suffered to hang on the railway-station as an ornament. His costume, half uniform and half fatigue-dress, compromised nobody, and was surmounted by a skull cap. His pantaloons were short, his figure was paunchy, authoritative and German. His German, however, was spoken with a French accent. As I mused in stupefaction upon the hint he had uttered, he pointed with his hand. "The train is starting," he observed.

The reader probably knows Prudhon's great picture in the Louvre, originally painted for the Palace of Justice, and entitled "Divine Justice and Vengeance in Pursuit of Crime"? This picture, which I had not thought of, I suppose, for an age, suddenly seemed to be realized before me, but the heavenly detectives were changed into mortal gendarmes. The porter and the nondescript threw back the gate, preventing my passage. The terrors of Prudhon's avenging spirits were all expressed, to my thinking, in the looks which these two official people exchanged in my favor, and then bent on me. We stood in a triangle.

"One moment: I propose a plan," I cried in desperation. "I do not know a soul in Strasburg, and the friend who brought me here is gone, I cannot tell whither. But I have an acquaintance in the British consulate at Carlsruhe—Berkley, you know," I explained with an insane familiarity, "my old friend Berkley's nephew. Admit me to the train, and we will telegraph to him. His reply will come in ten minutes, and will show you my responsible character. I have come fifteen minutes in advance of the starting-hour."

"The wire to Carlsruhe," said the porter, "is under repairs."

"The train to Paris," said the second man, "is off."

Some fate was pursuing me. Rudely rejected at the wicket, and treated as a man without a nationality, I felt as if I had but one friend now available on earth—the friend who had come into my head while conversing with the railway guard. Old Mr. Berkley, Mr. Sylvester Berkley and I had once breakfasted together at Brighton, the first sitting in a tub, the second eating nothing but raw macerated beef, and I for my part devouring toast and Icelandic poetry. The nephew had since gone into diplomacy to strengthen his bile. I had not seen him for years.

I approached the schedule of distances hanging on the wall. My movements were those of a man prostrated and resigned. I ran my forefinger over the departures from Kehl to Carlsruhe.

In three hours I was in the latter city.

It was not in beggar's guise that Paul Flemming would fain be seen in the capital of the grand duchy—the most formal capital, the most symmetrical capital, the most monumental capital, as it is the youngest capital, in Europe. Nor was it as a vagabond that he would wish to appear in that capital, before a friend who happened to be a diplomatist. I recollected the engaging aspect in which I had offered myself

to the reflections of the Rhine when last beside that romantic stream—a comely youth, with Stultz's best waistcoats on his bosom and with ineffable sorrows in his heart. Frau Himmelauen used to say, at Heidelberg, that my gloves were a shade too light for a strictly virtuous

SUSPICIOUS BAGGAGE.

man. The Frau has gone to her account, and Stultz, the great Stultz, is defunct too, after achieving for himself a baronetcy as the prize of his peerless scissors, and founding a hospital here in Carlsruhe. Not to insult the shade of Stultz, I determined to renew my youth, at least in the matter of plumage. A shop of ready-made clothing afforded me lavender gloves, silk pocket handkerchief, satin cravat, detachable collar and a cambric shirt: the American dickey, in which some of my early sartorial triumphs were effected, is not to be had in Rhineland. My ornaments purchased, the trouble was—to change my shirt. The great hotel, the Erbprinz, was no place for a man without a passport and without baggage: not for the world would I have faced a hotel-clerk with his accusing register. Yet the street was not to be thought of: only cats are allowed by etiquette to freshen their linen on the doorstep.

A resource occurred to me. In ransacking the city for my ornaments I had observed the castle-park, with its clumps of verdure and almost deserted walks. Hurrah for the leafy dressing-room!

At the gate a sentinel stopped me. Would he demand my passport? No: he taps with his finger the lid of that faithful botany-box, my sole valise. Aware that it contained nothing contraband, I opened it innocently and demonstratively. At the sight of that resonant

CARLSRUHE: THE GRAND-DUCAL PARK.

cavity, gaping from ear to ear and belching forth gloves, kerchiefs and minor haberdashery, the dragon laughed: his mirth took the form of a deep, guttural, honest German guffaw. He still, however, rapped sonorously on my box, shaking his head from side to side like a china mandarin. In his view my box was luggage, and luggage is not permitted in any European park. Relieved to find that my detention was not more serious, my first thought was to comply with the conditions of entrance. I begged to leave my package in the sentry-box, to be reclaimed at departure. The amiable Cerberus, smiling and nodding, closed his eyes significantly: at this moment I recollected that my only motive for entering the park lay in that feature of my paraphernalia, and caught it up again, with a gesture of parental violence, in the very act of depositing it. The sentry, watching with increasing delight my evolutions and counter-evolutions, evidently thought me a nimble lunatic, Heaven-sent for the recreation of his long watch. He no longer opposed any of my demonstrations, and finally, with a hearty chuckle, saw me slink past him into the groves, wardrobe in hand. Most accommodating of sentinels, why were you not in charge of a Paris barrier during the siege?

Once within the park, I found that my sight had deceived me: the day was hot, and the public, driven from the sunny walks, were concentrated in the shade. Not a bough but sheltered its group of Arcadians. I wended from tree to tree, describing singular zigzags on the

THE GENTLE CERBERUS.

sward. The guardians began to eye me with lively interest. Finally, Fortune having guided me to a beautiful thicket, a closet curtained with evergreens, I prepared to use it for my toilet, and relinquished a sleeve of my coat. At that moment one of my watchmen suddenly showed himself.

Looking at him with extreme seriousness, I slowly re-entered my sleeve, and walked away with unnecessary dignity, giving the guardian my patronage in the shape of a nod, which he did not return.

Forbidden the green-room, what if I tried the bath-room? Hastily making for the Square of the Obelisk, I took a carriage, engaging it by the hour, and directing it to the nearest bathing-establishment. The driver immediately ran off with me outside the city.

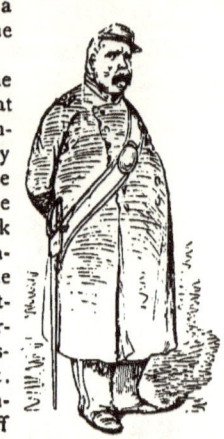

THE EYE OF ARGUS.

Carlsruhe is an aristocratic construction, whose princely mansions are supposed to be supplied with their own thermal conveniences. The locality suggested for my bath proved to be a vast suburban garden, buried in flowers, with amorous young couples promenading the alleys, and tables crowned with cylinders of beer, each wadded with its handful of foam. At the extremity, on a square building, five lofty letters spelled out the word *Baden*.

A waiter showed me a handsome bath, decorated with a tub like some Roman mausoleum. I instructed him as to the temperature of my desired plunge. He nodded quietly, and left me. Twenty minutes passed. I thought of my friend Sylvester Berkley, of the document I hoped to obtain by his aid, and, most fondly, of the hour when I could return from Carlsruhe. I thought of the little group who at Marly were expecting and reproaching me. Charles now, for the twentieth time, would be brushing my morning suit and smoking-cap: Josephine, in the act of whipping a mayonnaise, would draw anxiously to the window. The baron, my galling and indispensable old Hohenfels, would have arrived and scolded. My home-circle

BIER UND BADEN.

was like a ring without its jewel, while I, an undenominated waif in search of a *visé*, was fluttering through the duchy of Baden. Thirty minutes passed, and the bath-house retained the silence of a ruined monastery, while outside, among the perfumes and shadows of twilight, there began to arise strains of admirable harmony. I looked out of the window. Some lanterns placed among the trees were already beginning to assert their light among the shadows of evening. A chorus of fresh and accurate voices was pouring forth from the garden, the pure young tenors and altos weaving their melodies like network over the sustained, vibrating, vigorous bass voices. It was the antiphony of the youthful promenaders to the drinkers, the diastole of the heart above the stomach, the *elisire d'amore* in rivalry with beer. Amid this scene I recognized my waiter, illuminated fitfully like some extraordinary firefly as he sprang into sight beneath the successive lanterns, and pouring out beer to right and left. To my indignant appeal he turned, lifting his head, and stood in that attitude, finishing a musical phrase which he was contributing to the chorus. Then he told me that my bath was being made ready. The Teutonic placidity of this youth confounded me. Quite disarmed, I closed the shutter, changed my linen in the dark, and drew on my gloves over a pair of hands that decidedly needed the disguise. The lateness of the hour alarmed me, and I fled down the stair in three jumps. At the bottom I met my musical waiter, still tranquilly singing, and armed with a linen wrapper and a hairbrush.

"What do I owe?" I asked.

"Is der Herr not going to take his bath?" asked this most leisurely of valets.

"No."

"Very well: it will be half a florin, including towels."

I gave him the half-florin, and was getting into my cab, when he came rambling up.

"And the palm-greaser," he cried, "the trinkgeld?"

In ten minutes I was at the offices of the national representative, but it was now dark, and the porter, without waiting for my question, told me that the offices were closed and everybody gone to the opera.

"The theatre!" I shouted to my charioteer.

The ticket-seller was asleep in his box, and was much astonished at my application for an orchestra-seat. The last act of some obscure German opera was being

AN EXHAUSTED TRAVELER.

shouted in full chorus. At Carlsruhe the theatre opens at five o'clock, and closes virtuously at half-past eight. There was no sign of my friend, no indication of a box for members of the diplomatic body. I was very hungry, and would willingly have re-entered the boulevards in search of a supper; but the express-train going toward Paris would start at ten-fifteen, and I could afford to think of nothing but my passport. I drove to the national office again, my new costume quite shipwrecked and foundered in perspiration.

I was more explicit with the porter this time. I asked if Mr. Sylvester Berkley had returned from the opera. I was answered by that functionary that Mr. Pairkley was living at present in the city of Heidelberg, where he was trying a diet of whey for the benefit of his liver.

I became flaccid with despair. I was

THE SUNNY GROVE.

without a refuge on the habitable globe; my slender provision of funds would be exhausted in paying for the carriage; I was unable even to seek the friend who for the moment represented to me both country and fortune. The driver, witness of my dejection and recipient of my history in part, proposed to me a temporary refuge in a private hotel on the avenue of Ettlingen, where I would find chambers by the day, and a family table. The landlady, he believed, was a Belgian and a widow.

We drew up before a small house of neat appearance. I was shown a chamber, where, no longer dreaming of supper, I fell across a cushion like an overthrown statue. I felt as if a good month must have passed since I possessed a home.

I had in pocket about thirty sous. The philosopher was right enough when he said, "Traveling lengthens one's life;" only he should have added, "It shortens one's purse."

On awakening next morning the linnets and finches communicated through the window a pleasanter sentiment. Nature was gay and inspiring on this lovely May-day. By a perversity quite natural with me, my letter to Berkley, which it was my first care to write and post, contained but a slight reflection of my woes. My need of a passport only appeared in a postscriptum, wherein I begged him to arrange that little affair for me in some way by correspondence. The bulk of my communication was a eulogy of May, of youth, of flowers, of birds, all of which were saluting me as I scribbled from the beautiful little grove outside my casement. Treating the diplomate as an intimate friend—a caprice of the moment on my part—I begged him to go back with me to Marly, promising him the joys described in old Thomas Randolph's invitation to the country:

> We'll seek a shade,
> And hear what music's made—
> How Philomel
> Her tale doth tell,
> And how the other birds do fill the choir;
> The thrush and blackbird lend their throats,
> Warbling melodious notes.
> We will all sport *enjoy*, which others but *desire*.

I engaged to furnish him his regimen of whey, and did not omit to quote from the same poem, apropos of that mild Anacreontic drink, the lines which happen to introduce his name:

> And drink by stealth
> A cup or two to noble *Barkley's* health.

"The cup," I continued, "shall be at once your toast and your medicine, and the whey shall be fresh. If you want to make a Tartar of yourself, and feed on koumiss, I will have the milk fermented." To the baron of Hohenfels I wrote with equal gayety, begging him to plant the stakes of his tent in my garden until my own nomadic career should be finished. A third letter, as my reader may imagine, was directed to the Rue Scribe, and addressed to the American banker, the beloved of all money-needing compatriots — Mr. John Munroe.

My letters committed to a domestic, I felt absolutely relieved from care. I breathed freely, and recovered all my self-possession. Sing loud, little birds! it is a comrade who listens to you.

With two days, perhaps three, of enforced leisure before me, I undertook in a singular spirit of deliberation the criticism of my surroundings. I began with my bed-chamber. It contained both a stove and a fireplace. The fireplace was like all other fireplaces, but not so the stove. Stark and straight, rising from floor to ceiling, it was fixed immovably in the wall, a pilaster of porcelain. No stove-door interrupted its enameled shaft: only a register of fretwork for the emission of heat, and quite dissociated from the cares of fire-building, relieved the ennui of this sybaritic length of polish. It was kindled—and that is the special merit of this famous invention—from without, in the corridor which borders the line of rooms. If you put the idea to profit, O overtoasted friends of Flemming, I shall not regret my forced inspection of Carlsruhe.

I would distinguish less honorably that small oblique looking-glass inserted in the bevel of the window-jamb, and common to all the dwellings of Carlsruhe—

THE MILK OF HUMAN KINDNESS.

a handy article, an entertaining distraction, a discreet but immoral spy, which places at your mercy all the mysteries of the public street. This contrivance, which enables you to see the world without being seen, certainly gives you a tempting advantage over the untimely caller or the impertinent creditor; but it encourages, in my opinion, a habit of vision better adapted to a sultan's seraglio than to the discreet eyes of Western folk.

This reflection, by which I satisfied my perhaps exalted moral sense, was no sooner made than I found myself peeping to right and to left in my double mirror, not without a lively sense of curiosity. At first I saw—what Flemming, indeed, was wont to see when he consulted the Fountain of Oblivion—only streets and moss-grown walls and trembling spires, like those of the great City of the Past, and children playing in the gardens like reverberations from one's lost youth. Soon a nearer image approached. From a troop of blond girls, who dragged after them little chariots resembling baby-wagons, one damsel drew apart, allowing the others to pass on. She neared my window. Who is the maiden with the anachronic baby-cart? She is the milkmaid of the country. Here in Germany Perrette does not poise her milk upon her head or weigh it in a balance, in order to afford by its overthrow a fable to La Fontaine. She can dream at her ease as she draws it behind her. My fair-haired neighbor paused. A tall lad thereupon emerged from the neighboring trees, and, replacing Perrette at her wagon, he fitted himself dexterously into her maiden dream and into the shafts of her equipage. As the avenue was deserted for the instant, his arm enlaced her figure, with the obvious and commendable purpose of sustaining her in her walk, and with his lips close to her smiling, rosy ones he contributed a gentle note to the hymeneal chorus that was twittered from the trees.

Who could remain long shut up from such an out-of-doors? Directly I was in the open air, scenting the fresh breath from the parks. I inspected the streets,

THE FLY-BRUSH.

the factories, the people, the houses. A prolonged and deliberate examination of Carlsruhe enables me to assert that it is the most easy-going, slow-paced, loitering, temporizing, procrastinating capital outside of Dreamland.

A young workingman was assisting some bricklayers in an extension adjacent to the foundry of Christofle and Company. I saw him going, with a slow and lounging pace, toward the brick-pile, stopping by the way to quench his thirst at a hydrant, whose stream was so slender that a good many applications of the cup of Diogenes were necessary to allay the heat concentred in the fellow's thick throat. Arrived finally at the heap of bricks, the goal of his promenade, he took up precisely six, and proceeded with a lordly, lounging step to bear them back to the masons. Then, folding his arms, he watched the imbedding of those bricks in their plaster with a sovereign calm like that of Vitellius eating figs at the combats of the gladiators. When he consented to take up again his serene march, it was the turn of the bricklayers to fold their arms. At each errand he consulted the hydrant, and the builders watched all his movements with sympathy and approval.

THE TALE OF BRICKS.

I photograph the moving figures in the street with the same simple fidelity which I have employed to represent the trouble-saving conveniences of my chamber. Take another hero, equally worthy of Capua. The placid personage who assisted me to a bath in my room was as happy a dullard as my waiter in the *Baden*, and both of them caressed their job as Narcissus caressed the fountain.

A large cart drew up before the door, containing twelve kegs, thoroughly bunged. Any stranger would take the load for one of beer, but a tub among the kegs acted as interpreter. The young man from the baths in the first place saw to his horse. He walked around it: the drive having heated the animal, he covered it with a cloth, and guaranteed its head against the flies with several plumes of foliage, beneath which Dobbin, blinded but content, showed only the paralytic flapping of his pendulous, negro-like lips. These indispensable cares despatched, the young man from the baths brought up the tub after a short gossip with the kitchen-maid, who was going out to market. He asked her if there were a stable attached where he could put up the horse during the taking of the bath: being answered in the negative, he then, with an almost painful inconsequence of argument, chucked the girl under the chin. He next inquired if she had any soap-fat. At length he consented to lumber up the steps with one of his little kegs: the tenacity of the bung was so exemplary that a long time was consumed in getting the advantage

THE KNIGHT OF THE BATH.

GANYMEDE.

over it, and the water on its part was but tardy in leaping toward the tub in a series of strangulations. This formula, interrupted by minute attentions to the horse, had to be repeated twelve times, and the bath, which commenced as a warm bath, received its guest as a cold one. Such was the result when to the languor of the individual was added the national complication of apparatus.

The deliberate spectator—or, if you will, the imprisoned spectator like myself, with his artificial leisure—asks himself how long a time was consumed by this little country of Baden, by this people so lumpish in its labor, so restricted in its movements, so friendly to its own ease, in building its elegant metropolis of mansions and palaces? There is something piquant in learning that the city is the hastiest construction on the continent. It only dates from the year 1715.

Carlsruhe reminds the American traveler of Washington. In place of the tortuous plan and picturesque inconvenience of the antique capitals, it offers a predetermined and courteous radiation of broad streets from the grand-ducal palace, much like the fan of avenues that spreads away from the Capitol building. Formal as it is, and recent as it is, Carlsruhe affords as pretty a legend as any fairy-founded city of dimmest ancestry.

The margrave Charles of Baden, hunter and warrior, returned from victory to bathe his soul in the sylvan delights of the chase. One day, as he coursed the stag in the Haardt Forest, he lay down with a sudden sense of fatigue, and fell asleep: an oak tree shadowed him with its broad canopies. Dreaming, he saw the green boughs separate, and in the zenith of the heavens descried a crown blazing with incredible jewels, and inscribed with letters that he felt rather than spelled: "This is the reward of the noble." All around the crown, hanging in air like sculptured cloudwork, spread

ARRESTED MOTION.

a splendid city with towers: a noble castle, with open portal and stairway inviting his princely feet, stood at the centre, and the spires of sacred churches still sought, as they seek on earth, to pierce the unattainable heaven. When he awoke his courtiers were around him, for they had searched and found their lord while he slept. He related his dream, and declared his ducal will to build on that very spot a city just as he had seen it, with a splendid palace for

THE PIPERS.

central point, and streets like the spokes of light that spread from the sinking sun. So he said, and gave his whole soul to building this graceful capital and developing it with the arts of peace; for heretofore he had thought only of war, and had meant to patch up a seat of government in the little town of Durlach.

The Haardtwald still spreads around Carlsruhe ("Charles's Rest") to the eastward, but the bracken and underbrush have given way to beaten roads, which prolong with perfect regularity the fan of streets. An avenue of the finest Lombardy poplars in Germany, the trees being from ninety to a hundred and twenty feet high, extends for two miles to Durlach. Around the city spread rich plum and cherry orchards, yielding the "lucent sirops" from which is distilled the famous Kirschwasser.

The reputation for drunkenness, in my opinion, has been very erroneously fastened upon the German population. During my sojourn in Carlsruhe I have paid many a visit to the beer-shops, from the petty taverns frequented by the poor to the lofty saloons where Ganymedes in white skirts shuffled with huge tankards through a perfect forest of orange trees in tubs; for, worse luck to my morals, I have not seen a single frightful example, not one individual balancing dispersedly over his legs. In the grand duchy of Baden the debauch is punished by a law of somewhat harsh logic, which commits to prison both drunkards and those who have furnished the wherewithal to excess. The common people form a nation of drinkers, not drunkards. The beer-tables are usually placed in the open air, with shelter for the patrons in case of bad weather. The out-door air

INCENSE AT THE ALTAR.

is almost indispensable to correct the evils which might proceed from such an artillery of pipes all fired in concert.

For Germany, if not a land of intoxication, is certainly one of fumigation. The face of a German is composed invariably of the following features: two eyes, a nose, a mouth, and a pipe. Whichever of these features is movable, the pipe at least is a fixture. Fortified by this vital organ, he lives, loves and moves.

PART VI.

SHALL AULD ACQUAINTANCE BE FORGOT?

MY first dinner in the avenue of Ettlingen followed upon the twelve-barreled bath, but was far from being so glacial a refreshment. As I descended, quite pink and glowing, I found eight or ten individuals in the dining-room. They were French and Belgians, and exchanged a lively conversation in half a dozen provincial accents. The servants too talked French in levying on the cook for provisions: for this, as I have since learned, the domestics of my snug little boarding-house were deemed somewhat pretentious by the serving-people of the vicinity, who considered the tongue of Paris a sort of court language, for circulation among aristocrats only, and supposed that even in France the hired folk all talked German. My reception at the cheerful board was as cordial as possible.

Placed opposite me, our young hostess was looking in my direction with an intentness that struck me as singular. My passport was uppermost in my mind. I was not, however, very uneasy, for the reply of Sylvester Berkley would soon arrive and put an official seal upon my

THE REGISTER.

standing. It occurred to me, however, that I was a traveler accompanied by no other baggage than a tin box and an umbrella, and introduced by a coachman who had no reason whatever for forming lofty notions of my respectability. The landlady, whom I had scarcely seen on my arrival, was pretty, neat and quick, and an argument suggested itself that seemed adapted to her station and habits. I was base enough to take out my watch, a very fine Poitevin, and make an advertisement of that pledge under pretence of comparing time with the mantel-clock. This precious manœuvre appeared quite successful.

Very soon my ideas of apprehension and defiance were followed by other thoughts of a very different kind. The expression of the youthful housekeeper was not only softened in continuing to watch me, but it took on a look of great kindness and good-humor—a look that the finest watch in the world would never have inspired. On my own side I furtively examined this gentle yet scrutinizing physiognomy. Surely those gentle glances and my own faded old eyes were not entire strangers.

When Winckelmann was filling the villa Albani with antiques, it often happened to him to clasp a fair Greek head in his arms and go pottering along from torso to torso till he could find a shoulder fit to support his lovely burden. Such was my exercise with this pleasant head in its neat cambric cap; but in place of consulting my memory with the proper coolness, I am afraid I questioned my heart.

Immediately after the coffee my pretty hostess, passing my chair, with a quick motion in going out made me a slight gesture. I followed her into a small office or ante-chamber adjoining. The furniture was very simple; the indicator, with a figure for every bell, decorated the wall in its cherry-wood frame; the keys, hanging aslant in rows, like points of interrogation in a letter of Sévigné's, formed a corresponding ornament; and a row of registers on the desk completed the furniture. One of these books she drew forward, opened and presented for my signature, still flashing over my face that intent but benevolent glance.

"Monsieur, have the goodness to inscribe your name, the place you came from, and that of your destination."

I took the pen, and, with the air of complying exactly and courteously with her demand, folded the quill into three or four lengths, and placed it weltering in ink within my waistcoat pocket. I was looking intently into my hostess's face.

I think no American can observe without peculiar complacency the neat artisanne's cap on the brows of a respectable young Frenchwoman. This cap is made of some opaque white substance, tender yet solid, and the theory of its existence is that it should be stainless and incapable of disturbance. It is the badge of an order, the sign of unpretending industry. The personage who wears it does not propose to look like a "dame:" she contentedly crowns herself with the tiara of her rank. Long generations of unaspiring humility have bequeathed her this soft and candid sign of distinction: as her turn comes in the line of inheritance she spends her life in keeping unsullied its difficult purity, and she will leave to her daughters the critical task of its equipoise. If she soils or rumples or tears it, she descends in her little scale of dignities and becomes an ouvrière. If she loses it, she is unclassed entirely, and enters the half-world. The porter's wife with her dubious mob-cap, and the hard, flaunting grisette with her melancholy feathers and determined chapeau, are equally removed from the white cap of the "young person." To maintain it in its vestal candor and proud sincerity is not always an easy task in a land where every careless student and idle nobleman is eager to tumble it with his fingers or to pin among its frills the blossom named love-in-idleness: Mimi Pinson has to wear her cap very close to her wise little head. To herself and to those among whom she moves nothing perhaps seems more natural than the successful carriage of this white emblem, triumphantly borne from age to age above the dust of labor and in the face of all kinds of temptation; but to the republican from beyond the seas it is a kind of sacred relic. The Yankee who knows only the forlorn aureoles of wire and greased gauze surrounding the sainted heads of Lowell factory-girls, and frowsy ones of New York bookbinders, is struck by the artisanne cap as by something exquisitely fresh, proud and truthful.

My landlady's cap was as far removed from pretence as from vulgarity. Her hair was brown, smooth, old-fashioned and nun-like. I looked at her hand, which, having replaced the pen, was inviting me with a gesture of its handsome squared fingers to contribute my autograph. I made my note, pausing often to look up at my beautiful writing-mistress: "PAUL FLEMMING, American: from Paris to Marly—by way of the Rhine."

I had not finished, when, lowering her pretty head to scrutinize my crabbed handwriting, she cried, "It is certainly he, the américain-flamand! I was certain I could not be mistaken."

"Do you know me then, madame?"

"Do I know you? And you, do you not recognize me?"

"I protest, madame, my memory for faces is shocking; and, though there are few in the world comparable with yours—"

She interrupted me with a gesture too familiar to be mistaken. A tumbler was on the desk filled with goose-quills. Taking this up like a bouquet, and stretching it out at arm's length to an imaginary passer-by, she sang, with a mischievous professional *brio*, "Fresh roses to-day, all fresh! White lilacs for the bride, and lilies for the holy altar! pinks for the button of the young man who thinks himself handsome. Who buys my bluets, my paquerettes, my marguerites, my pensées?"

It was strangely like something I well knew, yet my mind, confused with the baggage of unexpected travel, refused to throw a clear light over this fascinating rencounter.

The little landlady threw her head back to laugh, and I saw a small rose-colored tongue surrounded with two strings of pearls: "Very well, Monsieur Flemming! Have you forgotten the two chickens?"

It was the exclamation by which, in his neat tavern, I had recognized my brave old friend Joliet: it was impossible, by the same shibboleth, to refuse longer an acquaintance with his daughter.

My entertainer, in fact, was no other than Francine Joliet, grown from a little female stripling into a distracting pattern of a woman. Twelve years had never thrown more fortunate changes over a growing human flower.

The acquaintance being thus renew-

A VIRTUOSO.

ed, I could not but remember my last conversation with Joliet—his way of acquainting me with her absence from home, his mention of her godmother in Brussels, and his strange reticence as I pressed the subject. A slight chill, owing perhaps to the undue warmth of my admiration for this delicate creature, fell over my first cordiality. I asked a question or two, assuming a kind, elderly type of interest: "How do you find yourself here in Carlsruhe? Are you satisfactorily placed?"

"As well as possible, dear M. Flemming. I am a bird in its nest."

"Mated, no doubt, my dear?"

"No."

"You are not a widow, I hope, my poor little Francine?"

"No." She blushed, as if she had not been pretty enough before.

"They call you madame, you see."

"A mistress of a hotel, that is the usual title. Is it not the custom among the Indians of America?"

"The godmother who took care of you — you perceive how well I know your biography, my child—is she dead, then?"

"No, thank Heaven! She is quite well."

"She is doubtless now living in Carlsruhe?"

"No, at Brussels."

"Then why are you here? why have you quitted so kind a friend?"

My catechism, growing thus more and more brutal, might have been prolonged until bedtime, but on the arrival of a new traveler she left me there, with a pen in my hand and a quantity of delicious cobwebs in my head, saying gently, "I will see you this evening, kind friend."

The same evening, after a botanizing stroll in the adjoining wood—a treat that my tin box and I had promised each other—I found myself again with Francine. Full of curiosity as I was concerning her adventures, I determined that she should direct the conversation herself, and take her own pretty time to tell the more personal parts of the story.

The stage grisette is perpetually exploring the pockets of her apron. Francine, who wore a roundabout apron of a white and crackling nature, adorned her conversation by attending to the hem of hers. When she asked about my last interview with her father, she ironed that hem with the nail of her rosy little thumb; when she fell into reminiscences of her mother, she smoothed the apron respectfully and sadly; when she proposed a question or a doubt, she extracted little threads from the seam: at last, perfectly satisfied with the apron, she laid her two small hands in each other on its dainty snow-bank, and resigned herself to a perfect torrent of remarks about the horse, the van, the little cabin among the roses, the small one-eyed dog and the two chickens. Conversation, a thing which is manufactured by an American girl, is a thing which takes possession of a French girl.

All the while I remained uninstructed as to why my little Francine had left her protectress, why she was keeping house at Carlsruhe, and on what understanding her customers called her madame.

I was obliged to take next day a long alterative excursion among the trees of the Haardtwald: in fact, her gentle warmth, her freshness, her nattiness, the very protection she shed over me, were working sad mischief to my peace of mind. I came upon an old shepherd, who, with his music-book thrown into a bush in front of him, was leaning back against a tree and drawing sweet sounds out of a cornet-à-piston.

"Even so," I said, "did Stark the Viking hear the notes of the enchanted horn teaching every tree he came to the echo of his true-love's name."

But the churlish shepherd, the moment he caught sight of me, put up his pipe, whistled to his dogs and rejoined the flock. I was dissatisfied with his unsocial retreat. I felt, with renewed force, that a note was lacking to the full harmony of my life, and I threw myself upon a bank. I tried not to see the artificial roads of the forest, alive with city carriages. I believed myself lost in a primeval wood, and I examined the state of my heart. I perceived with concern that that organ was still lacerated. The languid, musical pageant of my youth streamed toward me again through the leafy aisles, and I remembered my high aspirings, my poems, my ideals: the floating vision of a Dark Ladye passed or looked up at me through the broken waves of Oblivion; she listened to my rhapsodies with the old puzzling silence; she confided to me certain Sibylline leaves out of her diary; then she receded, cold and unresponsive, a statue cut out of a shadow. I was obliged to untie my cravat. Finally, I fell asleep and dreamed of Mary Ashburton crowned with the neat workwoman's cap of Francine Joliet. I returned to dinner considerably exalted, and just touched with rheumatism.

The soup was glacial, the roast was steaming, the conversation was geographical. "Pray, M. Flemming," said my neighbor (he had been stealing a look at the register of visitors' names), "can cattle be wintered out of doors as far north as Pennsylvania, or only up to Virginia?"

"Pray," said another, "is not New York situated between the North River and the Hudson?"

The prayer of a third made itself audible: "Ought we to say ' Delightful Wyoming,' after Campbell, or Wyoming?"

"We ought to eat with thankfulness the good things set before us," I replied, with some presence of mind. "Excuse me, gentlemen," I added, to carry off my vivacity, "but I think informing conversation is a bore until after the nuts and raisins. A Danish proverb says that he who knows what he is saying at

DELIGHTS OF THE VERLOBTEN.

a feast has but poor comprehension of what he is eating. On my way hither, breakfasting at Strasburg, I enjoyed a lesson in geography, and I aver that though the lesson was elementary, I breakfasted very badly."

"Who was the teacher?" asked the explorer of Wyoming, a German, in the tone of a man to whom no professor of Geography could properly be a stranger.

"The teacher," I answered with a smile, "was one Fortnoye—"

I did not finish my sentence. At that name, Fortnoye, a kind of electric movement was communicated around the board. Every eye sought the face of Francine, who, troubled and confused, fell upon the cutlet placed before her and cut it feverishly into flinders. Evidently there was a secret thereabouts. When coffee was on, I applied myself to satisfying the topographic doubts of my neighbors, but the name of the geographical professor was approached no more.

When dinner was over, and only two stranded Belgians remained at table, discussing whether the Falls of Niagara plunge from the United States into Canada, or from Canada into the United States, I stole into the narrow office, believing I should see Francine.

She was not there, but the register was lying on the desk. I fell to turning the leaves over furiously: I felt that I was on the trail of Fortnoye. I was not long in amassing a quantity of discoveries. Going back to the previous year, I found the signature of Fortnoye in March and April; in July and September, Fortnoye bound up and down the Rhine; in the depth of the winter, Monsieur Tonson-Fortnoye come again! Evidently one of the most frequent guests of my delicate Francine was the interpreter of *Cosmos*

THE CHURCHYARD LOVER.

in Strasburg, the white-bearded mystifier of the champagne-cellar, the finest singing-voice in Épernay.

Toward ten o'clock, as I paced the little grove called the Oak Wood, I saw at the miniature lake four persons, who were regaining the bank after trying to detach the little boat moored by the shore. They were just the four from our social table with whom I best agreed. I joined the party, and, hooking now a friendly arm to the elbow of one, now to that of another, I soon obtained all they had to communicate on the subject which occupied my mind. Each knew Fortnoye intimately: the result of my quadratic amounted to the following:

First. Fortnoye, educated at the Polytechnic School in Paris, is a man of grave character and profound learning.

Second. Fortnoye is a roysterer, latterly occupied in extending the connection of a champagne-house at Épernay. He is a Bohemian, even a poet: he can rhyme, but strictly in the interests of commerce—he composes only drinking-songs.

Third. Fortnoye is an exploded speculator, dismissed from the French Board: obliged to beat a retreat to Belgium, he soon found himself in Baden, where he had good luck at the green table shortly before the war.

Fourth, and last. (This was from the man of Wyoming.) Fortnoye only retreated to Belgium as a refuge for his demagogic opinions. He belongs to the innermost circle of the Commune and to all the French and Italian secret associations. He is represented in the background of several of Courbet's pictures. He has been everywhere: in Italy he joined the society of the Mary Anne, where he met the celebrated Lothair. This order has a branch called the Society of Pure Illumination. If he has liberty to return into France, it is because he is connected with the detective police.

The information, extensive as it was, did not altogether satisfy me. I made little of the inconsistencies betrayed by the various counsels of the Areopagus, but I closed the whole solemnity with one crucial interrogatory: "What the dickens does Fortnoye come prowling around Francine Joliet's house for?"

The answer was not calculated to please me: "She is young and attractive: Fortnoye advanced the funds to set her up in the house."

But my morose thoughts were distracted by the scene around us. The moon burst up above the trees of the Oak Wood—a fine ample German moon, like a Diana of Rubens. Close to our sides passed numerous young couples, holding hands, clasping waists, chattering gayly, or walking in silence with a blonde head laid on a burly shoulder. One of my companions pointed out a specially stalwart and graceful young apprentice, whose elbow, supported on a rustic bench, was bent around a mass of beautiful golden hair.

"An eligible *verlobter*," said he.

I thought of Perrette and the tall young man who had helped pull her milk-cart. My friend continued: "Betrothal hereabouts is a serious institution. The girl who loses her *verlobter* becomes a widow. Woe betide her if she dreams of replacing him too early! She will find herself followed by ill looks and contemptuous tongues: she even runs the risk of having nobody to marry better than a dead

man, if we may believe the history of Bettina of Ettlingen."

"The history of Bettina of Ettlingen? That sounds like the title to a ballad."

"It is a recent history, which you would take for a legend of the twelfth century."

I cannot help it. In face of that word

ON THE FIRST STEP.

legend my mind stops and stares rigidly like a pointer dog. The moment was favorable for a good story: the sky was covered with flocked clouds, behind which the ample German moon, shorn of half its brightness, took suddenly the pale gilded tint of sauerkraut. The wandering lovers, half effaced in the gloom, looked like straying shades in an Elysium.

"Ettlingen is between Carlsruhe and Rastadt, an hour's walking as you go to Kehl. The flowers grow there without thinking about it, and sow their own seed. It is therefore a simple thing to be a gardener, and Bettina's father, the florist, attended entirely to his pipe, leaving the cares of business to his apprentice, whose name was Nature. Bettina, as became the daughter of a gardener, was a kind of rose: Wilhelm, the baker's young man, would have thrown himself into the furnace for her. But there came along Fritz, the dyer, who had been in France and who wore gloves. She continued a while to promenade with Wilhelm under the chestnut trees which surround the fortifications of Ettlingen, but one night she suddenly withdrew her hand: 'You had better find a nicer girl than I am: I do not feel that I could make you happy.' Wilhelm disappeared from the country. His departure, which was the talk of Ettlingen, caused Bettina more remorse than regret. For six months she shut herself up: then, hearing nothing of her lover, she reappeared shyly on the promenade, divested of rings, ear-drops and ornaments. The beautiful Fritz, in his loveliest gloves, intercepted her beneath the chestnuts, and, armed with her father's consent, proposed himself for her *verlobter*.

"'Not yet,' she answered: 'wait till I wear my flowers again.'

"In Germany, as in Switzerland and Italy, natural flowers are indispensable to a young girl's toilet. To appear at an assembly without a blooming tuft at the corsage or in the hair is to indicate that the family is in mourning, the mother sick or the lover conscripted.

"With an exquisite natural sense, Bettina, daughter of a gardener, would never

THE LEGAL PROFESSION AND PROFESSION OF FRIENDSHIP.

wear any flowers but wild ones. About this time there was a grand fair at Durlach: almost all Ettlingen went there, and Bettina too, but as spectatress only, and without her flowers.

"The dances which animated the others made her sad. She left the ball and wandered on the hillside. There, beneath the hedge of a sunken road, she recognized her beauteous Fritz. Poor Fritz! he was refusing himself the pleasure of the dance which he might not partake with her. Ah, the time for temporizing is over! Bettina determines that to-day, in the eyes of every one, they shall dance together, and he shall be recognized as her *verlobter*. She looks hastily around for flowers. The hill is bare, the road is stony: an enclosure at the left offers some promise, and Bettina enters.

"It was a cemetery. Animated with her new resolve, she thought little of the profanation, and crowned herself with flowers from the nearest grave. In an hour the villagers from Ettlingen saw her leaning on Fritz's shoulder in the waltz. That night the shade of Wilhelm stood at her bed-head: 'You have accepted the flowers growing on my grave and nourished from my heart. I am once more your *verlobter*.'

"Next day Fritz came, radiant, with a silver engagement-ring, which he was to exchange for that on Bettina's finger, returned by Wilhelm at his departure. But the ring was gone. At night Wilhelm reappeared, and showed the ring on his finger. Some time passed, and Bettina lost a good part of her beauty, distracted as she was between the laughing Fritz in the daytime and the pale Wilhelm at night. She was a sensible girl, however, and persuaded herself, with Fritz's assistance, that the vision was created by a disordered fancy. But she caused inquiry to be made about the grave in the cemetery at Durlach: the answer came: 'Under the first stone in the line at the right of the gate lies the body of Wilhelm Haussbach of Ettlingen, where he followed the trade of baker.'

"Then she knew that she had robbed her lover's grave to adorn herself for a new *verlobter*. After this the ghost of Wilhelm began to invade her promenades with Fritz, and she walked evening after evening beneath the chestnuts between her two lovers.

"The gardener's daughter never looked fairer than on her wedding-day. Armed with all her resolution, and filled with love for Fritz, she presented herself at the altar. The priest began to recite the sacramental words, when he came to a pause at the sight of Bettina, pale and wild-eyed, shivering convulsively in her bridal draperies.

"Wilhelm was again at her side, kneeling on the right, as Fritz on the left. He was in bridegroom's habit, and he offered a bouquet of graveyard-flowers—the white immortelle and the forget-me-not. When Fritz rose and put the ring on her finger she felt an icy hand draw the token off and replace it by another. At this, overcome with terror, and making a wild gesture of rejection both to right and left, she ran shrieking out of the church.

"Such is the true and authentic story of Bettina," concluded my narrator. "You may see Bettina any day at Ettlingen, a yellow old maid forty years of age. Every Sunday she goes to mass at Durlach, where she employs the rest of the day in tending flowers on a grave, the first grave in the line to the right of the gateway."

I returned to the house with this grim and tender little idyll crooning through my brains. I took my key and bed-candle, and asked the porter if a letter had arrived for me from Sylvester Berkley. Not a line! This silence became inconvenient. Not only did I rely upon Berkley for my passport, the certificate of my character, but likewise for the revictualing of my purse. As I passed the small throne-room of Francine, where she sat vis-à-vis with all her keys and bells, a light, a presence, an amicable little nod informed me that a friend was there for me, and sent a bath of warm and comfortable emotion all over my poor old heart.

It was late. Francine, at a little velvet account-book, was executing some fairy-like and poetical arithmetic in purple ink. I had the pleasure, before a half hour had passed, of making her commit more than one error in her columns, do violet violence to the neatness of her book, and adorn her thumb-nail with a comical tiny silhouette. My gossip, which had this encouraging and proud effect, was commenced easily upon familiar subjects, such as the old rose-garden and the chickens, but branched imperceptibly into more personal confidences. I found myself growing strangely confidential. Soon I had sketched for Francine my life of opulent loneliness, my cook and my old valet, my philosopher's den at Marly, my negligent existence at Paris, without family, country or obligations.

EFFUSION.

Her good gray eyes were swimming with tears, I thought. With a look of perfect natural sweetness she said, "To live alone and far from kin and fatherland, that is not amusing. It is like one of the small straight sticks of rose my father would take and plant in the sand in a far-away little red pot."

A delicious vignette, I confess, began to be outlined in my fancy. I cannot describe it, but I know Francine was in the middle repairing a stocking, while my own books and geographical notes, in a state of dustlessness they had never known actually, formed a brown bower around her. Somewhere near, in an old secretary or in a grave, was buried the ideal of an earlier, haughtier love, wrapped up in a stolen ribbon or pressed in a book.

She continued simply, "I am very much alone myself. Without the visits of Monsieur Fortnoye I should be dead of ennui. I am so glad to find you know him, monsieur!"

This jarred upon me more than I can say. I assumed, as one can at my age, an air of parental benevolence, in which I administered my dissatisfaction: "Fortnoye is a roysterer, a squanderer, a wanderer and a pétroleur. At your age, my child, you are really imprudent."

SELF-CONTROL.

"He is a little wild, but he is young himself. And so good, so generous, so kind! I owe him everything."

"On what conditions?" said I, more severely perhaps than I meant. "Your relations, my daughter, are not very clear. Is he then your *verlobter?*"

She looked at me with an expression of stupefaction, then buried her face in her hands: "He my intended! Has he ever dreamed of such a thing? Am I not a poor flower-girl?"

And she was sobbing through her fingers.

My nights were sweet at Carlsruhe. My slumber was ushered in with those delicious dream-sketches that lend their grace to folly. Each morning I wondered what surprise the day would arrange for me.

The little wood was hidden from my window by an early fog: the birds were silent. I was meditating on my singular position, in pawn as it were under the care of Joliet's good daughter, when I heard my name pronounced at the bottom of the stairs. It was Sylvester Berkley.

The briskness of our friendships depends on the time when — the place where. To men in prison a familiar face is the next thing to liberty.

Some years ago I had an absurd dispute with a neighbor about a party-wall at Passy, and was obliged to go to the Palace of Justice at ten every morning for a week. My forced intercourse with those solemn birds in black plumage had a singular effect on me. While among them I felt as if cut off from my species, and visiting with Gulliver some dreadful island peopled with mere allegories. As the time passed I grew worse: I dragged myself to the Cité with horror, and before returning home was always obliged to wash out my brains by a short stroll in Notre Dame or amongst the fine glass of the Sainte Chapelle. One day, pacing the pale and shuffling corridors of the palace, waiting for an unpunctual lawyer, and regarding the gowns and caps around me with insupportable hate, at the turning of a passage—oh happiness!—a face was revealed in the distance, the face of a friend, the face of an old neighbor. At the bright apparition I made an involuntary sign of joy: the owner of the face seemed no less pleased. We walked toward each other, our hands expanded. All of a sudden a doubt seemed to strike us both at the same moment: he slackened his pace, I slackened mine. We met: we had never done so before. It was a little mistake. We saluted each other slightly and gravely, and separated once more, as wise in our looks as that irreproachable hero who, after marching up the hill with his men, pocketed his thoughts and marched down again.

My meeting with Berkley Junior was not precisely similar, but connected with the same feelings and associations. I dashed down four steps at a time, precipitated myself on him like a bird of prey, and wrung his hands again and again with fondest violence.

Now, up to that date my relations with Sylvester Berkley had been of a frigid and formal description. I had met him two or three times with his hearty old relation, and had borne away the distinct impression that he was a prig. While the uncle would breakfast in his tub, like Diogenes, off simple bones and cutlets, Sylvester ate some sort of a mash made of bruised oats: while the nephew made an untenable pretension to family honors, the elder talked familiarly of the porcelain trade, freely alluding to the youth as a piece of precious Sèvres that had cracked.

He met my advances with a calmness, imprinted with astonishment, that recalled me to myself. Against such a refrigerator my heart and fancy recovered their proper level: I had been caressing an iceberg in a white cravat. I examined my emotions, and found, to my shame, that my warmth had a selfish origin in the fact that I was alone in Carlsruhe, greatly in need of a passport and a purse.

"Do you intend shortly to quit the archducal seat?" asked Sylvester, by way of an agreeable remark.

"I have the strongest obligations to be at home," I returned. "I only await your kind assistance about my passport."

"It is expected at the office, but I fear it will not be received in time for you to take the next train. I fear we shall be obliged to keep you with us until thirty minutes past one."

He conferred on me, with his neck and his hand, a salute which had the effect of being made from a distant window. Then he departed.

To ask such a man for money was not easy. I dressed myself and marched in great haste to the gay quarter of the town, having made up my mind to depend on the mercies of the chief jeweler and the merits of my Poitevin watch. It had cost a thousand francs, and would surely, after many a service rendered, help me now to regain my home.

Another disappointment—not a pawnbroker to be found in Carlsruhe! I was ready to look upon myself as a fixture in the town, when a brilliant idea flashed upon me. One of my neighbors at table was transportation-agent at the railway dépôt. What so opportune for me as a credit on the railway company? With his recommendation my watch would surely be security enough.

Delighted with the thought, and with my own cleverness in originating it, I made briskly for the Ettlingen Gate, before which the road passes. Glancing at the clock on the dépôt, I regulated first my watch by the time of the place, in order that no doubt might be cast on

LOSING TIME.

its perfect regularity. I was holding it in my hand, my eyes still riveted on the great clock, as I stepped over the nearest rails. A shout, mixed with imprecations, was audible. My coat was seized by a vigorous fist, I was rudely pushed, my watch escaped, and the train from Frankfort, which was just entering the dépôt, only rendered it to my hands crushed, peeled and pounded. Instead of a thousand francs, my old friend would hardly bring five dollars.

After such a catastrophe what remained for me to do? Evidently to humble my pride and beg an obolus of young Berkley. I represented to myself that the victory over my own false shame was worth many watches, and I began to compose a little speech intended for his ear, in which I compared myself to Dante at the convent door.

I found him in his office clasping a hand-valise. "I am about to go away by your train," he said, without waiting for me to speak or remarking my shabby-genteel expression of heroism. He added, as he handed me a great sealed envelope, "There is your passport. Nothing imperative requires my stay here: I shall accompany you, then, as far as the station of Oos, and while you are continuing your route toward your beloved metropolis, I will go and finish my leave of absence at Baden-Baden, where I am claimed by certain conditions of my liver."

I was so nervous and uncertain of myself that this little change in the horizon upset me completely. For the life of me I could not, at that moment, and at the risk of seeing him drop his bag and rain its contents over the official courtyard, rehearse my awkward accident and disreputable beggary. On the other hand, it was much to gain a friendly companion and pass arm-in-arm with him to the ticket-office. Leaving every other plan uncertain, I determined to start from Carlsruhe in his diplomatic shadow.

I dashed with surprising agility into the house to ask for my account with Francine. I was about to explain that I would quickly settle with her from Paris, when the thoughtful little woman anticipated me. "Monsieur Flemming," she said, with her sweet supplicating air," you left the city without meaning it. If you would like a little advance, monsieur, I am quite well supplied just now. Dispose of me: I shall be so thankful!"

The money of Fortnoye! the thought was impossible. It was impossible to resist taking her bright brown head between my hands and secreting a kiss somewhere in the laminations of the artisanne cap.

"Dear infant! I shall be an unhappy old fellow if I do not see you again very soon."

—And I was off, dragged by those obligations of the time-table which have no tenderness toward human sentiment.

At one o'clock I was at the railway with Sylvester. I was uncertain of my plans, and the confusion of the dépôt added nothing to the clearness inside my head. Berkley advanced first to the ticket-seller's window. "A first-class place for Baden-Baden," said he.

GRAND DUKE'S PALACE, BADEN.

"How many?" briskly asked the clerk, seeing us together.

At that moment Sylvester heard a ghostly voice at his ear: "You may get a couple." The voice was mine.

Berkley got them and paid. I had reflected that my letter of credit from Munroe & Co. would undoubtedly be drawn on Baden-Baden, and had suddenly taken a resolution to try the effect of the springs on my unfortunate stoutness.

We got down at the Gasthaus zum Hirsch, but I had already sold the ruins of my chronometer, and was twenty-five francs the richer for the transaction.

I cannot call Baden-Baden a city: it is a stage. It is a perpetually set scene for light opera. Everything seems dressed up and artificial, and meant to be viewed, as it were, in the glare of the footlights. But instead of the shepherds in white satin who ought to be the performers in this ingenious theatre, it is the unaccustomed stranger who is forced into the position of actor. As he toils up the steep and slovenly streets, faced with shabby buildings that crack and blacken behind their ill-adjusted fronts of stucco and distemper, he cheapens rapidly in his own view: he feels painfully like the hapless supernumerary whom he has seen mounting an obvious step-ladder behind a screen of rock-work on his way to a wedding in the chapel or a coronation in the Capitol. The difference is, that here the permission to play his rôle is paid for by the performer.

But I, as I sat hugging my knee in the hotel bed-room, was possessed by loftier feelings. If there is one faculty which I can fairly extol in myself, it is that of displaying true sentiment in false situations. My thoughts, with incredible agility, went back to Francine. A knock came at the door, and my emotions received a chill: my visitor could be none but Berkley, in whose face I should see a reminder that I owed him for my car-fare.

In place of frigid politeness, however, the diplomatist wore all that he knew of good-fellowship and Bohemianism. He was now clad in tourists' plaid, and stood upon soles half an inch thick—a true Englishman on his travels.

"Come, old boy!"—old boy, indeed!—"you must taste the pleasures of Baden-Baden: it is but four o'clock, and we can see the Trinkhalle, the Conversations-Haus, and plenty besides before dinner. Is there any place in particular where you would like to go?"

I looked solemnly at him. "I would fain visit the Alt-Schloss," I said.

"With all my heart!" replied Sylvester, tapping his legs and admiring his boots. This unpromising comrade was wearing better than I expected.

THE WOOD-PATH.

SCENE OF MATTHISSON'S POEM IMITATING GRAY'S "ELEGY."

"Shall we have a carriage?" he pursued. At this question my face contracted as by the effect of a nervous attack. I thought of the few pence I possessed. I assumed the determined pedestrian.

"For shame!" I cried: "it is but three miles. Where are your tourist muscles? I should like to walk."

"Nothing simpler," said the man of facile views: "we shall do it within the hour."

I breathed again. We set off. We had before us cliffs and hills, with small Gothic towers printed on the blue of the sky; but the mountain-path beneath our steps was sanded, graveled, packed, rolled, weeded, and provided with coquettish sofas at every hundred steps. I, who happened that afternoon to feel the emotions of Manfred, would gladly have exchanged these detestable conveniences for precipices, storms and eagles.

"How ridiculous," I said with a little temper, "to go to a ruin by way of the boulevards!"

"Ah," said my companion of complaisant manners, "you like Nature? It is but the choosing."

And Berkley, perfectly acquainted with the locality, directed our steps into a narrow path hardly traced through the woods. Here at least were flowers and grass and sylvan shadows. No sooner did I smell the balm of the pine trees than my heart resigned itself, with exquisite indecision, to the thoughts of Francine Joliet and the memories of Mary Ashburton. I glanced at Berkley: he seemed, in Scotch clothes, a little less impenetrable than he had appeared in white cravat and dress-gloves. I cannot restrain my confidences when a man is near me: I buttonholed Sylvester, and I made the plunge. "I used to talk of the Alt-

"WINE OR BEER!"

Schloss," I murmured, "with one whom I have lost."

"Ah, I comprehend: with my late uncle, perhaps."

"No, sir, not with any cynic in a tub, but with a maiden in her flower. It was one of the best points I made with Miss Ashburton."

"The Alt-Schloss is indeed a picturesque construction," said the diplomate, by way of generally inviting my confidence.

"We were conversing about the poems of Salis and Matthisson," I pursued. "I had in my pocket a little translation of Salis's song entitled 'The Silent Land,' and endeavored to bend the dialogue in a suitable direction, but these allusions are incredibly hard to introduce in conversation, and we happened to stray upon Baden-Baden. I asked Miss Ashburton if she had been here, and she answered, 'Yes, the last summer.' 'And you have not forgotten?' I suggested— 'The old castle,' she rejoined. 'Of course not. What a magnificent ruin it is!'"

"What tact your friend displayed," said Berkley, "to feign utter unconsciousness of the green tables, and see nothing but ruins in Baden-Baden!"

"Permit me to say," I replied quickly, "that it is not agreeable to me to have that lady alluded to, however distantly, in connection with gambling-tables. The Ashburtons had been probably drinking the waters, for her mother was noticeably stout and florid. But to continue with the poets. I explained to her that the ruins of the Alt-Schloss had suggested to Matthisson a poem in imitation of an English masterpiece. Matthisson made a study of Gray's 'Elegy,' and from it produced his 'Elegy on the Ruins of an Ancient Castle.' Miss Ash-

ENTRANCE TO THE ALT-SCHLOSS.

burton became nationally enthusiastic, and said she should like very much to see the poem. Her wish was usually my law, but the translation of the other song being in my pocket, I was obliged to palm it off upon her; and after conceding that Matthisson had written his 'Elegy' with unwonted inspiration, I sailed in upon that tide of feeling—with a slight inconsequence, to be sure—and

declaimed my version from Salis. Miss Ashburton, sir, was obliged to turn away to hide her tears."
"I used to hear from my uncle of your attachment," said Sylvester, with his politest air of condolence, "and I assure you my opinion ever has been that your feelings did you honor. Nothing, in my view, is so becoming to gray hairs and the evening of life as fidelity to a first passion."
"Lord forgive you, Berkley!" I exclaimed, startled out of all self-possession by his impertinence. "What on earth do you mean? You are completely ignorant of what you are talking about. I have hardly any gray hairs, and some excellent constitutions are gray at thirty. You are partly bald yourself: I know it from the way you turn up your love-locks. And it was not Miss Ashburton I was talking about. That is, if I did derive my reminiscences from her, it was with an object of a very different character at the end of the perspective. I have adopted other views; that is, I have lately had presented to my mind—"

"KELLNER!"

With these rhetorical somersaults, like the flappings of a carp upon the straw, did I express the mental distractions I was suffering from, and the tugs at my heart respectively administered by Francine's cap-strings and Mary Ashburton's shadowy tresses. Berkley, diplomatically approving the landscape before us, would not get angry, would not be insulted, and offered no prise to my difficult temper.
"Tell me now, Sylvester," said I after a few minutes' silence. "You are young, yet you have seen the world. What is the best refuge, in your view, for a man of delicate sentiments and of ripe age? Would you recommend such a person to shut himself up for ever in a hermitage of musty books, and to flirt there eternally with the memories of his young loves, who are become corpulent matrons or angular maids? Or, don't you think, now, that an autumnal attachment—provided some sweet and healthy intelligence comes in contact with his own—is a capital thing in its way? The crackling fireside instead of the lovers' walk? The perfection of rational comfort subservient to, rather than dominating, his early dreams? Respectful affection, fidelity and fondest care as the conditions surrounding one's character, and upholding it in its best symmetry? Cannot the poet think better if his body is kept snug? Cannot the man of feeling remember better if his slippers are toasted and his buttons sewed? In fact, is not one's faith to a beloved ideal best shown by acquiring a fresh standing-point to see it from?"

"No doubt Hamlet's mother thought so," said Sylvester rather brutally, "and married King Claudius solely to brighten her ideal of her first husband." A more appropriate remark, it seemed to me, might have been found to chime in with my speculations. "But here," pursued the statesman, compromisingly, "are old memories protected by modern conveniences. Here is the 'Repose of Sophie.'"

We had mounted a terrace from whose eminence the whole spread of the valley was visible. Profanation! No sooner had we attained the plateau than a covered gallery appeared, and a Teutonic voice was heard with the familiar inquiry, "Will the gentlemen take wine or beer?"

Was ever a man of delicacy and feeling so ruthlessly treated as I? To be tempted by circumstances into pouring out one's most intimate confessions to an icy person to whom one owes money, and then to have even this imperfect confidence interrupted by a tavern-waiter in an apron! Miserable hireling! give us solitude and meditation, not beer!

Flying the "Repose of Sophie" without the concession of a glance, we mounted toward the ancient castle, whose ruins seemed ready to roll on us down the hillside. It was indeed romantic. The wind, in plaintive, melodious tones, searched our ears as it came perfumed from the tufted walls. We penetrated through a scene of high and mossy rocks, bound in the lean embrace of knotted ivy, and finally by a dismantled postern we intruded into the castle. Sacrilege again! The stone-masons were tranquilly working here and there, solidifying old ruins and very probably fabricating new ones. The wind, whose sighing we had admired, was the cat-like harmony of the æolian harps: these harps were artlessly stretched across each of the old vaulted windows. We arrived at the high portal of the ancient manor, a genuine Roman construction of Aurelius Aquensis — a gateway with a round arch: it was obstructed by hired cabs, by whole herds of venal donkeys saddled and bridled, and by holiday-makers of Baden in Sunday clothes preserved for ten or fifteen years. The old pile itself is transformed into a hostelry. Gray was wrong: the paths of glory lead not to the grave, but to the *gasthaus;* and Matthisson could have imitated the "Elegy" about as well in the gaming-hall as among these rejuvenated ruins.

The modern idea of a wood is a graveled chess-board on a large scale, flooded at night with gas: the modern idea of a ruin is a dancing-floor, with a few patched arches and walls lifted between the wind and our nobility. We shave the weeds away and produce a fine English turf: we root up the brambles and eglantines which might tear the skirts of the ladies. Our lovers, our poets and romancers must fly to distant glades if they would not walk in the shade of trees that have been transplanted.

I was considering the sorry triumph of the stage-machinists of Baden-Baden, when Berkley, who had disappeared, came in sight again. Our dinner, he said, was ready—ready in the guards' hall. I retreated with a sudden cry of alarm. I had rather dine at the hotel; I had rather not dine at all; I was not in the least hungry. It was the emptiness of my pocket that caused this sudden fullness of the stomach. Berkley made light of my objections.

"Listen! You can hear from this mountain the dinner-bells of the city. We should arrive too late. Although you hate restored castles, you need not refuse to dine with me in one."

The noble hall was a scene of vulgar festivity, where the ubiquitous kellner,

TYROLEAN.

racing to and fro with beer and plates of sausage, solved the problem of perpetual motion. It was not easy, in such circumstances, to maintain the flow of poetic association, but I accomplished the feat in a measure. As the shades of evening closed around the hill, and the bells of twenty dining-tables ascended to us through the still air, I thought of Gray's curfew—of that glimmering Stoke-Pogis landscape that faded into immortality on his sight. I thought of Matthisson's "Elegy" on this forlorn old dandy of a castle. I thought of the sympathetic chest-notes with which I read to Mary Ashburton the "Song of the Silent Land."

I thought of Francine, and of the condition of base terror I was in when I ran away from her with the man who momentarily represented my solvency, my credit and my respectability. May the foul fiend catch me, sweet vision, if I do not find thee soon again! A Tyrolean, who entered by stealth, persuaded a heart-rending lamentation to issue from his wooden trumpet: although the acid sounds proceeding from this terrible whistle set my teeth on edge and caused me at first to start off my seat, yet I rewarded him with such a competency in copper as made his eyes emerge from his face. A singing-girl and some blonde bouquet-sellers had equal cause to rejoice in my generosity. It is when a gentleman is landed finally on his coppers that he becomes penny-liberal. I glanced defiance at Berkley, my creditor, as I showered largess on these humble poets.

We descended under the stars, and I began to think that illuminated gravel-roads were, at night, susceptible of some apology. We returned to the city by easy stages, with a halt at the "Repose of Sophie." At the hotel there was given me, re-directed in the pretty hand of Francine, an unlimited credit from Munroe & Co. on the house of Meyer in Baden-Baden. I was a freeman once more.

PART VII.

THE SEDUCTIONS OF BADEN-BADEN.

THE ANCIENTS AND THE NEWS.

THE supreme delight we take in being racked, tortured and suspended over chasms by the fickle tenure of a rotten plank is one of the most unselfish traits of human nature. For my part, I have never been so happy as when held, by the strong power of imagination, right over the depths of a mediæval *oubliette*, at the bottom of which the roaring of the sea or of a brace of gor- mandizing lions was distinctly audible. The first question asked by Paul Flemming of the baron of Hohenfels, when at Heidelberg, was one about that tradition of the castle according to which Louis le Débonnaire was frightened by an apparition of Satan and the Virgin into delivering up his brother Frederick to the two Black Knights representing the Vehm-Gericht. "Ha! that is grand,"

I said, inexpressibly refreshed with the allusion to the thrilling Vehm-Gericht. "Tell me the whole story quickly, for

ELICITING TRUTH.

I am curious as a child." Ah! that indispensable Vehmic Council — true grammar-school in which the genius of Radcliffe and Ainsworth was formed— was there ever a contrivance so admirably adapted for pleasantly crisping the scalp and icing the veins! I am not ashamed to say that even in these latter years of mine there are certain stormy evenings when I draw forth the coals over the hearth, practice my geomancy, lock out all interlopers, and invoke the powerful Wizard of the North. He plunges me into a dream that is the very acme of sweet terror: a voluptuous swimming sensation overcomes me as my bed, in whose integrity I should elsewhere have perfect faith, sinks down, down, down, fathoms deep. The damps of dungeons are around me: around me also are black and awful forms, from one of which a solemn voice proceeds, asking if I know where I am. I am drilled in my lesson: "I believe that I am before the Unknown or Secret Tribunal called the Vehm-Gericht."

"Then are you aware," answers the judge, "that you would be safer if you were suspended by the hair over the abyss of Schaffhausen?"

I enjoy it immensely, for I have recognized the voice, slightly broken with inward laughter, of the Wizard himself. I know perfectly well that he cannot afford to lose a hero in the very middle of the second volume, and I know, too, that he is a dear old hypocrite of a mediæval, with a mask of terror and a heart of butter. "Now, by my halidom!" says the great Vehmic Wizard in his finest chest tones, "mockest thou me, caitiff? Off with him, then, to the profoundest bastiles of Breisach!"

And there I am, on a sheaf of fresh theatrical straw, with a bottomless pit in the floor, in which I can see the subterranean scene-shifters. And my name is not Paul Flemming, but Arthur Philipson, and I hear footsteps. They come, they come, the murderers! O Lady of Mercy! and O gracious Heaven! forgive my transgressions! And when the footsteps approach, there, robed in angelic white muslin, is Anne of Geierstein. "Can these things be?" I cry fatuously; "and has she really the powers of an elementary spirit?" And she, taking my hand, wafts me forth, as blissfully and easily as would a morning dream, into the daylight.

"I knew she was coming," observes the Wizard at my e l b o w, "and that was the reason I dumped y o u there."

When, however, I examined the underground portions of the Neues Schloss at Baden-Baden, I found the relics remaining there endued with a ferocious realism that took away my confidence. Sylvester Berkley in evening-dress—

"KNOW THYSELF!"

for he had some people to meet at dinner—myself in my garden-cap, and a guide with a torch, committed ourselves to the exploration. We had hurriedly got over the examination of the palace for the sake of these famous sub-constructions. 'Tis there, they say, in the Middle Ages sat the terrible Vigilance Committee called Vehmic, formerly the terror of Europe, and more recently the cause of many a melodrama and opera.

We descended innumerable steps, formed of slabs of rock scarcely connected together, and worn by the steps of ages. Tottering or sliding under our feet, they threatened death for the least false balance. Relieved of this peril, we passed through ten vaults, each more sepulchral than the other.

A door, made of a single stone, presented itself. After long efforts the stiff portal opened—not by means of a key, but of powerful levers which we ourselves helped to move.

We were in the grand chamber of the Secret Tribunal. The form of the seats from which the judges spoke was still visible on some of the stones that rose out of the ground. After a silent examination, followed by a procession through numerous corridors, we were suddenly ushered into a large hall, more forbidding than all the rest. Bolts of iron, chains and rusty clamps adorned the blackened and slimy walls. "This is the inquisition-chamber," said the guide solemnly, moving his torch along the stones still spotted with blood: "here the victims, placed on the rack, were tortured with the pincers, their foreheads

"WHEN WE SHALL MEET AT COMPT."

compressed by a constantly narrowing band of iron, and their feet set on a furnace."

I fairly choked in such an atmosphere, and at the presence of these visible, palpable irons rusted with blood, a cold perspiration stood out on my forehead. I looked at Sylvester. Smiling, white-cravatted, he was kissing the pommel of his cane.

"You are good-natured," he said, "to devote so much valuable emotion to such a small affair."

"A small affair!" repeated I, pointing to the tortures.

"In former times," he answered with the most perfect self-possession, "when enemies invaded the country, these big cellars were used to fold the sheep and oxen, as well as those less valuable beasts of burden, the women. You see the chains and fastenings for the cows. Up

ROMAN CAPTIVES DELIVERED TO THE VANDAL.

to this point, dear Mr. Flemming, I have not contradicted your errors—you seemed to feel a need for a Vehmic Council, and I indulged you—but now that it has brought out the perspiration over your temples and nose, thus including you among the tortured, I suppress it. No Vehmic Council ever sat here."

Even painful feelings are sometimes not without their sweetness. I felt like keeping mine. I observed that the magnitude of these terrible halls witnessed

EX VOTO.

that they were constructed for some awful purpose. The guide, furnished only with the name and definition of each room, declined to take part in the discussion. After having made us pass over a little bridge, whose gaping planks allowed a damp, tomblike air to ascend to our nostrils, he turned suddenly. "The oubliettes!" he said in his hollowest tones.

I took a stone, and let it fall through a crack in the boards: it was ten seconds arriving at the bottom.

I crossed my arms and looked firmly at Sylvester. "Well?" I said.

"A well, certainly," he answered.

I was put out at having the word thus taken from my mouth to my disadvantage.

I asked the guide if he knew no story of the dark old times, with the name of some illustrious victim plunged into the oubliette.

He confessed to knowing, of his own memory, that formerly, a long while ago, when he was quite young, a little dog, that had stolen in at the heels of its master, had disappeared between the planks of the bridge. The animal's name was Love. The owner was an Englishman, and therefore very rich. He offered enormous bribes for the body of his dog, living or dead. With the dog, which was got out alive, but sneezing, they brought up a kind of dust, half white and half red, which evidently proceeded from human bones and weapons reduced to rust.

I did not consider that the adventure of the aforesaid Love was tabulable in a class of historical events sufficiently grave to allow me to make a weapon of it against Sylvester.

The more I studied the character of the latter, the more it puzzled me. With his correctness, his measured phrases, his politeness, he united a strange obstinacy and an obvious exaggeration. As we emerged from the dungeons of the Neues Schloss, our discussion still proceeding, he combated my views with a vivacity and a personal strenuousness that surprised me. Here evidently was no man, like Flemming, content to hold his dearest opinions by a thread of fable or sentiment. But the trait was hardly noticed ere it was handsomely apologized for. Berkley, his own accuser, complained of a temper the reverse of diplomatic. "My poor uncle was just so," he observed, "and has been known to dance on his own chinaware like a dervish. He tried cold tubs, and I am trying whey. Every one, as Socrates observes, should know himself."

It appeared to me that there were depths in Berkley which I had not sounded. I took his arm and returned with him to dinner. Habituated to Baden-Baden, the dinner was for him a continual series of bows, compliments, sending off of brimming glasses to bowing and complimenting people at a distance. Of two especial friends of his, one was a German literary gentleman, so famous that I do not venture to mention his name—the other a landscape-painter.

After dining, I, for my part, discovered an acquaintance, one of the disputants of the table at Carlsruhe. After asking for a few points, such as whether the St. Lawrence River did not keep its color for a long time after running into Lake Superior, and whether Washington Territory were not synonymous with the District of Columbia, he gave me a chance for a question, to hear whose answer my ears were throbbing. I asked, as indifferently as possible, after Francine Joliet.

It appeared that since my departure Francine did nothing but sing from morning till night. Exceedingly dissatisfied with this reply, I turned to Sylvester, who

THE CHAPEL OF THE POOR

with his friends intended to drop in at the Casino of Holland, a rendezvous for the archæologists and curiosity-hunters of the country. There is at the Casino a library of limited numbers, but composed exclusively of works connected with the traditions of the grand duchy. I found there several persons of my own kidney, capital fellows, Germans of that noble stomach that digests science equally with beer.

The next day I counted, of course, on returning to Paris, but the thing was not feasible. The clothes in which I stood would hardly bear the journey, while my funds, though unlimited in the letter which I carried in my pocket, were practically reduced to a few coppers. To change these conditions a little time was absolutely necessary.

For the matter of pocket-money, however, small change is perfectly useless at Baden-Baden. Once deposited by the train at the station of Oos, you become a privileged subject of the proprietor. He takes charge of your pleasures, treats you to balls, races, hunts and concerts, and will not let you pay so much as a cab-driver or a washerwoman. For these, again, there is a formal tariff of charges, regulated by city ordinance. Of those wasps of the traveler's life you hear nothing until the day of your departure, when they make a feeble rattle in the hotel-clerk's bill.

The persuasions of my acquaintance, the claims of my affairs, and, above all, a certain assonance and sympathy I found between this sentimental watering-place and my feelings, prevented my immediate departure. I therefore began to explore the locality. I dashed through the Black Forest like the Black Hunts-

THE GALLERY OF LEGENDS.

man of Fontainebleau—in a cab, however. I faithfully attended the concerts. I took part in the promenade — easily planted in a garden-chair. I frequented the Conversations-Haus. I enjoyed the Casino, with its books and its maggots. I even condescended to visit the reading-room of good Frau Marx, where, plunged into all the papers and all the reviews of the day, were noses of old club-men from half the countries of Europe, not to speak of the frosty ones belonging to German school-mistresses, who pottered round the tables in impossible bonnets. I became reconciled to Baden-Baden, and no longer called it a theatrical decoration.

At the Old Trinkhalle, where is found the principal or father fountain, I would watch Sylvester, armed with a little thermometer, testing the water, which has the singular faculty of burning the hand, but not the lips. O simple problem, but too much for a diplomatist!

Berkley drank like a dolphin, and was probably the most superstitious believer in all the baths.

Opposite the Old Trinkhalle is the old drinking-gallery, now become the general shelter for all the broken statues, all the Roman potsherds, left from the ancient Aurelia Aquensis. There I saw a Mercury with ass's ears, found on the summit of the Stauffenberg, which owes thereto its modern name of Mount Mercury. With Berkley I visited the Stauffenberg aforesaid, the Fremersberg and many others. The old cemetery itself received our visiting-card, though there is no record of tourists having gone thither before us. We were rewarded by the sight of its calvary and cross, where the Saviour appears life-sized, while behind him, on a mountain two yards high, perches an angel in the most innocently-diminished perspective. At this grotesque monument Sylvester, to my surprise, crossed himself. Abstaining, for my part, out of respect for art, if for nothing else, I asked him frankly the cause of his un-English action. "My views may be peculiar," said he, "but as I think a diplomatist is the mediator between different nations, I consider that he ought to observe all religious practices that are not in themselves immoral."

We next entered a little cell decorated as a chapel. The walls were covered with *ex voto* offerings, such as little twisted arms and clubbed feet, modeled in plaster: small paintings of many kinds, each with the story of a miraculous cure, told of the intercession of the saints, more powerful here, it would seem, than the thermal springs. In the chapel and around the door were good simple peasants, men and women, muttering their paternosters as they knelt. Sylvester knelt with them, and like them muttered a prayer.

It was after our promenade in the cemetery that I bethought me of a mundane but agreeable resurrection, that of my wardrobe. I dropped Berkley, with rendezvous at the New Trinkhalle, and in the discreet shelter of a tailor's shop caused my old scarred habit to disappear under a neat spring surcoat, with some further transformations of like character. I also procured varnished shoes and a silken hat, so strong upon me was the influence of watering-place vanity and the fear of hotel-stewards. Making then for the Trinkhalle, I found in its vicinity a knot of my philosophic friends from the Casino, together with the painter and the literary man.

Opposite the New Trinkhalle, which is not to be confounded with the old one, rises an edifice in the form of a classic portico, presenting a long gallery upheld by Corinthian pillars. On the wall between each pair of columns is painted in fresco some legend of the country, to the number of fourteen pictures. One of these allegories the painter was demonstrating to his friends, like a geometrical theorem, with the aid of his cane. I joined the group. "It is the story of young Burkhardt Keller, a noble knight. On two different evenings he met, as he was riding through the forest of Kuppenheim, a lady veiled in white, who sank into the ground at his approach. He caused the ground to be dug up in the place where she had disappeared, and found there the remains of a Roman altar, then the fragments of a statue, of which the bust alone remained uninjured. The features were of great beauty, and the gallant Keller would fain have had it play for him the part of Galatea before Pygmalion. In the

THE MARBLE VEIL.

same wood, at the hour of midnight, Keller met the veiled lady for the third time. On this occasion she did not sink into the earth: leaning against the altar, she slowly raised her veil. The face was that of the statue, but animated and alive. Keller

THE PAGAN ALTAR.

advanced ardently, and she opened her arms. When they closed again upon that perfect breast they had returned to stone. Next day the youthful knight

THE CONVERTED PRE-RAPHAELITE.

was found dead at the foot of the ruined altar, a pool of blood flowing from his mouth. The veiled dame was one of the devils."

We politely applauded the artist's story, though I think we all knew it, and I for my part had been reading it the day before in a volume found at Frau Marx's.

The literary man, however, showed no marks of approval. "See how you have spoiled," said he to the narrator, "a fable bearing most pointedly on your own artistic and vagabond profession. Now listen to me. I have found the same episode in the Chronicle of Otho of Freissingen: I shall narrate it for your benefit, introducing a few details from that of Gunther. A good legend deserves a title. I shall call it 'The Unhappy Pre-Raphaelite.' It goes back as far as the twelfth century.

"In the court of the margrave Herrmann, sitting contemptuously on an overthrown saint in the chapel, might have been seen a comely young man biting the ends of his moustache with vexation. 'Why has the margrave made me his minister of the household and of fine arts?' he said. 'I am out of my element here. We make nothing but angular saints and angels in mediæval positions. They will call us purists, and worship us in the future, I know very well; but I am a born romanticist. Why has the school of Delacroix not arisen, that I might join myself to his standard?'

"The young man's name was Keller. He had accompanied Frederick Barba-

A BIT OF PRE-RAPHAELITE REALISM.

rossa on his first crusade, but, although brave, he had not disemboweled a single Saracen. 'The Oriental schools of 1840,' said he, 'will need them all for their *Turkeries*.' He brought home with him simply a raging mania for inlaid armor and palm-leaf shawls. You perceive, gentlemen, a veritable Decamps of the Middle Ages! Although of a meek and humble spirit, he could not attend mass before the hideous high altar, emblazoned with all the jeweled hideousness of Gothic statuary. Yet he had been in Rome to attend the coronation of the same emperor Frederick Barbarossa! What attracted him at Rome were not the processions, the pope, nor the Byzantine frescoes in the basilicas. 'They will do very well for Ruskin,' he said, 'but I wish to record myself as decidedly renaissance.' So he used to sit on fallen capitals and beweep the lost noses of heathen deities.

"Returning home, his behavior was remarked in church. Poor lover of plastic beauty, simple line and artistic suavity! he was obliged to turn away his eyes from the images of the saints. Whatever was angular, disjointed or grimacing affected him with nausea; and he used to groan when the licensed sculptor of the court, who was also the bellows-mender, set up a new saint with flutes for legs and a high seraphic expression.

"The margrave Hermann loved Keller like a father, having raised him from a simple page. As there was some danger of his being burnt for sacrilege by the pure-minded and devout pre-Raphaelites around him, an aristocratic match was hit upon. The daughter of the provost of Kuppenheim, known for the strictness of her Catholicism, would lead him back to a better way and to æsthetic principles more safe for the preservation of human life in a pious age. When Miss Kuppenheim, however, was paraded from her convent for his inspection, he found her long-footed, goose-necked, violin-breasted and ecstatic, much like the statue of Saint Ottilia; but he consented to visit her two or three evenings in guise of a suitor.

"Just at this period his secretary, knowing him curious about old broken china, Roman cement and such things, came

A SUBJECT FOR THE BATHS

to announce that the foresters, in uprooting an oak somewhere about the pleasaunce, had uncovered a stone vault, built with mortar so hard that the roots had hardly succeeded in penetrating it. Keller caused an opening to be made, and descended with a torch.

"He was in a Doric chapel, in the middle of which was a statue so beautiful that it betrayed the chisel of Phidias. "You know the collector Sauvageot spent a quarter of a year in cleaning with a needle the splendid purse-clasp of Henri II., which was bought for three francs as old iron. Keller undertook a similar service for the white daughter of

TREASURES OF "LA FAVORITE."

Phidias, in removing with the point of his dagger each mossy film from her marble skin. When a month had slipped away in this delightful labor, he passed many further days in measuring, analyzing and studying her soft perfections, to the complete neglect of Miss Kuppenheim.

"Now it was not so very long since the soldiers of the Cross, after incessant struggles, had obliterated paganism in Germany. Some obstinate heathens, in the recesses of the Black Forest, were supposed to be still attached to their idols. The Vehmic tribunals were yet daily looking out for opportunities to drive back to the fold, with holy violence, the estrays both of politics and theology. The provost of Kuppenheim presided at one of these tribunals. He was heard to remark that the slight put upon his daughter had no influence on his legislation, but that the moral elevation of pre-Raphaelitism must be preserved.

"The temple was one day found overthrown and the daughter of Phidias shattered. The saint-maker, possessing himself of one of her legs, observed that he could make three or four out of it for the new group of Saint Ursula and her virgins commanded by Miss Kuppenheim. It is unnecessary to add that Burkhardt Keller was discovered lying among the fragments, pierced to the heart. The dagger was his own, but on it was perceived the seal of the Vehmic judges: they used to hide their hand, but they signed their works."

A DANDY SKELETON.

We received with suitable edification

this history of an early martyr for the Renaissance. Sylvester Berkley emerged from the Trinkhalle, his last drop of whey on his lips, at the moment when the literary gentleman was bringing in his Vehmic judges. I took care not to interrupt him, but at the moment of his conclusion I said: "So the Vehmic tribunal has held its sessions in this region? They occupied, then, the subterranean chambers of the New Castle, since, under the presidency of one Kuppenheim, provost of Baden, they could pronounce and execute sentence upon Burkhardt Keller?"

I regarded Sylvester sarcastically as I delivered this crusher. I supposed him annihilated. Berkley considered a few seconds; then, with a parliamentary gesture, addressing the others rather than myself, he poured forth a little history of the Vehmic institution from its foundation by Charlemagne, so lucid, rapid, fluent and bright that Clio in person could not have acquitted herself better. These courts, to believe him, had rendered in their time a service to religion as great as that of the Inquisition, which he praised in passing as having saved Spain and Italy from the bloody religious wars which raged contemporaneously in France, England and the Netherlands. The Vehmic judges, especially powerful in Westphalia, had successively fixed themselves in Frankfort, in Rastadt and in Baden. But they had never sat in the cellars of the Neues Schloss: he would answer for it.

To my profound surprise, the savants of the Casino were of his opinion, and even the author sustained him. To such a vacillating condition does a course of drinking at a fashionable watering-place bring a man's backbone!

Another picture in the Gallery of Legends helped to re-establish me after this humiliation.

A dispute sprang up about the powers of the natural springs taken as a bath. Sylvester, a headlong bather and a willing orator, pronounced a discourse in their favor. I opposed him, armed with complete ignorance of the subject, and adorning my arguments with botanical flowers derived from my small study of simples.

"Mr. Flemming," said Berkley, concealing a smile, "you, in this age when

A FRIEND IN CHURCH.

legends are receiving their eternal quietus, remain one of the faithful. For you a story has only to be wild and improbable to receive the most ardent support. I will argue with you simply by means of another painting in yonder gallery." And, borrowing the artist's cane, he pointed to the picture of the *Baldreit*.

This was the name of one of the most celebrated old hotels near Baden-Baden. Cured at the spring, an ancient prince of the Palatinate leaped up early one morning, leaving his gout behind him in the wash-basin. He ordered a horse and pranced about the courtyard in his joy, awakening landlord, ostlers and servants with his din. Waving his hand to them, the prince said: "See how soon I can ride." But the noise was such that "soon ride" were the only words they could hear, and "soon ride" remained the sign of the house. In the fresco, animated and blithe, he leaps to the saddle, while the landlord thrusts his nightcap from a window, the chambermaid lifts her arms to Heaven, the servants stare, the knight's "nurse curses in the pantry, and everything is in extremity."

My answer was ready. "What is the picture about?" I asked of Sylvester. "The palatine comes to Baden with a

HERCULES-CUPID.

palsy, and is instantly cured. Why, then, as the painting shows you, it is a special miracle, a fact without precedent. By their surprise, amounting to terror, yonder Boniface and servants testify that they have never seen or heard of such a thing. It is, then, not the habit of the water, but the exception, that is commemorated by the artist—"

"Herr Goetzenberger," put in the landscape-painter.

"Mr. Goetzenberger's picture is the only one in the gallery of which the programme conceals the date and hero's name. The plumed hat and the yellow boots he puts on his knight indicate the thirteenth or fourteenth century for the miracle. Be assured it has never happened since."

I got the laughs that time, and Berkley had an aspect decorously diabolical.

Meanwhile—such an enigma is the heart of man—I felt less and less like returning home. My imperious longings to depart were strangely mitigated when I held in my hand the key of deliverance.

With the first application I made to Meyer on the strength of my letter of credit I felt the swelling need of disporting a day or two on the strength of my funds, away from the chains of home and the tyranny of my faithful Charles and Josephine. To increase the congeniality of my surroundings, I found myself in a perfect saturation of legendary romance. I could hardly put my head out of window but a poem or a fable was unerringly darted at me, like the bouquets with barbed pins which are shot at you by the flower-girls of Naples. If I examined some faded print in a bookseller's window, and idly wondered who might be the hero of that triumphal entry or civic reception, an obliging Teutonic voice was ready at my ear: "It is the return of the margrave Ludwig-Wilhelm to Baden-Baden, sir, after conquering the Turks. What do they think of our hero in your country, sir?" the voice would add.

"He is highly esteemed," was the necessary reply, upon which I would fly like a scared child to the good Frau Marx or to the Casino of Holland for the purpose of mending the deplorable ignorance from which, in company with my good fellow-countrymen, I suffered in regard to this particular immortal.

The snare thus laid, it was impossible to get rid of the heroic warrior, who stuck to me like birdlime. The library of the

EXTRAVAGANCE.

Casino informed me that he was brought up like a girl, after the precedent of Achilles at Scyros, his mother having exacted solemn oaths from his tutors that never a weapon should touch his hands. One day the unfeminine girl kissed her governess like a trooper, and then leaped from the window to box with the porters in the courtyard. Become margrave of Baden, Ludwig made twenty-six campaigns, conducted twenty-five sieges, appeared in forty fights, shared with John Sobieski the glory of delivering Vienna from the Turks, and died peaceably in bed. A few hours after it would be the tomb. Here, having unwittingly strayed into the collegiate church of Baden - Baden, I was fascinated for an hour by the allegories piled up in honor of this same Ludwig-Wilhelm by Pigalle, and the pompous Latin in which his glories were celebrated: *Atlas Germaniæ—Imperii protector — Hostium terror—Infidelium debellator — Quoad vixit, semper vicit, nunquam victus.* O illimitable glories of this world! how small a part of its geography do you really cover!

It was from the tomb of Ludwig that I was excavated by a waiter from the hotel, who had been sent out by Sylvester to search until he found me. There was project of an excursion to Ebersteinburg, *La Favorite*. Every tourist visits the *Favorite*, a mile from Baden-Baden, and it harmonized well enough with my thoughts of the instant, for it was built in 1725 by the margravine Sibylle-Auguste, Ludwig-Wilhelm's eccentric spouse.

In approaching the favorite residence of Ludwig's widow, kept intact, in furniture and upholstery, since her death about 1733, I assumed my behavior of propriety: my head bent, my nose in my hat, I prepared to enter a palace which was in some sort a mausoleum.

THE CELESTIAL MASS.

What I actually found was an endless curiosity-shop. The shelves were stuffed with Venice glasses, Bohemian crystal, hard-paste, soft-paste, Chinese crackle and Limoges enamels. The glass cases were filled with carved rock-crystal and jade. Similar baubles were accumulated on the walls, the cornices, the chimney-pieces and the stoves.

Berkley, my cicerone, had told me that I should find the portrait of my hero Ludwig, and even under several different types. I passed rapidly over

THE UNWILLING LISTENER.

the faience and majolica, searching eagerly for that warrior; for, in my opinion, there is no historical document equal to the simple physiognomy of the individual faithfully copied without flattery by an artist. Lost among the memorial gimcracks, I failed to find a likeness of the margrave, and consulted in despair a multitude of miniatures representing a whole nation of women.

Among these ladies some were in court costume, some in mourning robes, the majority in many different travesties, as of gypsies, dancers or jugglers with pointed caps or fanciful turbans. On a closer examination, all these faces had a look of relationship, an air of resemblance. I had in fact under my eyes, in this extravagant German seraglio, a single woman, the margravine Sibylle-Auguste, nun, odalisque, marchioness or witch at pleasure!

Berkley, who joined me, showed me a series opposite, representing a good, vulgar, burgher's face adorned with as great a variety of costumes as its neighbor's. This good burgher, unfortunately for himself, was the dashing hero, the Turk-slayer, Ludwig-Wilhelm himself!

There were seventy-two margravines, seventy-two margraves—in all, one hundred and forty-four portraits from two models. How the ghost of Ludwig must have haunted the painter who seventy-two times slandered him!

Was the extraordinary Sibylle a lunatic, a poetess or a saint? We visited next the cell of the same princess, constructed in a corner of her park. Here, during every Lent, she repented of her sins for the year, sleeping on earth and straw, causing her maids to flagellate her with leaded thongs, and dining in company with waxen statues of the Virgin and Saint Joseph. Easter arrived, she flung her nun's cap up the chimney, and began again those orgies prolonged till daylight which were the scandal of the land.

But it is the country of lady eccentrics. What tourist has not had pointed out to him, but a few years back, the extraordinary concurrence of female celebrities gathered around the green tables of Baden-Baden? A woman now playing the violin is far from an every-day spectacle. A nun stroking the same instrument is, one would say, a still rarer sight. Yet that was what was seen formerly at the convent of Lichtenthal. At present you do not see the pious fiddlers, but you hear them still.

Soothing my homeward-yearning conscience by the assurance that I had some very important notes to take on the history of Ludwig-Wilhelm, I went for one last time to the Casino of Holland. When I observed neatly tacked upon the door the legend, "Shut on account of Sunday," I remembered what day it was. I then followed one of the prettiest Sabbath promenades of Baden-Baden by strolling over the pleasant walk to Lichtenthal.

The little church of the Augustine nuns at Lichtenthal was founded in the thirteenth century by the widow of Margrave Hermann V. It still retains the fine Byzantine Madonna which once marched to the door and offered the keys in heavenly sarcasm to a band of marauders. On either side of the altar I saw the glass cases in which are preserved the bones of Saint Pius and Saint Benedict. Better-dressed skeletons are seldom met in mortuary circles. Collars of lace, rosettes of velvet and pearl on each rib, on the bald ivory skulls rich caps in plumes—they are altogether what Victor Hugo has well called "troubadour skeletons."

Another singularity struck me. Twenty minutes before the mass the candles were blazing on the altar, and the sounds of distant music, like heavenly viols,

NUN VIOLINISTS.

seemed to celebrate aërially a service that was invisible to the eye. Probably the Sisters, in their cloister, were tuning their violins. The congregation, not yet diluted with the throngs of curious travelers who attend later in the season, was completely German, silent and absorbed. Not far from me I recognized, seated in his stall, one of my savants of the Casino: he was a fine little gentleman, asthmatic and short-stemmed. On his right was a villager, or perhaps my friend's servant, mumbling over his breviary. This learned man had obliged me, the day before, with a crabbed manuscript, so insufferably fine that I had incontinently stuffed it in my pocket. Now, as if there were a system of dumb-show established between us, this man of learning began to make signs to me, pointing out the altar and one of the skeletons, his head all the while playing a perfect fountain of nods. I nodded in my turn, without a particle of comprehension, and in due time yielded myself to the enjoyment of the Sisters' music. After service I approached to ask an explanation, but he was encircled by a bevy of ladies. As I passed, however, he flung me out a kindly ejaculation: "There, you see—it was the invisible mass—the legend—you know," and sent me back quite bewildered to the hotel.

On my walk, however, it occurred to me to examine the manuscript. I passed the happy promenaders with my face quite shut up in the book, of which the writing was so close that the eyes could decipher it only by a sort of contact. There I found question of my warrior Ludwig-Wilhelm; of the fiddling nuns; of one of the canonized skeletons by the altar; of the wild penitent Sibylle-Auguste; the whole playing around the person of a relative of the margrave's—none other than Margrave Charles of Carlsruhe, he who had dreamed in the forest, and sketched that fair city as the delineation of his dream.

This prince was in his youth extreme-

A FOREST DRIVE.

ly wild. At the same time he was the pride of his father, Margrave Frederick VII. of Baden-Durlach, and so handsome and vigorous that the historian Schoepflin says of him that "Nature, hesitating whether to form a Hercules or a Cupid, made both the one and the other." He was called to Stockholm to see if he would answer for husband to the queen-dowager's granddaughter. But his conduct was so wild in Sweden that he was not invited to prolong the visit. He fought with Ludwig at Landau, and came back wounded to the baths, where Sibylle-Auguste received him honorably and lodged him in the Neues Schloss. Hercules-Cupid's unhappy reputation soon began to gather around him again like a cloud, and one day an Augustinian nun ran pouting to the abbot Benedict and complained that the devil had kissed her. The good abbot arranged that the devil should not return, and took his measures so well that Charles conceived against him a deep feeling of spite.

At this time, in the general state of poverty consequent upon war, the Church was threatened with bankruptcy. The nuns feared being obliged to abandon the orphans whom they were educating. In such an extremity the abbot, although eighty-seven years old, took the field and begged from door to door, arriving finally at the New Castle.

His young enemy, Charles, promised ten thousand florins on condition that he, the abbot, should say a mass for the success of his enterprises; and this not once nor twice, but ten times a year for ten years. The abbot pointed out that such an engagement, for a nonagenarian, would be unsuitable and impious. The young margrave held firmly to his condition that the mass should be performed by the abbot alone, even should he have to return from the other world to do it. Upon this the good man crossed himself as if he were conversing with the Fiend in person, and retired to pursue his quest elsewhere. Soon, however, he returned: the citizens were impotent, the nuns were weeping. He signed the bond, and hurried back to the convent with his ten thousand florins. That very night, after so strange an excitement, he was seized with apoplexy and died.

Already revenged on the abbot, the pitiless Charles pursued the Church. Refusing the masses of any substitute, or even of the bishop, he instituted a suit. The princess Sibylle-Auguste threatened him with her anger, but he was unyielding. The Sunday arrived at length for the first of the ten annual masses. Sibylle and the nuns were in their chapel, the hour passed, and the bishop did not appear. The princess sent a page for him, when, to the great surprise of the congregation, the doors of the church rolled back of themselves on their hinges: a man appeared, haggard, gasping, and staggered toward the choir as if impelled by superior force. It was Charles.

The door closed behind him, and immediately the church was filled with eerie music, vibrating from harps and violins in the upper arches. At the altar now could be heard the holy mutter of a man's voice—a voice that made Charles tremble. Bending his starting eyes upon the spot, he easily distinguished there the shade of Benedict going through the office as of yore, while angels swung the censers. For the congregation it was an invisible mass: they only saw the stirring of the altar-laces, the book opening of itself, the sacred wafer entering voluntarily into the tabernacle.

Mass over, the pale witnesses of this miracle found Charles leaning against a pillar of the doorway, panting. He had wished to fly, but a superior force withstood him at the portal.

Charles stopped his suit. The elegant and pious Sibylle, struck with the celestial harmonies she had heard, and was not quite certain of hearing again, conferred an endowment providing for a choir of violins to be played on Sundays and feasts by the nuns. Charles, or Carl-Wilhelm, the hero of this prodigious history, became very brave, but never lost his gallantry. After the peace of Rastadt, renouncing his residence at Durlach, he laid out Carlsruhe, as we have seen, on the model of a lady's fan.

It was still early in the day, the weather was delicious, and I felt ashamed of my inertia as I flung away the little manuscript book. Sylvester Berkley had refreshed himself at the sermon of an Anglican divine, the first of all that flock of curate-tourists who would brighten the atmosphere of Baden-Baden during the summer—an edification which seemed to express itself in the enhanced whiteness and accuracy of his cravat and the transfigured effulgence of his highlows.

We arranged a drive to New Eberstein, on the Murg, a castle eight miles off, inviting the artist and the literary man, who had been sacrilegiously devoting the morning to chess.

It was a beautiful excursion along the bases of the hills and under the tasseled

THE DISCONTENTED ARTIST.

shadows of the Black Forest. However, when, walking up an ascent for the ease of the horses, I burst into exclamations at the view, I could get no response from the landscape-painter. He stood digging his cane into the bark of one of those immense trees called Hollanders, because they are chosen for the Holland marine. As I expatiated on the scene, he gruffly said, "Humph! Light badly distributed, sky improbable."

Who ever knew a landscape-painter to approve a landscape unless it were on canvas?

Long rafts of felled timber were slowly coiling their way along the Murg. It was Birnam wood coming to Dunsinane —the Black Forest moving in serried ranks down upon the Netherlands. From far up the little stream—from the cloudy recesses of its humid forest cradle—come pouring the uptorn, helpless trees, caught in its eddies, precipitated over its cascades, trying with dumb fidelity to learn the fluidity of water.

We were unable to enter the Eberstein, it being occupied. The visitors were disposed to complain of this disappoint-

THE MURG RIVER.

ment, with the exception of one, who sat down muttering quite cheerfully under a tree. That one was Flemming, and he sat as contentedly as possible, crooning ballads of Uhland and Schiller, and filling his reverie with Black Knights and ghostly battles. Was not the Grafensprung, the Count's Leap, before him? Were not those the toiling whirlpools of the Murg? Was he not free to penetrate the Eberstein at the advantage of some centuries in advance?

A great poet and a great painter have blended their genius over the .fortunes of Count Eberhardt and his family. It will not improve the romance of the situation to explain their ancestral tree, but a few words will place the works of these two immortal artists in harmony with each other.

Schiller's ballad and Scheffer's canvas celebrate a sister and a brother, children of Count Eberhardt II. of Wurtemberg. The son, a youth of promise, for yielding the victory to some troops of the palatinate, was reproached by his father, who cut the tablecloth in front of his place, signifying that the young knight had not gained his bread. Afterward, on a day of splendid victory, the boy was slain, and his father retired weeping to his tent amid the general acclaim. His name was thereupon changed from Eberhardt the Fighter to Eberhardt the Weeper, and his mourning over the gallant dead is the subject of Scheffer's picture in the

Luxembourg, of which a magnificent replica by the artist is visible to my American reader in dear old Boston Athenæum.

The sister, Lida, was forced by her father to marry her cousin Conrad; but the bride was placed upon the noble horse Tador, which had been taken from her own true love, Count Wolf of Eberstein. Obeying some impulse quite worthy of Pegasus, this steed, in the ballad of Schiller, flies like the wind with Lida to the castle on the Murg where Wolf is hiding. He leaps with her upon the horse, braves the pursuers as long as possible, and then wildly dashes with his two loves, his horse and his affianced, over the steep cliff into the river.

With much converse over the German ballad-form between the author and myself, we returned to Baden-Baden. The painter and the diplomatist, disgusted with our frivolous sentiment, fell to talking on the subject of skimmed milk, upon which theme they met with equal enthusiasm, the fluid serving the one as a varnish for his charcoal-sketches, the other as an occasional diet.

Our horses were good, and we arrived quite early in the afternoon. I felt like taking advantage of the weather, and asked the landlord how I should put in my time. As I approached him with this question, my vision of a stay in Baden-Baden was extended over several days at least. His reply set me to packing my new pantaloons and trifles as if my life depended on it. At the moment when I felt most assured of some settled fixity my incomparable enthusiasm of temper set me flying off like a projectile. He spoke—and it was disinterested of him—of an amusing conference going on at Achern, a station on the road to Kehl. The catchword of Kehl reminded me of Strasburg, Épernay and home.

SCHILLER AND SCHEFFER.

As for the attraction, it was a congress of all the philharmonic and orpheonist societies of Alsace and the grand duchy. This Sunday night would be their grand *pot pourri*.

The temptation was too strong for me. The train was just attainable. Wringing Sylvester's hand until the glove split, and settling my landlord's bill, I—went to Achern on the route to Kehl.

PART VIII.

THE MUSIK-FEST AT ACHERN.

"SHUT UP!"

I WAS never a dancing man, having been in youth so absent as to forget the figures while I whispered poetry into my partner's ear, and in age too obese; but I love the concord of sweet sounds, and, like Henry of Ofterdingen in Novalis's story, Paul Flemming thinks to music. I become so absorbed at the opera that I have been eyed in my box by the principal lady in the female choruses, with an absolute certainty that I was a conquest. I still repair with the baron to representations of *Don Giovanni;* and when Faure is serenading the prima donna, guitar in hand, I ob-

serve to my good Hohenfels, "How that melancholy chord he plays vibrates through the gayety of the air! So in the noisy crowd do I hear the mournful string of my own heart."

"You are addled eternally, my poor Paul," the baron replies. "Don't you know that Faure's guitar is a dummy, and that his accompaniment is really played by that squinting young man at the large harp?"

The baron, an excellent fellow, is too prosaic to perceive that my imaginative way of hearing is the best. It was with genuine anticipation, then, that I rolled along to hear the orpheonists at Achern: these choral reunions are superb affairs in Germany.

On my way I took the towns of Ottersweier and Sassbach: unless a route has something of vagabondage it is no route for Flemming. At Ottersweier I had been told I could find some curious documents — removed thither from the great historical stores of Heidelberg — about Ludwig-Wilhelm, my scourge of the Turks and husband of the frivolous devotee Sibylle-Auguste. Greatly interested in recovering this biographic trace, which I had only lost at Baden-

115

Baden for the vile reason of the Casino being closed for Sunday, I presented myself eagerly at the bureau of archives.

THE ASHES OF TURENNE.

Still the same baffling privacy and the same dominical excuse—"Shut up on account of Sunday!" My Sabbath had truly been a day of prayer, but of prayer ungratified. The church, though, was open, and among its mural paintings and stucco angels I got the better of my chagrin.

Nor was Sassbach a very satisfactory success. I wished to see the monument to Turenne, who fell here in 1675, having before him, for adversaries, Montecuculli and my hero Ludwig-Wilhelm of Baden, then a boy twenty years of age. I had vaguely heard that at Sassbach, by international consent, the death-place of Turenne was considered as having been conquered to the French nation by the warrior's fall—that the scene was, in fact, a miniature France, defended by an army of a corporal and four zouaves, still commanded by the ghost of the mighty Turenne. I might have known that since the disasters of 1871 no such martial courtesies could be claimed by France. The real tomb of Turenne is at the Invalides, happily safe from the reverses of war. His monument, which covers nothing, and the relics of the tree under which he died, are in the custody of an honest Teuton, who warms his feet in his little box while he waits for patriotic tourists. He showed me the bullet which killed the great soldier, and I could but secretly wonder how many of these authentic balls he might have sold to eager French purchasers. The vicarious bullet, however, had been inspected by more credulous eyes than mine. On the visitors' register I saw, under date of April 4, 1832, the names of Hortense, "duchesse de Saint-Leu," and of Louis Napoleon Bonaparte, the latter then a wandering actor, with his greatest comedies and tragedies yet to play, but believing in his star even before the missile which killed Turenne.

I was chased out of Sassbach by a volley of large drops, precursors of a sullen and determined storm which almost literally floated me into Achern. The streets, however, were as flush with people as though the Acherners, like garden flowers, were in the habit of coming out to get the shower. It was not the deluge which attracted them.

I found Achern a city of silken and gingham domes, on which the rain thumped its funeral marches perseveringly. A thousand umbrellas surmounted two or three thousand human heads:

"NEITHER BED NOR BOARD!"

these canopies, however, might have been more impartial, for they did not protect the sculptured heads of Haydn and Mozart, which in turn surmounted them: the lyre of Strasburg, the Belgian lion, the civic arms of Heidelberg, of Colmar, of Mannheim, of Mülhausen, tore their way on a dozen banner-staves through the world of umbrellas. Worse than the crowd or the flood, the landlord of the Golden Crown met me with that overdone air of politeness which announced, even before he spoke, that he could offer me neither bed nor board.

My situation would have discomfited

"WAITER! WAIT!"

Turenne himself. The overstocked Golden Crown would naturally be the type of other hotels; besides, my hat, a curly silken leaf of the Baden-Baden parterre, did not invite me to a journey of exploration. No more did the absence of my stout umbrella, which I had left behind: it was probably still plunging in quest of the bottom of some bottomless *oubliette* of the Neues Schloss. There is nothing which awakens the careful and tender instinct of a man's heart—no, not one's first-born—like a perfectly new hat: you shelter the vanity from a wind to which you willingly expose the baby. To be sure, the loss of your heir excites commiseration, but that of your hat scorn. I naturally put up my hand to examine mine as I stood in the porte-cochère amid a group of unfortunates as sad and shelterless as myself, with not a dry cheek among us. Jupiter Pluvius! the hat was gone!

I had hit upon a method, of specious but fallacious cleverness, to reconcile my smart chapeau and my rustic garden-cap. On the road, ugly and sympathetic, it was my bonnet that crowned the situation: in the street—that is to say, among marts and cities—I wore my hat. Inside it I had found a cunning way to secrete my cap, reduced to its simplest expression, or, in other words, deprived of the whalebone that gave it a circular bent. This proof of penetrability in matter, at least in matter of costume, had not a little set me up. I was less proud of it now, when the deceptive clasp of the whalebone had treacherous-

THE RECOVERED HAT.

ly lulled my poor old head in false security, and when my volatile hat was probably flying back to its native Baden.

I must seek repose, and it shall be elsewhere. I am already quite willing to follow my hat. I am quite disgusted with Achern, which has become the merest bog, and with its landlords,

> Who are indeed a bog that bears
> Your unparticipated cares,
> Unmoved and without quaking.

I apply for instructions. The landlord, who appears again, and who evidently disapproves my costume and me, reiterates, "No room! no room!" when I ask

THE DOOR-MAT.

him the way to the station. I fancy he is responding to his own thought rather than to mine: in a Baden railway there is always room. I try his subordinates: there are plenty of waiters, who, stimulated to the utmost height of their talents, with ardent eyes and with the gait of hunted ostriches, are vaulting in a covey into the dining-room, loaded with plates and dishes. I try to bring one down on the wing, but he describes a loop around me with the quickness of a lasso, and shoots through the doorway, within which a hundred growling voices are calling for him.

If it was hard that I could not enter, I thought it still harder that I could not get away. I believe I am not naturally uncharitable, but in that dark, damp hour I could almost have drowned in the gutters of Achern my Baden landlord who had sent me there, Berkley who had brought me to the baths, the customs-officers of Kehl who had despatched me for Berkley, the engineer who had driven me over to Kehl, the conspirators of Épernay, and the wretched James Athanasius Grandstone, whose birthday had tempted me from the outskirts of Paris. While I was musing thus, full of spleen and misanthropy, a carriage approached like a sail to a shipwreck. It was depositing a load of visitors, but it would suffice to conduct me to the station. As the driver was closing the carriage door I leaped inside before him.

The cabman, with a calm gesture of a heavy arm, put me aside like a feather. Extracting a glossy hat from under the seat I was about to occupy, he observed, without seeming to open his mouth, "Stout old foreign gentleman in a cap: perhaps it is you, sir. Lost hat, handed to me by a comrade of mine. Would you stand a trifling trinkgeld?"

Thus it was that after a more or less voluntary abdication I recovered my crown. But the restoration brought me little happiness, for the landlord, who ran up once more at the noise of the carriage, informed me that the train would not stop at Achern until ten. It was striking four. I pressed my property upon my brow—as if I were not sure to lose it at the first possible opportunity —and resumed my thoughts, while the

COURTING SLEEP.

driver, certain of better jobs than mine, rumbled off without trying to mend my indecision. I was tired and humble: I

sat doggedly upon the stairs, crowned indeed with my novel splendors, but resigning my coat-tails as a door-mat to every stranger who chose to tread upon them. I believe it was the hat and the humility, combined perhaps with my involuntary liberality to the coachman, which converted the landlord. The hat of ceremony, indeed, is a kind of passport on the Continent. Boniface, at any rate, came to me for the fourth time, made me a fourth long-bodied bow, and invited me to a large chamber on the topmost floor. The apartment was soaked with the tobacco-smoke of years. "I give you the bed-room of my daughters," he said for explanation; and I tried to believe him.

In a quarter of an hour I was at dinner. To dine alone is with me an impossibility. My meal, like an Egyptian banquet, was made in the company of two mysteries—one a friend and one an enemy—Francine and Fortnoye. The sweet stewardess and the enigmatic commission-agent helped me to my rations and seasoned my sauces. I determined to hunt down the whole chimera, and for that purpose to go home again by Épernay and Noisy.

"You will call me in time for the train at ten," I said to the waiter: he promised. "You will not forget, on any account," I insisted: he repeated his vow. It was a broad-boned, colorless waiter, with two buttermilk eyes, far apart, at the bottom of two caverns tufted with white bristles.

I sought my chamber for a little repose. At first the tumult of bands in the street, a veritable conspiracy between the musicians of Baden and those of Alsace, and the rehearsals going on in the house itself, made slumber impossible. I tied a handkerchief over my ears to exclude the clamor, wrapped my nose in the sheet to get rid of the odor from the pillows—on which the innkeeper's daughters seemed to have strewed *caporal*—and sat for some time in bed, upright and agonized. I was soon, however, prostrated by sheer fatigue.

Hardly had I closed my eyes, as it seemed, when the glimmering, far-apart bluish eyes of the waiter appeared in the doorway, and I was summoned to the railway-station. The night-train arrived with supernatural whiz and roar. At

THE ENCHANTED STEED.

last I found my face turned toward the dear lares and penates! At the rate of a mile a minute the engine flew toward Paris. At the metropolis what changes since my departure! The new avenues and boulevards had developed like magic. The belt-railroad surrounding the city took possession of me: there was no stopping, and with an ever-increasing speed I was borne quite around the capital, and eastward again, by way of Charleroi, Luxembourg and Metz, to Strasburg. As I was flying, still in the train, over the bridge to Kehl, I suddenly saw two horsemen riding by my side. They kept up easily with the locomotive, both mounted on the same apocalyptic steed, and necessarily running on the water. They were richly dressed, but the wind plunged with hollow murmurs under their waistcoats, as in empty space. There was no flesh on their ribs, long spurs were attached to their bony heels, and their skeletons rattled at every bound

riders turned their eyes, filled with pale flame, upon me. They gave their names. One was Ludwig-Wilhelm, the scourge of Islam, the original of the seventy-two miniatures I had seen in the *Favorite* of Sibylle-Auguste; the other was Margrave Charles of Baden, founder of the city laid out in a fan.

Charles, in evident allusion to his forced entry and detention in the church of Lichtenthal, said sneeringly, "Very well: you see how it is to be drawn by a power stronger than yourself. How do you like legendary adventures by this time, Mr. Paul Flemming?"

Addressing myself immediately to Ludwig, whose worthy burgher attitude invited confidence, I asked where this unslackening race should end.

"At Achern," he replied.

"But why must I return thus upon my point of departure?" I demanded.

"Because you have forgotten to settle your account with the landlord," he retorted, with his broad skeleton grin.

This appeal to my sense of duty shocked me so that I awoke. It was broad day: the train was lost, with a witness! I was ready to raise a shout of distress, or at least to summon for vengeance the inculpated waiter. A new incident deterred me. A spectre again! Something clad in white was passing around the chamber. I thought for a moment, with bachelor horror, of the landlord's daughters. Supposing this should really be their boudoir! A glance through the curtains reassured me: the spectre wore

THE MIRROR.

of the horse. The latter had joints of steel in sockets of copper, and I heard the sound of pistons and the rush of steam as he moved: it was my enemy the locomotive in a new disguise. The

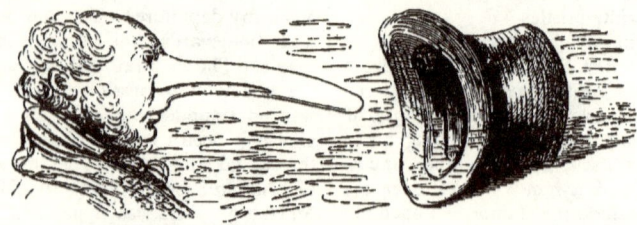

WHO KNOWS?

boots. Another glance showed me a gentleman tying his cravat at the glass. The host had simply used his right to dispose of the vacant bed. The new

tenant was no ghost: the face I caught for a moment in the mirror was comely and ruddy. I fell back somewhat comforted, letting go the curtains.

The lodger having departed, I leaped to the floor and made a hasty toilet. As I went to crown the edifice by putting on my hat, a name written on the lining of the article arrested me. It was "FORT-NOYE." We had changed hats! With this sphinx, then, I had passed a whole night unconsciously. No wonder my dreams were bad. Descending, I asked some time-table questions of the landlord, and added, "Do you know a certain M. Fortnoye, whom you have given me for fellow-lodger?"

"Do I know him? He is our champagne-merchant—mine and all the hotel-keepers' within twenty leagues. And a

MOTION SUSPENDED: RESOLUTION TABLED FOR AMENDMENT.

fine man, sir, with his joke always in his cheek! You see, the trade makes the tradesman, for champagne-sellers keep the ball a-rolling: the business lets no man be dull. As for this one, he is always in good temper: he has it bottled in his brains. You should have seen him last night. Four students from Carls- ruhe and Heidelberg—he had them all under the table in no time, and at his own expense. But that is his style of increasing the connection: they come back to it sure enough, sir."

Mine host, so miserly with his words the night before, chatted this morning like a parrot: I took advantage of his

THE TAILBOARD.

loquacity to get the probable route of Fortnoye.

At some miles from Achern, in a romantic landscape, rise the solemn ruins of All-Saints' Abbey — *Allerheiligen.* It is a refuge fit for Carlyle's Eternal Silences. Hither, nevertheless, were bent the combined noises of Baden, Belgium and Alsace. Achern had been the focus, but Allerheiligen was the Mecca of the philharmonic pilgrimage. All the musicians and singers, as well as all the rest who were merely secular and auditory, would pour to-day into the ruined abbey. I hesitated but a minute: I took a seat on the tailboard of a terrible cart, and I followed the world—followed the drivers, followed the walkers, followed Fortnoye, followed my hat.

Every ten minutes we passed a pretty village, whose inhabitants, probably augmented by neighbors from the inner country, passed us in review. The peasants here are not like those whom you

BLACK FOREST FLOWERS.

see in Carlsruhe and Baden - Baden. You are already in the Black Forest. The countrymen were in ample red waistcoats and broad hat-brims, the blonde girls bare-headed, with floating ribbons. As we filed through these ranks of rustic spectators, the red waistcoats, alternating with the golden heads, shone like poppies in a field of wheat. The quantity of yellow tresses I saw on this excursion was truly edifying. I am certain that Germany produces a sufficiency to sur-

THE TRYSTING-PLACE.

round the globe with a ringlet of gold—a precious ecliptic, worthy enough to mark the course of the sun.

After passing through several hamlets —I think Ober-Achern, Furschenbach, Ottenhofen were among them—and consuming two hours of time, we descended from the cart to clamber up the hills.

Fifty minutes' climbing, and we paused in a little grove, which seemed to have been appropriated as point of reference for all the strayed revelers and disjointed couples who attended the concert. Here those who had lost their friends, girls who missed their lovers, and husbands divorced from their wives, met by mutual agreement. It was a concourse of Plato's half-souls, seeking their affinities anxiously and clamorously. Odd sounds, agreed upon no doubt as signals, made the little wood vocal: some crowed like cocks, some hooted like owls, some bellowed like all the herds of Bashan—a singular concert, preluding the genuine one. Every fatigue-cap, felt and kepi collected in the grove passed under my inspection, but I could not detect my own hat or the countenance of Fortnoye. The throng gradually dispersed, moving together in a particular direction, and I followed the rest. Every one went to buy tickets at a box-office temporarily set up behind a high rock. I secured a card with a lyre on it, a first-class place, and the change for a half-florin. A hundred paces farther, as the path descend-

SHADES OF THE BLACK FOREST.

ed through the trees, a view burst upon us of the ruins and their site.

Seated in its rocky funnel, with an amphitheatre of noble scenery around, and the echoes of the Grindbachs cataract muffled in the tufted woods, the abbey of Allerheiligen was of old a nest of learning, famous for the sapience of its sylvan monks. Here Elmy the gypsy, whose student-lover had climbed to the crow's nest to recover her betrothal-ring saw the brave boy dashed to pieces at her feet, and only obtained the precious token from his dead hand. The betrothed couples of the present day I found more comfortably engaged: the lasses were pouring out beer for the lads, and family groups, perched everywhere on the hillside, were regaling themselves with viands frugally brought from home. Those heads of families who missed the shadow of a tree or a thicket tranquilly dined in the sun. Indeed, they were not entirely deprived of shelter, seeing that the breadths of felt with which they shaded their own brows cast a liberal and grateful penumbra over the whole group. Nowhere else can you find mankind wearing such solid and ample parasols: if these honest Black Foresters could measure their height by the circumference of their brims, they would be giants. What was strange, neither in the field at the bottom of the funnel nor on the sides was there a sign that these pilgrims of melody thought of anything but eating and drinking. I should have argued the concert to be postponed *sine die* if I had not accidentally perceived two fat bass-viols and several slender coffins containing violins proceeding toward the ruined abbey, the latter still closed to the public, even to those with tickets for the first place.

It was an animated sight. The extemporized tables, the bar arranged along

GENTLEMEN OF THE ORCHESTRA.

a low ruined wall, whose fallen stones offered seats to the drinkers, were occupied by moving throngs, amongst which I ceased not to pursue the trail of my fugitive hat, and of that unaccountable Fortnoye for whose discovery my hat-hunt was but a pretext. For a quarter of an hour, with my eyes wide open, did I turn to the cardinal points of this mighty funnel, boxing the compass of Allerheiligen, when the sound of popping champagne-corks arrested my ear. No better indication of my man could be thought of. I posted myself near the drinkers, who turned out to be a party of students, and sought an excuse to enter into conversation with them, not despairing of finding in the group some who had disgraced themselves with Fortnoye the night before.

A quick young collegian anticipated me. Instantly observing my tin box, he said very courteously, "Are you a botanist, sir?" As I was about to profit by the interview to lead up to the subject of Fortnoye, he continued: "I am a botanist myself: I am studying for the profession of drugs. If you would find an excellent field, go five miles from here, to the base of the Tiberg. The *Anagallis Arvensis* grows there in abundance. Your health, sir!"

The whole party rose, touched glasses and trooped off laughing, not without reason: the plant adorned with so much fine Latin is no other than the chickweed, oftener sought by canaries than by botanists. But I remembered how mercilessly I had hoaxed MacMeurtrier with the tobacco plants and pineapple fruits, and felt that I had no right to be too much put out.

The vacated students' table offered itself invitingly, and I seated myself. These tables were under the agency of the chief forester of the estates, transformed on Sundays and holidays to an innkeeper. With an eye to business, this functionary offered no alternative to his guests but rabbits killed in his demesne or the ever-prevailing and monotonous ham. Among the waiters—whom I suspected, from the dignity of their chief, to be wood-choppers and charcoal-burners on ordinary days—I succeeded in making one excited individual listen to me. I ordered rabbit and Affenthaler wine: he reappeared after a long time with ham and beer. But I took care, after the first mouthful, not to complain, for the beer was Bavarian and the ham Westphalian. As I tasted the one and the other with the gusto of an epicure, suddenly my table, with the plates and bottles, resounded to a tinkling hail—a hail of money. Whence came this Danaë shower? No one knew, but its effects, satis-

AURI SACRA FAMES.

factory to some, were for others, and especially myself, most deplorable. The peasantry from the heights around us, hearing the metallic ring, plunged upon our tables, our benches, our feet and our dishes, to collect the small change falling from the skies. It continued to rain, not kreutzers only, but little coins of silver. The instinct of avarice spread through all the throng; the crowds poured down the hill like a landslide; men and women, young girls, lads and children, all eager for the quarry, fought hardily for this uncelestial manna. Woe to the girl who received a kreutzer in her bodice! she was not to remain the possessor. The waiters, sent up to pacify the fray, yielded to the game with avidity, and seemed to find themselves in a new California. The dogs, even, plunged into the loot, disdaining indeed the silver, but not the ham-bones and little saddles of rabbit. In the confusion the benches turned over on their sides, the tables on their backs, followed by some of the diners. My own lot was cast among these latter.

I got up bareheaded and shamefaced, but no one had noticed my reverse. The rain of silver had taken another direction, and the world, as of old, had run after the money. A playful dog was shaking and worrying a hat a few feet off: he readily rendered me my head-covering, or more properly that of Fortnoye. A bell gave signal that the concert was beginning. Hurrying up to the ruin, I posted myself outside the door,

THE DÉBRIS.

where all the holders of first-class places necessarily defiled before me: not a single Fortnoye!

What an unfortunate notion was mine, to chase this invisible and possibly chimerical enigma into the ruined wilderness of All-Saints! Had I taken the morning train, I should be already at Strasburg. The interior of the abbey, now overflowing with music, tempted me to enter.

Truly, the picture was original. The orchestra and the orpheonists filled the sacred apsis. Despoiled of their stained glass, the long Gothic windows were painted instead with the distant landscape and the gilded summits of mountainous crags. The audience was divided into two portions or categories: the first occupied impromptu benches, laid from base to base of the fallen pillars; the second stood up behind. Authorized by my ticket to mingle with the first, my entrance among the hindmost obliged me to content myself with the last.

The overture to Mendelssohn's *Antigone* had already been executed, as well as a fine choral of Louis Lacombe's, and I had a brief glimpse of the collected performers—a tableau full of piquant German character, and worthy to rank with Hogarth's picture representing the opera of *Judith*. My view was a short one, for, the sun coming out from behind a cloud, every lady in the parquet opened out the implement she carried, which was no circumscribed and feeble sunshade, but a liberal umbrella, provided in view of a possible storm like that of yesterday. The men delayed not to imitate the example, and my inspection of the performance was intercepted by a bubbling sea of variegated hemispheres. Meantime, my own position among the poorer multitude was flooded with hot sunshine: I lost no time in changing it; and a lusty elder tree, clinging to the ruined wall just behind me, offered me a natural sunshade more agreeable than the circular shadow of the best *regenschirm* in Germany. The perch offered me another advantage. It placed me in a post of observation where I could interpret the secret of the mysterious shower of gold.

At the base of the hillock which I occupied a group of students were whispering and busying themselves over some stealthy preparation. In the ringleader I recognized my disciple of drugs, the same who had suggested a botanizing tour after chickweed. He held a sack, containing probably a provision of copper change, and each of the band, rummaging in his pockets, added a supply of small moneys, and even of silver: as for my druggist, he drew forth a handful of gold, whose opulent gleam was clearly visible to me in my hiding-place. When he had mixed a portion of this in

PLAYFULNESS.

the bag, the whole conspiracy of tempters busied themselves in flinging it over the wall amongst the mass of second-class auditors, whose ranks I had just left. And the scenes of dinner-time were not tardy in recurring—the scramble, the bickering, the topsy-turvy and the chaos.

Poor Germany! I thought: is it thus she distributes the gold just wrung from bleeding France? With her *nouveaux riches* tempted only to senseless freaks, and her lower classes famished as ever, it is little profit she will get from her undigested wealth. The spectacle, testifying to nothing so much as to the misery of the German populace, saddened me more than it diverted me. I was still thinking about it when the sun, having seen all it cared about of the concert,

HOGARTHIAN GROUP.

re-entered its tent of clouds, and every umbrella, with simultaneous promptness, changed from a hemisphere to a straight line. I passed into the enclosure once more, just before the *finale*. I got a better place than at first, and enjoyed a full view of the singers and the instrumentalists.

Among the former I remarked a performer who gesticulated a good deal more than he sang, and whose looks were constantly turned toward myself. His countenance seemed American in its outlines, and bore a likeness to the countenance of James Athanasius Grandstone. But how was it possible to suppose that individual amongst these professionals? Nevertheless, it was strictly and identically he.

I had known many students of pharmacy: never had any of them fed the multitude with gold. I had met many an American wine-seller: never one who had fitted himself to compete with German musicians. It was a day of surprises. After seeing Jupiter raining gold under the metamorphosis of a Heidelberg student, it remained to me to see my compatriot, who could hardly hold his own at college in a "*Gaudeamus igitur*," in the guise of an orpheonist. At the side of Athanasius, singing or not singing, but with mouths wide open all the same, and in every hand a scroll of music, stood his whole dinner-table of Épernay.

THE PARASOL.

The circle that had enjoyed the Eleusinian mysteries of the wine-cellar, even to the little caustic hunchback, and that had started with Grandstone to pass his birthday at the Falls of Schaffhausen, was reunited here at Achern, needing only myself to form the clasp. Near the witty dwarf, and bending over the same sheet, I recognized a pale face, with a red boss in the middle: it was palpably MacMeurtrier, the homœopathist, preceded by his ardent nose. How came this Scotchman in the group?

But I was not at the end of my astonishments. As I made my way through the dispersing crowd which separated me from the performers, I ran against an individual. Looking up, I recognized my hat: the obstacle was Fortnoye! I quickly had an explanation of all these wonders.

In the railway-carriage which had conveyed the birthday party to Strasburg, Grandstone and his friends had formed a plan with Fortnoye to meet all together at the musical festival of Achern. The homœopathist, for his part, bound likewise for Schaffhausen, had run upon the whole convivial group in the Krone Hotel at that spot. The embossed dwarf—whom it will be more civil to call hereafter by his real name of Somerard—had attacked him in a moment as lawful prey. Strange to say, the encounter begun in jest had terminated confidentially: something imperturbable and canny about the Scot proved attractive to the hunchback, subject himself to all the irregular vivacities so often noticed in his kind. MacMurtagh or Meurtrier, having disarmed his waspish opponent by dint of stolid calm, was destined to yet another victory: at the close of a long evening's conversation on homœopathy, Somerard, always ailing and doctor-hunting, declared himself a convert. The famous combination of vegetable magnetism with *similia similibus curantur* had fascinated him. This target of the wit's former scorn, this heron on stilts, this man with double knee-pans, recognized from a sketch of Hogarth's, had become his veneration and comfort.

Grandstone, over a cigar, confided to me the details of this strange partnership: "I don't know what to think. They'll persuade me that I have seen the cure with my own eyes. This Scotch-

AMATEUR PERFORMERS.

man, who doesn't look particularly like the devil, pretends that he can make the force of the sap in young trees communicate itself to his patients. He makes his magnetic passes all the while, you see. Now, I myself have been with Foster when he read letters through his forehead: I'm not prepared to say there is not something in magnetism. But you ought to hear the rigmaroles that Murtagh says over his patients: the greatest rot you ever listened to! And he says he can straighten up any case of spinal curvature. I have seen Somerard hugging a young poplar tree by the hour. When he came away he said he felt perfectly full of sap. What I'll ask you to explain is, that the tree certainly drooped and turned out the wrong side of its leaves."

It appeared to me that my mercantile young American was half a convert himself. Having remarked that Somerard, who was rich enough for the luxury, had actually engaged the Scotchman as professional companion, he proceeded to account for the presence of his band among the performers rather than among the audience. It seems they had come on foot through the Forest from Freiburg in the Breisgau, whither the railway had transported them from Bâle. On their tramp they had fallen in with a contingent of the grand orpheonist army. They had dined with them, supped with them, slept in the same barn. Next day they had awaked to find themselves fast friends, and it had seemed good to all hands to remain united, even within the precincts of art.

While Grandstone, in satisfying my surprises, suggested so many new ones, I did not lose from view Fortnoye, the man of mystery, and my rival in the pretty hotel at Carlsruhe. He was speaking with the forester, no doubt on the subject of champagne. Their colloquy finished, I approached and offered him his hat.

"Ah, monsieur," he said, laughing pleasantly, "you are, then, my unknown room-mate? You must have taken me for a thief. But where have I seen you ere now?"

VEGETABLE MAGNETISM.

I replied promptly: "At Strasburg, where I sat at the same table with you and your new Masonic convert, Mac-Meurtrier here. Possibly, also, you saw me last night when you put *hors de combat* your friends the students, and diverted all the hotel-waiters from attending to me."

"A truce to these follies," he replied. "I am winding up my bachelor life."

"Are you thinking of marriage?" I asked with unnecessary interest.

"Who knows?"

"Pardon!" said I, "but I have heard much of you lately: it was at Carlsruhe, at the boarding-house—"

He blushed faintly: "You know the lady who keeps the house where I put up?"

"Francine? I knew her as a baby: I brought her news of her father, whom I had just left at Noisy."

"Hullo!" (The French for the exclamation, I think, was "Tiens! tiens!") "I saw him the same day as you. I know you now, monsieur: you are the man with the two chickens."

9

PART IX.

ASTRAY IN THE BLACK FOREST.

THE LAKE OF UNDINES.

YOUR vilest matchmaker is Death. Year after year he weds the tender and the base. His call, even as Keats's purer bird, is heard through every age "alike by emperor and clown." What avails our protest? From time to time some delicate prince, first conscious of the natural, helpless antipathy, shall idly ask, for humanity's Cæsars and Alexanders, whether they must come to this fashion i' the earth; and Death's groomsman the gravedigger sings twice or thrice, "Oh, a pit of clay for to be made for such a guest is meet." Again and again some wild Constance, morbid bride of corruption, shall shriek, "Arise forth from the couch of lasting night," and offer her maniac kiss to the "détestable bones," and put her eyeballs in the "vaulty brows." And Death, more horrible than any *duègne complaisante*, re-

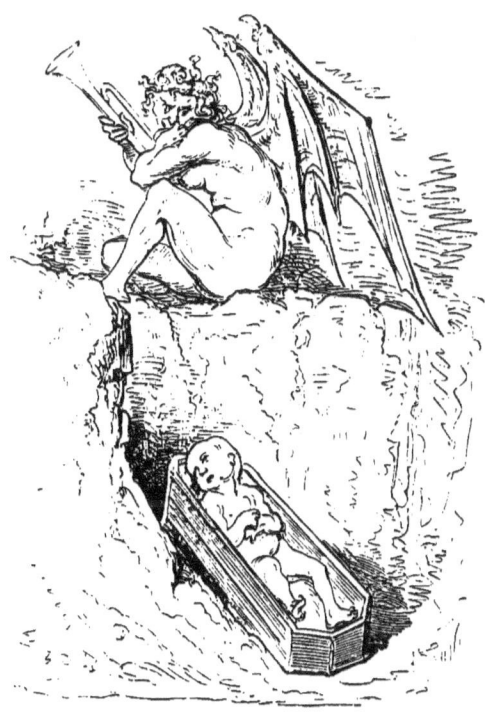

ILL-FAME AND INNOCENCE.

ceives with his own grin his pennies from the filmy eyes. Our fine delicacy is nothing, our choice is impotent.

And Beauty shall be laid in Yorick's bed, for innocence must slumber with the clown to-night, and in the grave is no device nor difference.

I am approaching the most serious part of my story. I should be sorry for the reader to think that Paul Flemming can occupy himself with only *dilettante* studies and ballads of travel. Fill thyself with angrier ink, O pen that long since wrotest the dirge of Emma of Ilmenau: do thy spiriting darkly, as when, by those lone banks of Neckar, there fell a star from heaven! I have no plain and easy tale to tell this morning, and I must needs fortify myself, as in the old time, with the old words, when I said, "O thou poor authorling! reach a little deeper into the human heart. Touch those strings — touch those deeper strings, and more boldly, or the notes will die away like whispers."

It is now four or five years since a lonely and beautiful woman, hurrying across the wealthy plains of Belgium with an infant in her arms, was forced to pause at Brussels. When she rose from a sick bed the angel of death had stolen from her bosom the little tender babe, and had laid the poor abortive being in the cemetery of Laaken. Just able at length to walk, she stole to the churchyard to bid a last adieu to the grave, for uncontrollable reasons urged her speedy departure from Belgium. "Take care of the poor flowers," she said, putting money into the hand of a stolid sexton. Then, in a voice all broken with sobs, "Ah, darling, darling little daughter! why cannot I stay near you? What gentle eye will ever dwell on your sweet grave when your mother herself abandons you? Who will tend these desolate little roses and violets?"

"I will!" said a voice which seemed to rise upon the wind. She looked around, but saw nobody: was the sound a lingering echo of delirium? She came in haste next day at an early hour snatched with difficulty from the routine of travel. The grave was already covered with fresh plants for all its petty length, and guarded with a grating of iron. "My prayers are answered," said the poor traveler. When she had gone a figure approached the tomb from the nearest clump of cypresses. It was a young man of vigorous proportions, but with a face worn and saddened with anxiety. He laid his hand upon the rail. "Poor baby!" said he, "it is in the name of maternity!"

After that no week passed by but the young philanthropist returned, darkly studying the bed where chance had laid the baby-bride of Eternity. He was a home-sick Frenchman, and truly few young men but those of the Latin race would be capable of an action generous, yet uncalled-for and slightly mock-heroic. Only briefly a resident of Brussels, and driven thither by a schoolboy's manifestation which had been viewed in a political aspect, he had formed the habit

FALLS AT ALLERHEILIGEN.

of promenading in the cemetery. The small creature, hidden in the grave without ever having met his eye, became for him an interest and an object in life. He visited no one else, avoiding even the other refugees tempted by bankruptcy or ill-fortune into the friendly territory. Sick for his native land, he established a parallel between himself and this tiny stranger withered on a foreign soil. It lived in his fancy as a pallid cherub, and alternated with imperfect visions of a graceful lady half seen among the trees. His constant visits were noticed, and with no friendly eyes.

"What would you think, yourself, Flemming?" said Grandstone, who recited, as we strolled toward the cascades of Allerheiligen, the history from which I have condensed this shadowy little idyl.

"I think he was Quixotic, but a fine fellow."

"They didn't think him very fine in Brussels," said my young countryman. "You see, they don't give a hearty welcome in Belgian society to French refugees, being more used to fellows that have jumped their bail or to gentlemen of the Rochefort order than they are to Don Quixotes. It was too bad, though, the things they dared to drop about that baby and its supposed father. 'We had better part,' said the landlord who lodged him near the cemetery: 'there are too many of your family in our faubourg.'

"Was he obliged to move away, then, from the grave he had tended so generously?"

"It was of the less importance, for his banishment from French soil was repealed. Before departing he came once

LADDER OR BRIDGE?

more to the churchyard of Laaken. He left a considerable sum with the sexton, making him promise to keep the place in his special care. Nothing could be more handsome of Fortnoye."

—For it was again of Fortnoye, the eternal, the inevitable Fortnoye, that the tale was told. I had been repeating to Grandstone his riddling words about an approaching matrimonal project on his part. The former continued:

"Do you fancy that even if he wants to marry, a girl who goes over the country with undecipherable and mysterious babies is the wife for our whimsical, scrupulous Paladin? It was a pure infamy, though, to invent that coarse slander about him and the child."

"But who is the supposed mother of the infant?"

"Why, don't you see? Her godmother is well known at Brussels, where she shut her door against the adventuress. Of course it is your pretty hostess of Carlsruhe."

"What! Francine Joliet? The infamy

is in attaching any kind of mystery to that lovely creature's conduct."

I was proceeding to defend my dainty Francine at greater length when our dialogue was interrupted by a simultaneous cry. It was a cry of delight, for we had now mounted the hills, those sunny summits which had filled so beautifully the arches of the ruined windows in the abbey, and the cascades of Allerheiligen were before us. From the eminence we had reached, stretched out in their silver length, were unfolded to our sight the multiplied cataracts, like twenty rivers standing story over story.

Our comrades were waiting for us a little farther on, Fortnoye among them: as we neared each other I stepped briskly up to him and grasped his hand, a manœuvre which seemed considerably to surprise him. It was a salute proceeding from the grave at Laaken.

Swelled by the tributes of the Murg, the Enz and the numerous water-courses that drain the Black Forest, the falls of Allerheiligen have torn their way through a rocky tract, whose points of resistance have looped up the stream into numerous draperies. Formerly, to trace these cata-

SAINT SATAN.

A CARTLOAD.

racts through their whole length, the forester or hunter was obliged to slide over dangerous crags at the risk of his life.

Later, a series of ladders was thrown from peak to peak, where travelers with strong heads might clamber at their slippery will. At present, the whole is arranged for the tourist with plank-walks, rails and bridges; yet many of the latter, in the history of the evolution pursued by Allerheiligen, remain in a state of partial development, and hesitate giddily between ladder and bridge.

The country-folk from the musical festival crowded the stairways, where the spray from the torrent baptized a wonderful variety of rustic costumes. I essayed a rude sketch of the scene, but the fantastic embossed man, Somerard, by dint of flying and capricoling about me, and professing ecstasy at the effect of the blank paper, destroyed my drawing before it was begun. As we crossed from the left bank to the right one I plucked a fine gentian, and opened my tin box to receive it: I found already in the cavity a sheaf of nettles. Evidently the dwarf about to become a giant had chosen me as his victim for the day. As I shook a finger at him he puffed up quite globularly with laughter: perhaps in elongating he would grow more wise; and so, with jokes and Joe Millers, we took leave of Allerheiligen, ever memor-

LAKESIDE REVERIES.

able for its processions of *buffo* characters trailing between the coulisses of a grand, austere landscape.

At the entrance to the little grove where I had found such a lively scene of rendezvous in the morning were numbers of cabs and carts. Grandstone, Fortnoye, the homœopathist, Somerard, two other champagne-feasters from Épernay, a chance friend whom Grandstone had seduced from among the orpheonists, and myself, formed a little drama of eight persons. We engaged two carts. Grandstone went to direct the peasant who drove. I supposed we were on the return to Achern.

"To the Mummelsee!" said Grandstone.

"Is that the place where we are to dine?" I asked, rather absently, with a regret flung backward at my breakfast, interrupted by the shower of gold.

"We dine at the Hirsch."

"Why not at Achern? I shall certainly take the evening train for Paris. My chum Hohenfels must be almost a maniac by this time."

"We take the Paris train too; at least, if not for Paris, as far along as Épernay. But, you innocent, do you suppose people come to Allerheiligen without going to the Mummelsee?"

"What is a Mummelsee?"

"The Mummelsee is the Lake of Undines," said Somerard.

"And where is this Lake of Undines?"

"At the Mummelsee."

It appeared unnecessary to prolong this circular argument. Besides, the term "Lake of Undines" had a soft ring to my ear. We rode through a gentle valley toward Oberkappel, exchanging the din of the Funnel for the completest pastoral silence, punctuated here and there by the notes of the birds. Our party did little to disturb the scene: some smoked, with the grateful taciturnity of smokers; some slept at the bottom of

ASPIRATION.

the carts, where even Somerard, rocked in the cradle of his back, forgot his pranks in a succession of falsetto snores. For my part, I mused on a certain artisanne cap at Carlsruhe. Surely that milk-white talisman was without a smirch, notwithstanding Grandstone's careless tales and a censorious world. Fortnoye had not spoken with blame of the gentle girl; and she, as I reflected with a pang,

FALLS OF SCHAFFHAUSEN.

was so shy, so grateful, so devoted in speaking of him!

Suddenly, as I saw the floating capstrings very distinctly before me, they gave a smart crack like a whiplash. We had arrived at the "Hirsch." I must have been nodding.

The Hirsch is a large *gasthaus*, an ordinary stopping-place for drovers, for clock-sellers, or for the intelligent tourist bound for the Lake of Undines. Placed between the route for Würtemberg and that for the Mummelsee, it presents on the side toward the latter the form of a large chalet, where you can enter by a human-looking doorway, and have the range of two stories of chambers. On the side of the Würtemberg road you

AN UNSOCIAL COMPANION.

find but one floor, and an entrance into a garret like a hay-mow: it is the loss of level between the Seebach valley and the slopes of the Black Forest. We entered a large, low, whitewashed room, furnished with limping tables and chairs of unassuming rustic-work. One ornament was on the wall, a tinted wood-cut of Waldhantz the Poacher.

Germany has plenty of legendary Wild

Huntsmen, but the jolly Waldhantz is the appurtenance of the Black Forest. This amiable being, the king of poach-

AN ACCIDENT.

ers, used to course the woods with an ingenious little gun, easily concealed, and Saint Hubert took good care to keep his gamebag filled. But one day he met a sinister-looking black-haired personage, resembling more the Prophet of Evil than the good Saint Hubert.

"Good-day, Waldhantz!" said the stranger sulphurously.

"Good-day, Satan!" replied the bold poacher.

"What is that droll little thing in your hand?"

"That? Oh, it is my pipe. Do you smoke?"

"Show me how to use it. Is your pipe filled?"

"It is." And Waldhantz, who had conceived the beneficent idea of ridding the world of its arch-enemy, put the barrel up to the smiling lips of his new acquaintance.

"Have you your flint there? Now light." With a prayer to Hubert, Waldhantz fired his fowling-piece. When the smoke cleared away Saint Satan was seen in good form, but coughing out clouds of buckshot. "What strong tobacco you use!" he said with a queer wink. Waldhantz had the glory of endeavor, but not of success. It sufficed him, however, for enduring fame.

The rays of the sun were getting level. We provided ourselves with alpenstocks, and with another bit of iron-shod wood called a guide. Our course lay along the rivulet which descends from the Mummelsee. I had intended to talk seriously with Fortnoye on the route, but the steepness of the ascent forbade conversation. Although I leaned affectionately on the scapulary angle of the guide, I panted like an August cart-dog. To add to my humiliation, as I painfully divided off the pathway I perceived overhead, leaping goatlike from rock to rock, a Titan scaling the mountains, the patient of our homœopathist, Somerard of the mocking eye. For one moment I was ready to believe in the vegetable-magnetic theory of the doctor, who toiled inadequately after on his interminable legs.

A grand basin turned by some puissant potter in the arid clay of the surrounding hills—leaden waters, stagnant and thick, without fish within or insects or flowers above,—such is the Mummelsee. Evidently as birds will only breed

THE REAR.

in an untouched nest, the Undines demand for their lodgment a massive laver sacred from profane company.

At times, however, the Mummelsee is stirred from its depths, and that too when no wind is breathing. The leaves do not flutter in the forest, the raven's breast is not curled as he sails motionless over the lake. The strange agitation is soul-thrilling and terrible. The nymphs who live below in bowers of coral (it is probably the only instance known of the coral-builder as a fresh-water polyp) come to the surface in the full of every moon. They come up like bubbles and disport on the surface, where their gleaming, moonlight-washed bodies seem to be lilies blushing into roses. When the cock crows the frolic and jest, the wanton diving and swimming, cease in a moment, and the nymphs plunge to wait for another full moon. Sometimes the dawn surprises them: then there appears a dreadful Uncle Kuhleborn, a dwarfish ugly monster, who threatens them and drives them headlong into the lake, and the waters are left dull and sullen. Once the lasses of Seebach were surprised at their spinning by a lovely apparition, a fair girl who sat among them and spun from her ivory wheel a threadlike fountain-spray. She always left them at one hour, but the son of the house set back the clock, and that night she went hastily to the Mummelsee and threw herself into the water. Then a complaining sound was heard, and the lake began to foam and boil. But the young

"FIZZ!"

nan, infatuated, flung himself into the whirlpool, and then the water was still, but the spinning Undine appeared no more.

We stretched ourselves on a hillock, as appositely as possible for the visit of any fairy with ivory wheel or a foam-spinning distaff, but our receptive state was not honored with an apparition.

THE SICK-BED.

We lay and caressed our alpenstocks beside this small parody of the Dead Sea, beside this flat frog-pond for whose sake we had gone aside from Achern and committed ourselves to a journey. Some of those green-coated musicians, the frogs, began to be audible in the sedgy banks, and reminded me for a moment of the young apprentice in green who had long ago sung to me to "beware." The worst of it was that MacMurtagh, the Scotch charlatan, began to take me, as if he might follow the lead of his employer, for the butt of his clumsy badinage.

"Oh!" I said casually, "this is a poor exchange for the cascades of Allerheiligen!"

"—Which are themselves a lame substitute for the falls we have just seen at Schaffhausen," said the Scot. "Ah, Mr. Flemming, you have seen nothing! If you had been privileged, like us, to be at Schaffhausen, while reading at the same time the matchless description of Ruskin!" And the doctor began to recite, through his red nose, and with the utmost disenchantment of a strong Scotch brogue, a long passage beginning "Stand for an hour at the Falls of Schaffhausen."

Grandstone, wearying rapidly of this entertainment, turned to me with a groan. "Don't you smoke?" said he.

The incense from a number of mouths was curling among the mists of the Mummelsee. MacMurtagh interrupted himself: "Mr. Flemming smokes only by proxy and with the aid of four negroes," he said ironically, alluding to my little quiz upon him at Strasburg.

I laughed good-naturedly enough. "You really must forgive me," I said. "When I popped that joke on you it was in remembrance of the duke of Mississippi, to whom my dear Frau Kranich introduced me at Ems, and who, she assured me, kept a private secretary to 'smoke to him.' As for the Schaffhausen falls, if you were acquainted with my former history you would know that I saw them in those same old times, before you were born. Since then I have grown lazy. I no longer take tobacco, even by proxy: in revenge I take my waterfalls infinitessimally diluted, at the hands of a homœopathist!"

TRUTH AND HER FAVORITE WELL.

Fortnoye, stretched apart from the rest, on his pelvis and his two elbows, formed a sort of tripod. To escape from the recoil of my shot at MacMurtagh, I went up and offered him a penny for his thoughts. He turned to me a face that was surprising for its depth and tenderness of expression. "I am thinking of a fairy," said he, "whom if I had the power I would bid arise this moment out of yonder lake." I know not why it was —I am sure I was torn with jealousy— but on that I gave him my hand for the second time.

In order to get an idea of the dignity of the hills on which the Black Forest is planted, our younger men had determined to ascend the Hornisgrinde, an excursion which would occupy the remainder of the day. This is the most elevated peak of a range which extends from Sassbachwalden to Oberkappel. For my part, I started in the rear of the party, but with a covert determination to botanize and sketch in such a manner as to be left entirely behind. The fatigues of the morning had already told on my knees, which felt curiously uncertain under me, and I was wiping my brow already when my companions had mounted the first hillock. As for the short gentleman, the lively Somerard, he departed for the loftiest peaks like an eagle, and as if the best the Schwarzwald had to show were all insufficient for his desires.

My own rearward location, however, soon became the most popular one. In a short time I saw our guide returning to the lake, and looking like a Savoyard with his monkey as he carried the ambitious Somerard on his shoulder. He had fallen all of a heap in the pathway. MacMurtagh, who with the rest followed the descending cortége, said that it was a superexcitation of the assimilative organs, the result of an overdose of young ash tree in the morning, aggravated by the rarer air of the heights.

At the Hirsch, where we hardly arrived before nightfall, the table was already

ONE OF THE CHORUS.

set, and we found to our wonder at each plate a noble bottle of champagne labeled Le Brun, of which house Fortnoye was a special agent. "The Le Brun brand," said he carelessly, as if to conceal the generosity of his handsome treat, 'you'll find the most honest and conscientious of all the champagnes." This surprise, arranged over-night by our invaluable companion, put us all in good humor and obliterated our fatigues, except those of poor Somerard, for whom a bed was laid in a corner of the great room. The invincible dwarf, sociable to

BROKEN SLUMBERS.

the last, feebly applauded with his hands when he saw the *sierra* of bottles stretched along the table.

As the repast proceeded some rather effervescent talk was heard, and witticisms and good things were not wanting. Fortnoye, the prophet and interpreter of the vintage, while continually adding to the fund of wit, maintained that the whole exhibition was due less to our natural ingenuity than to qualities inherent in the Le Brun brand. He argued that he could recognize its true effect in our gay but not silly repartees. This gift, he pleaded, was the special one of the champagne he represented, and thereupon he developed a most extraordinary theory, which he claimed to have been years in forming. Let him hear, he said, such and such a bright speech, such and such a sarcastic reply, and he could tell whether it were born under the influence of a sparkling or a still wine. At need he believed he could specify the very part of the Marne département where the speech or the sarcasm had been fermented and put in stock, whether at Rheims, Épernay, Avize or Sillery. In his opinion, Moët tended rather to imagination than to mirth, Montebello inspired musing rather than conversation, while Clicquot turned naturally to politics; and so on with twenty obscurer labels, which he ranged under general headings, such as "wines of wit," wines "patriotic," or

"POP!"

"anecdotic," or "hearty," or "jolly," or even "a little broad."

The theory amused us abundantly, and I gave with the rest my vote for the classification of Fortnoye, without letting him know how many prejudices I had been forced to conquer before coming over to his side. Fortnoye, in accepting our comments and administering some vigorous strokes of his own, had never got the better of a sort of dreamy gravity which seemed habitual with him.

This man had seemed to me at Épernay a mere proficient in vulgar horseplay: at the house in Carlsruhe I learned to think him a suspicious character. Engaged as I had been in his pursuit by a ridiculous accident and a peevish curiosity, I had him now face to face without the ability to see him clearly. Which was the true Fortnoye—the ambulant wine-agent, the poet, the philanthropist or the buffoon? They were all present in one, but the buffoon was disguised in the philosopher's mantle: his thoughts laughed oftener than his features. A keen, discriminating mind leaped up from the wine-cask, like Truth from her fabled well. As for the heart, I had but to trust the God's acre at Laaken for that. There remained but one more quality of Fortnoye's to test him in—that of bard.

At dessert I invited him to sing some of his own songs. He complied by rolling out more than one brindisi. They were transparently joyous, light-hearted and sincere, like fragments of Burns: at the moment of the most hilarious expression of gayety they were furnished with a penetrating note of pathos or sentiment, which, shaded in the most ex-

INTELLIGENCE.

quisite manner by the manly voice of the singer, sent the strangest thrill of sympathy into the pleasure with which we listened, and matched our delighted ears with an accompaniment of swimming eyes. We joined in the choruses with absolute fury: the German orpheonist contributed to these refrains some variations and Tyrolean jodels which enlivened if they did not entirely follow them; and the sick Somerard, determined not to be forgotten at his corner, piped in the choir like a friendly steam-whistle. The fairies must have heard it all in their lake with feelings of envy.

Already, at several attempts, our two drivers had striven to detach us from the table. The night, they said, was gloomy, and it would be perilous crossing the valleys of Kappel and Seebach after it was too late to see the heads of the horses before us. We paid small attention. "One song more!" we cried, and still Fortnoye, with his grave enthusiasm, sang of cheer and hospitality, and the German vocalist, lashed to his utmost endeavors, sent forth his voice in Tyrolean exercises that resembled a syrupy liquid *blobbing* forth from a gi-

THE BLACK FOREST.

gantic champagne-bottle. At last we rose, and the charioteers cracked their whips with the relish of anticipation

Doctor MacMurtagh, who had vainly endeavored to secure a hearing for certain effusions of Allan Cunningham and the Ettrick Shepherd, now declared his patient unfit to bear the jolts of the wagon. He refused to leave his charge. Grandstone, too, said it would be disloyal to quit Somerard's bedside. Fortnoye declared that wine-merchants should work in harmony, and governed his conduct by Grandstone's. The two natives of Épernay were glad of an excuse to stay with Fortnoye; the orpheonist, cracking a fresh bottle, found himself very well where he was, and promised to spend the night at table; and I, for my part—what could I do against such a formidable majority? "*Resolved*," said Fortnoye, "That to return to Achern without M. Somerard would be an act of treason which the remotest posterity would brand on us as a crime." ("Hear! hear!" said the congress.) "*Resolved*, As Doctor Meurtrier yonder promises to set his patient up again by morning with the aid of a few juleps of poplar and birch tree, that we engage in another little project. *Resolved*, That we gain on foot to-morrow, not Achern again, but Appenweier, a nearer town, and a station where the railroad to Baden makes a branch to that of Kehl. We thus save

RESTING IN THE WOODS.

time and improve our acquaintance with the Black Forest."

The majority became unanimity, and we sent the carts rattling back to Achern. The landlord, not unused to making a bed-room out of his dining-hall, threw a few mattresses over the floor, where we stretched ourselves, rather ill at ease. The orpheonist alone, true to his promise, remained all night stolidly upright at table, communing with a large pot of beer and a small bottle of Kirschwasser.

Bright and briskly we quitted the grand hotel of the Stag in the morning. We directed our course for the little town of Appenweier on the road to Kehl, and I thought of an early return homeward, and an encounter with Hohenfels at Marly. The cows were going out to pasture: they knew their way better than James Grandstone, who volunteered to guide us, knew ours. Ottenhafen and Lautenbach left behind, we admired the pretty valley of Salzbach, and passed various tiny and almost nameless hamlets, when a town came in sight—surely Appenweier and the Kehl railroad!

The town was Oppenau, and we had overshot the station. Grandstone was dismissed without arrears of wages: we sought a more experienced guide. Venturing into a handsome village-house and drinking a glass of beer, we asked the red-waistcoated owner for a cicerone. He pointed to a tall lout, a ferryman, who had just brought some countrymen over the stream which laved the cottage wall. We explained to the boatman our wish to go to Appenweier, and he replied by two gestures—one an affirmative nod,

LARGESS.

the other an invitation with his forefinger to get into the boat.

This Charon conducted us for an endless time along his little river, the Rench or the Ramsbach. Finally, leaping out and not looking behind him, he marched along a woody path, and then up a hill. We followed, our mutual conversation growing more and more sparse as our confidence decreased. This was our history from six o'clock A. M. until two in the afternoon. More than once I and my tin box sank to the ground for a little rest. Like the slave of some deceptive princess in the *Arabian Nights*, he led us through countless meanders, without answering our questions or ever once looking at us. At last he brought us to a town, and Grandstone, as the financial agent of the party, showered largess upon the guide and dismissed him, glad at last to have come to the termination of so long a walk. He made an exaggerated rustic bow and plunged into the recesses of the town.

At that moment I perceived on a signboard the name of the place. It was not Appenweier. It was Freudenstadt.

"Hurrah, boys!"—I could not forbear the joy of announcing our luck—" is not this delightful? We are lost in the Black Forest! Let us have adventures! Let us quote the vagabondage of Cervantes and the philosophy of Gil Blas! Let us adopt knight-errantry as a profession, charter our own association, and practice 'Exploration of the Black Forest, by a Company of Musical Amateurs, limited'!"

"Only hear the ancient boy!" Grandstone said in advance of me to the Scot, without thinking me so near. "Was there ever such a jolly old absurdity? He thinks he is still at the age when he used to walk around Heidelberg with his tiresome friend the baron."

We commenced our wilderness-life by getting a good comfortable dinner at the little tavern of Freudenstadt. The village proved to be a commercial centre, to the extent of irradiating upon a happy world the blessings of straw hats, glass mugs and musical boxes. There was a strange church here, constructed in some very remote antiquity on that cellular system which we pretend is most exclusively modern—the same system which Mr. Dickens so disapproved on his first visit among American prisons. The men and women at Freudenstadt worship in such privacy that they cannot see each other, though the preacher's desk is visible to every one of the congregation.

But I must render justice to the dinner. It was composed of cold sausage, of a salad, and a tart open and filled with Irish potatoes. It seemed to me preferable to the ordinary bill of fare at Delmonico's or Véfour's. But then I had been walking for it from six in the morning. It is proper, also, to celebrate the hotel bill: it bore not the slightest resemblance to my late one at Baden-Baden. It was computed in kreutzers, and cost us something like a dime each.

Again, then, we set ourselves in motion, having easily exhausted the commercial charms of Freudenstadt. Our guide, this time, was neither Grandstone nor the ferryman, but Accident. We were determined to have our souls thrilled with adventure.

The fact is, the Black Forest, so far as we could see it, appeared about as safe and quiet as the route from Boston to Cambridge, and we fancied we could have our adventurous experience at a very reasonable outlay in actual risk Behold us lost in the Black Forest!

PART X.

A WALK TO WILDBAD.

TIME PASSES.

"A SAW-MILL IN THE BLACK FOREST, May —.

'MY HOHENFELS: I have passed through such vicissitudes that I do not know the day of the month. I have sought in vain to turn my face toward my beloved hearthstone. I have drained the last drops of a bitter cup, which shall never be set to these lips again. I refer to the cup they gave me this morning for breakfast, the beverage in which was of so vile and wooden a quality that nothing shall tempt me to try its like while beer is to be had: I believe there was sawdust in the grounds. The bread, too, seems to be all bran here, or perhaps there is sawdust in that too. In fact, baron, I write to you this morning in the full disenchantment of a satisfied endeavor. 'Why must I be haunted' (I have always said) 'by this persistent, importunate *Me?* Why cannot Paul Flemming lose himself?' And now I *have* lost myself, and I cannot tell you what a poor triumph it is.

"Too tedious the tale to give you the recital of my repeated failures to meet you at Marly! Since the day when I started to rejoin you, with no greater eccentricity of direction than the characteristic one of going eastward when you and my rendezvous lay westward,—since that fair start there has not been a morning when I have not been rushing to find you, not a night when I have not prepared to throw myself upon you at railway speed. The accursed railway! that and the perfidy of seeming friends have kept us apart. At this moment I do not know where I am, nor have I an

144

idea how to get home. I do not know whether Appenweier or Freudenstadt is the nearer town, nor in which of them I want to be, could I get there. I am passing through the Black Forest, desperate and restless, with a motion in my wooden head like the perpetual motion which Wodenblock had in his timber leg, and which made him travel on through distant lands, a never-resting skeleton.

"Freudenstadt was the last village that had its baptismal appellation written up on a guide-post. Since that, I have been stringing village on to village without knowing or caring for their names. Everybody speaks a kind of jargon which is just enough like German for me to get it exquisitely wrong and set myself off on the wildest goose-chases. Yesterday, in a dim and lonely forest road, I was fairly frightened, for methought I heard eleven o'clock strike from twenty steeples at once: I feared my wits had fled. Going on a few steps, I found that the illusion proceeded from a wandering clock-seller, who had seen me first, and had stopped to advertise himself by setting all his mechanism in motion. While I paused to talk with him a cuckoo flew out from his breast, where he had hung his finest timepiece: the ghostly bird, unpleasing even to an unmarried ear, chimed in impertinently with our conversation, and the twenty clocks continued to strike as I asked my way of the fellow. He answered in patois, and the result of the whole chorus was indeed distracting. To make him talk better, I went so far as to buy a clock. He did indeed speak more loudly, and I understood him to say that beds and nourishment could be obtained at a neighboring mill. It has proved to be a saw-mill, and the beds are filled with sawdust. If you can think of any more incongruous and absurd figure than a lost man carefully carrying a clock through the recesses of the Black Forest, you must find it in Arnim's 'Wonder-Horn.' I no sooner had the automaton in my arms—there was a neat glass globe over it, and the utmost delicacy of carriage was required—than my one object in life was to find a place where I could set it down.

THE EAR DISPLEASED.

"Soon after dismissing my clock-seller —and indeed his prices were moderate —I heard a shot in the thick of the forest. I paused to listen, and directly a shadow was seen, faintly recalling old religious pictures of Saint John in the wilderness bearing the lamb. The Shadow fled at sight of me with extreme rapidity: I could but remark the lusty grace of the poacher as he made off with the goat dangling at his back. The incident was rather reassuring than otherwise, as a poacher argued proprietary rights, even here in the woods, and promised a vague connection with homes and haunts of men; but he was not an available person of whom to ask the way, being more ready to show me his heels than his tongue. The valley which led to Freudenstadt I have called the Valley of Rasselas, for it seems impossible to get out of it, and I believe I am all the while going round in a circle. I often hear, behind the green draperies of the forest, the songs of young girls, or the laughter of women washing clothes around a spring, or the lowing of herds: it is like dreaming. It is an enchanted vale, peopled only by echoes, or by such quaint and picturesque types as my freischütz and my time-bearer. Still, remembering the coffee and the bread, I am far from satisfied, and am convinced that losing the omnipresent Ego is not so fine as German poets have said it would be.

"Here there are no inns. The pilgrim deposits his staff in what corner soever he can. I asked one or two other people for the mill—a stout young woman who walked along braiding some fine and puerile-looking straw lace in her clumsy fingers, and a cowherd. I pursued this idea of the mill with some eagerness, for how could I forget, my own baron, that charming night we passed together in what we called the enchanted valley of Birkenau, when you sent the postilion right past the Weinheim landlord, who stood in his door solicitous to bless, and when we put up at the old mill on the Wechsnitz, where by the droning wheel we recited Goethe's

A POACHER.

'Youth and the Millbrook'? Ah me! that incident occurred while my life was comparatively unclouded. It was before I had met the Dark Ladie, and before some other and perhaps superior attractions had impinged on my course Well-a-day! I hope she is happy; but I am bound to confess that I do not know Mary Ashburton's present name, nor aught of her history since she married that traveling valet who convinced her that he was the Lord of Burleigh in disguise. I may have changed my views, I may have selected a very different type of female excellence; but time enough for that when we meet.

"The clock-vender's mill proved, as I have told you, a saw-mill. A pair of honest fellows were playing at draughts inside it, with pieces two inches broad hastily sawn off from sticks of brown and white timber; their table was a plank, rough from the mill, standing upon round and barky legs which had

A SAW-MILL IN THE SCHWARZWALD.

doubtless been trimmed to make the chequers, and rudely chalked over the top in a large chessboard pattern. The mill was stopped for the moment, the hungry teeth of the saw resting fixed in the heart of a pine. I was not put out too much when I found what kind of a laboratory it was. Have I not somewhere confided to you my notion of writing a poem to match Goethe's, and to be called 'The Song of the Saw-mill'? have I not enlarged to you on the beautiful associations of flood and forest that branch out from the theme?

STRAW-BRAIDING.

At least, I have included, among the lessons of American poetry I have dinned into your ears, Bryant's capital translation of Körner's little lyric on the 'Saw-mill.' I accepted the substitute, then, and took shelter under the substitute's roof of long and fresh-made boards.

I am a bird upon whose age you are always insisting, but I am for ever being caught with some variety of sweet-flavored chaff; so I fluttered confidingly in to the lure of the two friendly peasants.

THE FLOWER-SPIRIT.

The lure was a bed filled with atoms of wood—as was also the coffee. I have postponed my poem.

"Risen with the sun, I am writing to you, my Hohenfels, upon the primitive table just described, which is worthy of the patriarchal ages. My wanderings must add immortal facts to my essay on Progressive Geography, though it is embarrassing not to be able to find out the names of any of the places I encounter. —But what—what is the agitation which at this moment alarms my senses? The chamber seems to be whirling around me! The table is escaping from my elbows, and grates over the floor in a series of thrills or vibrations! Everything in the room is dancing and leaping, and a tremendous roar has begun to come in at the window! They have started the mill! I must seek elsewhere to finish this scrawl."

The fact of being leagues away from any probable post-office was just the incitement I needed to write to the baron: my letter, which I never took out of my pocket, was but fairly begun when the pair of millers, having cleared away our poor breakfast of coffee and sausages, set the apparatus in motion, as I have said.

As I rose a group of my fellow-pilgrims burst into the chamber, which was still furnished with the row of sawdust beds on which we had passed the night. Grandstone and Fortnoye, finger upon lip, brought me to the window, which looked out on the stream and on a little savage garden. "Now you can surprise the doctor in the very act of administering his peculiar remedies," said the latter.

Poor Somerard, hardly recovered from his accident of the evening before, was to-day put on a regimen of mere abstinence. The influence of poplar-sap being far too drastic, he was restricted entirely to perfumes, and under their control we found him. Planted near the window, and standing up with much spirit to a garden-flower which by his side appeared a giant, he inhaled the fresh odor with all the ardor of a war-horse that breathes the smoke of battle; and Sawney, at his back, was cautioning and restraining him, murmuring scientific formulas whose vile Latin came imperfectly to our ears, and perhaps pointing to his own red nose as a warning against the reckless stimulation of the smelling organ. The litany took some ten minutes; at the close of which our homœopathist, dropping a grain of sugar out of a tube, administered the same to

CHARLATANRY.

his patient in water, and his surgical operation was for the present ended; the poor patient's back, to the ordinary eye, having much the same profile as before.

"What an invention!" said to Grandstone one of his guests from Épernay, his voice protected by the clatter of the machinery. "This doctor causes his client to drink through the nose—that same nose through which he doubtless makes him pay."

"Mysterious, though," said honest young Grandstone, doubtfully. "You'll find Somerard particularly light and airy this morning: it's the essential oil he gets out of those gilliflowers and things.'

"There is a need in humanity," said Fortnoyt in his slightly rhetorical way, "to which the race of charlatans responds. They are the parasites of the upper classes, just as the fortune-tellers subsist on our servants. There are metropolitan quacks

THE TRIPOD OF KNOWLEDGE.

and there are provincial quacks. In all the towns, and in the outskirts of great cities too, have we not encountered the same Proteus in his various forms of tooth-puller, pain-killer or corn-doctor? 'Heaven bless you, my fine fellow!' I think as the honest rogue

REFRESHMENT.

cuts his poor flourish with feathers, armor, music and fanfare : ' you are such a satire on the age that I would not part with you. We all have an aching tooth somewhere in the corner of our jaws, and we all try to temporize, instead of submitting to the regular dentist and the excruciating pull. While you are amusing the villagers, monsieur and madame are beguiled just as well with some Mesmer or Cagliostro adapted to their rank in life.'"

"And the scientific ranks, too!" added I. "You must not think that learning excludes credulity. Have I not seen, in my own rooms at Passy, grave members of the Institute, in their sacred coats embroidered all round with silver olives, bending their old backs over my card-tables or endeavoring to float up to the ceiling like Mr. Home? But let us leave quackery, and this frightful mill too, where the tables turn from causes more purely rational. It will be delightful to follow that hemlock-tinted brook, which looks like mead or metheglin spilled from the drinking-horns of Valhalla."

"The gentleman is fond of the Northern mythologies," said the German orpheonist, who entered now—the same who had sat up all night with his beer and kirsch in the hotel of the Stag. "I have found something better

than the milk or honey-mead of Valhalla. I encountered, in a cow-yard, the very woman whom we met braiding straw; and I have bought from her all this potful of first-rate kirschwasser."

The good pair of millers would accept nothing for our beds or breakfast : they were offended at the bare hint. But when we passed the kirschwasser round to them in a friendly way, they drank it almost all between them.

I had to take a gibe from Somerard as I left my clock dancing a *pas seul* on the shelf above the quadrille of seven or eight mattresses upon the floor, for the whole frame of the mill was shaken with the revolving wheel. I had no repartee ready for the sarcastic dwarf; and indeed my feeling for him was one of pity when I saw the look of trust and veneration with which he started off on the arm of Doctor MacMurtagh. I could but think of the proverb of the casuist Schupp, as reported by Heinrich Heine : " In this world there are more fools than persons."

My curiosity about Fortnoye being by no means satisfied, I sought occasion to enjoy his society as we walked, but he was the most popular member of the group, the pivotal member about whom the rest revolved in various combinations. He was never alone. I attached myself to him, however, and conversed indifferently amongst the rest while my arm was linked to his. Presently my chance came. The doctor, attracted by an echo, paused

TEACHING THE ECHO.

to hold a dialogue, it being, as he remarked, the only individual in the country that could speak a word of canny

Scotch: the rest, except Fortnoye, were willing to stop and hear the extraordinary duet. I carried off my man while the doctor was executing the song "Green grow the Rushes" for the echo's benefit, and our orpheonist, who could not catch the tune, and could make nothing of the words, added to the confusion by assisting in the chorus.

I made haste to report to Fortnoye the strange things I had heard about him from my fellow-lodgers at Carlsruhe—

THE LURLEIS OF BADEN-BADEN.

that he was at once a sage, a revolutionist, a bankrupt, a tradesman and a poet.

"There is a pennyworth of truth in all that," he answered, laughing. "But as we grow older we grow wiser. If you will but take me as I am to-day, I am no more a Communist than I am a bankrupt. My existence has been rather idle and aimless until lately, and I confess that there are adventures to be told of my after-college days that I do not like to remember. I will tell you a trifling incident. Some few years ago I was at Baden-Baden, sulky, homeless and alone. What does the traditional young man do at Baden-Baden when he is friendless and far from home?"

"He yields to the seductions of the games. The sirens of gambling allure him as they rise from the green expanse; and then the Lurleis sink with him and crunch his bones at their leisure under the—under the table."

"You are very right. One rainy evening I entered the rooms where, beneath a blaze of light, were assembled the roués of the Continent, the blacklegs of

THE DOUBLE ZERO.

England, the miners of Australia and the curious beauties of New York—"

"Of course it was your first visit?"

"No: that would be the proper way of beginning a story, but in fact it was *not* my first visit. I had risked fifty francs every Saturday for some months out of pure ennui, and had lost and won, with, of course, a slight tendency toward sacrifice on the average. I considered that I was paying very cheap for an extraordinarily interesting drama, and thought it would not be honorable to frequent the rooms unless I lost at least as much as I usually did. I laid down that night my fifty francs carelessly upon the O O, the double zero—the dangerous and fascinating spot affected by so many

GOING FORAGING.

players. The indicator went spinning round—in 'its predestined circle rolled,' as your Shelley has it. I lost, and the

THE CROUPIER'S FOREFINGER.

croupier curled his forefinger around my little pile and tucked it in as the elephant absorbs the unregarded apple of the wondering little boy. Nothing could be quicker and cleaner. 'Take the whole of me, then,' I said in a pet, and threw down five hundred francs upon the same cynical double zero."

"Without doubt," I observed, "you lost again, and were left without a hope in the world."

"Not at all, not at all! It was certainly all I had, but my quarter's allowance was coming in on the Monday, or you see I should not have run the risk. I never found any use in losing my head on these occasions. And then I won."

"You won!"

"Won, yes—a whole pocketful. And that was what frightened me. I was really afraid I should be bitten with the playing-fever. At home that night I wrote a short memorandum in my pocket-book: '*N. B. Never gamble again.*' Of course, I only had to be reminded of it. I dedicated the sum, every centime, to the next worthy charity that should present: I was not long in finding such a one, and, as it happened, that money, by an odd providence, went

SIGN-LANGUAGE.

to build a little monument in a cemetery —the cemetery of Laaken, in fact."

I did not reveal that I knew anything of the story. The babe, the wretched mother, the generous young stranger whose blushes I had had painted for me, whose sobbing words had been quoted in my hearing, the days of his tender watching by that poor child's last marble cradle, formed a memory too beautiful and delicate to be exposed. I grasped his hand, warmly enough, no doubt, and only said, "I've been told, too, that you are no stranger to Francine—"

"I should hope not!"

"And that you advanced the funds to start her in business."

"A bit, certainly — at six per centum. Besides, that little affair created a new centre of employment for my wines, and I had guarantees for my capital from old Father Joliet. Since those good fellows of your table choose to see in me a wild-cat speculator, was not this a reasonably good speculation?"

I was enchanted, for the easy commercial tone in which he spoke convinced me that he had never borne any relation toward Francine but that of her wine-agent.

However contented MacMurtagh might be with the lessons in Burns he was giving to the echo, the conviction became more and more deeply impressed on us that our lingual relation with the Black Foresters was not satisfactory. The orpheonist, whose nativity was in the Swiss direction, could understand about a word in forty of those which were addressed to us: I myself, with perhaps a broader education, a better knowledge of roots and a more philosophical way of listening, could usually pick up a word in twenty-five. We walked along the road with less and less assurance, until, at the sight of a man dressed in black, whose passage brought up all the little children to his knees and all the women to the gate-posts or door-sills, Fortnoye quietly left us.

As I drew near I found he was talking to the priest in Latin. I contributed my own tributary stream of erudition, and we held a biblic colloquy in a language strangely varied with the French

ENTRANCE TO THE HÖLLEN PASS.

accent, the German accent and the unreasonable accent that used to be taught at Harvard. From this extraordinary diet the best results came out.

We had been marching quite away from the direction of Strasburg: we were at the village of Wurzbach, between the Lentz Valley and the Negold Valley. To our right was shown the little town of Calw, situated at the extremity of the Black Forest, on its Westphalian side: on our left, at a two hours' march, was

Wildbad, the famous watering-place, from whence we could easily reach a railway-station. These items considerably encouraged the chiefs of the army and revived the spirits of the men. In truth, the whole troop was getting tired

FREIBURG IN BRISGAU.

of the Rasselas valley, which seemed to have no bound nor limit.

At half an hour from Wurzbach the fog that had accompanied us all the way from the mill condensed into positive rain. We hastened our steps, looking meanwhile to right and left for shelter. A large cowherd's hut, distinguished by a wooden cross and surrounded by whole hillsides of cattle, offered itself to our regards.

This time the hospitality we received was not effusive or voluntary. An old man and his daughter, the only guardians of the place, watched us taking possession with an expression of alarm. In fact, the rain increasing, the cows began to enter, and the strangers were eight in number: it was a large party for so small a place. We were obliged, however, to await the passage of the shower: the storm redoubled, and the interior was a mass of steam. It was noon. We were all hungry, and not a sign from our hosts announced a dinner. We were all ranged, damp and clammy, like frogs on a skewer, along a miserable shelf or bench opposite the empty fireplace. The old man and the girl looked in their laps.

Tired of this, Fortnoye got up and rang upon the table a broad écu of Brabant, ordering the girl, with a quiet and becoming air of authority, to kindle a fire and serve some food. His gestures and his fine manly tones were expressive enough: the damsel, looking to her father for permission, and receiving a nod, filled the oven with wood and quickly sent a volume of smoke rolling up the chimney. Fortnoye was not yet at the end of his resources. He had perceived a rabbit skin amongst the rafters, and, taking it down, he signified, with the assistance of another resonant écu, that we would take rabbit for our luncheon. The old man, when he comprehended this idea, nodded his head, put the two broad pieces slowly into his pocket, buttoned on leather gaiters and a thick felt overcoat, and doggedly vanished into the storm. He was gone an hour, but he did produce a pair of rabbits. Meanwhile, the idea of remaining for perhaps a day in a hovel without a larder, and where our Latin was not of the slightest advantage for social intercourse, became so intensely vexatious that we resorted to various expedients for shedding the light of intelligence on the mind of our young female companion. We named her Gretchen.

A kind of comical delirium seized on Somerard. As he desired eggs for dinner, he took to crouching on the ground and crowing like the morning cock in *Hamlet*. Gretchen regarded him with stupefaction. Grandstone upon this, feeling an inclination for mutton-chops, began bleating like a lamb. His Épernay friends had unequal tastes: one took to fishing with an imaginary line, the other to drawing an invisible ox by a rope, and to lowing expressively. I, for my part, thought with infinite regret of my faultless cook at Marly. The efforts of all our pantomimists were fruitless, and we starved on until the return of the old proprietor, except when one of us, imitating Alfred in another neatherd's hut, took to toasting brown bread at the cinders—an operation which he continued with patience and great effect—until our friend returned successfully with the rabbits, even as Alfred's henchman with news of the Danish defeat.

Our rude dinner finished, we lost no time in leaving this primitive hotel. The rain had abated, and soon ceased entirely. Before entering Wildbad we judged it necessary to enter a large gasthaus, in the form of a chalet, placed upon the right of the road, in order that the brushing, cleansing and pipe-claying proper to an entrance in form upon the Baths might take place. We had hardly gone in when one of the most familiar choruses of the Allerheiligen concert smote our ears: it came from the throats of a dozen orpheonists, who, after visiting the ruins and cascades, had plunged like ourselves into the Schwarzwald, and had described a very different circle through its recesses from ours. They had traversed the romantic Hell-vale, the Höllenpass; they had basked in the beautiful Paradise, or Himmelreich; they had touched long enough at Freiburg in the Breisgau to admire its fine cathedral, one of the few

THE MUTIVE.

completed edifices of its class in Europe; and here they met us on the outskirts of Wildbad. Our own orpheonist, who I believe was a law-clerk from Geneva, fraternized at once with these artists, and I saw him no more at the waters. Fortnoye determined to do a little stroke of business among the hotel-keepers of this favorite resort. Grandstone, after clucking together his brood of invited guests, busied himself with plans for their entertainment at the baths. I was the only one who wished to depart instantaneously. My motive for such intense haste, need I explain it to the reader?

We, who had been such great friends, dissolved like a summer shower. All were busy and preoccupied: Fortnoye was the only one who grasped my hand at the station.

PART XI.

THE NECKAR REVISITED: OLD FRIENDS AT HEIDELBERG AGAIN.

PURSUIT.

ROBERT BEVERLEY, in his *History of Virginia*, published in 1705, says that "at the mouths of their rivers, and all along upon the sea and bay, grows the Myrtle, bearing a berry, of which they make a hard brittle wax, which upon refining grows transparent." He goes on to speak of the uncontaminable sweetness of this bay or myrtle—a sweetness so obdurate that candles made of the wax go out with a fume that is a perfume: they die in an odor of fragrance, these tapers, like little saints; so that people blow them out for the pleasure of smelling the snuff.

The modest *Vaccinium myrtillus*, an unpretending member of the great family of the bays, grows abundantly in the shade of the trees and up the sides of the hills in the Black Forest and along the Rhine. Its berries are exported into France, sometimes to the figure of forty thousand hogsheads in a season; but that must be in a year when the vintage is bad, for the innocent *Vaccinium myrtillus* (or airelle-myrtille) changes in the hands of the cunning Frenchmen into grapes: those versatile chemists have found a philosopher's stone by which they can ferment a capital wine out of the myrtle. The plant which can render such service to humanity, which can

155

make glad the heart of man with its wine or cheer his nights with its light, deserves an illustrious recompense; and the myrtle has given its name to one of the grandest towns of the old Palatinate,

THE MEETING.

the university city of Heidelberg. The word Heidelberg signifies "Myrtle Mountain."

I wish I were writing these lines by the scented rays of a candle made out of the American myrtle. I wish this *romer* by my side were filled with bland bay wine. For I am in Heidelberg! I am at a little card-table in a beautiful bed-room, where the snowy sheets—the first I have seen for several days—extend an almost irresistible invitation to a tramper so tired as I. Yes, I am writing in Heidelberg! I wonder what the May moon is whispering to the old tower that lies prone on the mountain yonder, overthrown and calm—an Endymion in slumber, with ivy bound around its forehead. I should like to ask some poet: I should like to ask Hohenfels, with whom I have discussed rhyme and reason by the month together here in Heidelberg. I *could* ask him, and find out exactly what he thinks about the moon, for a parallel ray streams into the next room, where Hohenfels is sitting in the fauteuil, dozing probably. But I will go to bed. I will lay down my pen and try my pillows—I have seen none since those of Achern, on which the landlord's daughters had strewed tobacco instead of poppies. I will blow out my fat, gelatinous candle, whose snuff is by no means perfumed with myrtle. I would

like to read myself to sleep with a volume of Goethe, my faithful Charles being hard by to carry away the light when I dropped off, as was his style of old. I *could* summon Charles easily enough, for he is in the ante-chamber adjacent to my bed-room, snoring on a cot bed.

But what is all this? Heidelberg! And Hohenfels with me at Heidelberg, as if it were young Paul Flemming again who talked, and the baron were by, with thirty years' silver taken out of his long hair, to criticise and listen! And Charles himself present, the faithful retainer, as though the snug summer box at Marly, with all its comforts, had been wafted away to the shores of the Neckar! Heidelberg, and the baron, and the devoted Charles! It must be a witchery of the May moon. Let the pen fall, and let the morning correct what the night has dreamed.

Yet morning has come, and I am still at Heidelberg, but half in a dream. Let me recall how I have fared since I parted with Fortnoye and the Épernay revelers and started Parisward from Wildbad.

At the junction of Oos, as I emerged from the railway-car with the impression that I must take another carriage to get

THE FEMALE CRUSOE AND PETS.

upon the French line, a heated man stepped out of the terminus as I entered it. The heated man was Charles, my faithful Charles!

I hardly recognized him at first, I so little expected to meet him in the duchy of Baden. As he saw me his feelings expressed themselves in a complete inability to speak, and in a perspiration that set a tiara of pearls across his forehead: when he grasped my hand something fell splashing upon my boot, and I made no doubt but it was a tear.

For thirty-six hours, Charles, borrowing the wings of steam and the reflector-lantern of the locomotive, had been searching for me minutely, as Diogenes searched for a man or Telemachus for a father. A letter received by Hohenfels at Marly from some gentleman unknown, to Charles had given the former some account of my escapades. According to this epistle, I had just left Baden-Baden, seemingly without cash, and to all appearance owing board-money at Carlsruhe, and probably at other places. The baron, inexpressibly shocked to recognize such a vagabond in a friend of his,

THE DEAD CASTLE.

waited a few days for my appearance; then, unable to bear it, flew to my relief. Charles begged to go along with him. Josephine the cook was to write to them instantly if I arrived, and was left with narrow instructions to look well into the faces of all ragged persons who came begging at the gate, and turn no one away who could possibly be her master in a state of adversity. If I did not come, she was to write all the same and send a line of news every day.

Two of these epistles had reached Charles without any tidings of Monsieur. Hohenfels had become very morose at Baden-Baden, and went about muttering anathemas against young heads covered with gray hair. His correspondent, whom he met there, and who was of course Sylvester Berkley, was equally nonplused. He could not understand how I had obtained the sinews of war for any further campaigns, and was much surprised that I had not returned direct to Marly, since he had bidden me farewell at the station, with my baggage on my person in the shape of a battered tin box. I must then, he opined to Hohenfels, have gone back to Carlsruhe, where I seemed to have unlimited credit with a certain Francine. He took the trouble to accompany the baron thither, his curiosity undoubtedly piqued in the matter of Francine as well as of me. In fact, the two gentlemen had left this morning, and were doubtless now in Carlsruhe. Their instructions to Charles were to post himself at the Oos junction and watch at all the trains with the eye of a hawk and the ear of a lynx for any faded gentleman who should bear my stature, and who would probably be heard asking for a temporary loan to enable him to reach Paris. His story told, Charles looked me over, and his old protecting tone took an accent of pity as he said, "Monsieur must have suffered a great deal to be obliged to buy an old hat like

BURNING OF HEIDELBERG PALACE.

that." It was my new hat, which indeed had had its own little history.

"We will go to rejoin them together," said I. "I have a debt at Carlsruhe which I am glad enough to settle."

"Monsieur has run in debt?" There was a flood of reproach in the tone, and Charles, who is of my own age, yet likes to treat me as a schoolboy, made me feel as I did when I was at Cambridge and used to confess my debts in the vacations. At seven in the evening we reached Carlsruhe.

In search of Berkley, I approached the official bureaux once more, at about the same hour as before, and with the same question. The identical porter, like an automaton, gave me the identical reply of the previous occasion: "Mr. Berkley has gone to Heidelberg, where he is dieting on whey." I asked if he had not been in Carlsruhe to-day, returning from Baden. The answer was affirmative, without explanations. "If he has gone to Heidelberg, is there not another gentleman with him?" There was a new affirmative response, and the watchman went so far as to add, "I believe the gentlemen have gone there to hunt for something they have lost."

That something was I. Satisfied with my news, I ran around parenthetically to the house where I had been so comfortably lodged. In the pretty dining-room everything was confusion. The dinner-table, all entire, giving up its old researches in Progressive and Comparative Geography, was talking of the grand event. Francine had gone, Francine had been taken away—by an old gentleman, a servant added. I came just in time to attract every one's suspicions to myself. "What were you plotting together in the office yonder?" asked the man of Wyoming, pointing to the cabinet, where the keys still hung up like interrogation-points in a manuscript.

This gave me great concern, but I had leisure to think of nothing for the moment but to place myself as quickly as possible in the care of my keepers. Pigeon-holing Francine in my brain, to be thought about when I should have leisure, I hastened with Charles to the railway. The train which had just brought us was ready for departure. Carlsruhe is a dining-station, and while I was at the table of Francine our fellow-passengers were mingling soup and coffee in the brief agony of a railway meal.

Charles, sitting with me in a first-class carriage for the first time in his life, indicated his sense of the proprieties by maintaining perfect silence, and placing himself at the greatest attainable distance in the diagonal corner from my own. Under any other circumstances he would have been full of talk. I fell into a train of musing that agreed well enough with his taciturnity. I considered how I had abjured the Rhine, and was now skirting its mountain-walled borders. I thought of the insane concatenation that was flinging me upon Hohenfels once more, and at Heidelberg! A score and a half of years expanded their cloudy wings around me, and a lymphatic beauty smiled vaguely upon me in the general situation. The baron and I, though assuredly we never expected to see Heidelberg together again, might discuss Richter and Schiller behind that many-windowed mask of a ruined façade, and our criticisms would become juvenile again and unconventional, like those of the Brontë children when their father made them utter opinions from behind a mask on the great men of England. But the baron! I paused doubtfully. My very servant had been scolding me: what avalanches of reproach had I not a right to expect from Hohenfels!

We reached Heidelberg in the dark, and I made for the hotel of Prince Charles, where I knew that Berkley usually took his whey. I trembled with apprehension. I was about to meet

RUINS AND CABBAGE.

the man whom I had urged to pass the spring with me in my little country den at Marly. I had written him two letters: the first was from Carlsruhe, wherein I bade him await me. He had obeyed, but his waiting had been vain. The second letter, from the saw-mill in the Black Forest, was in my pocket.

Charles quickly discovered for me the little suite of rooms in which Sylvester and the baron were installed. I ordered him, with a dignity unusual with me, to go in first: I was shaking in all my joints. The door opened, and in an instant Hohenfels was hugging me like a lunatic in his long arms.

"Ah, you terrible responsibility! Have I got you safe?" he said. I felt his heart thumping against my own ribs.

Berkley left the chess-board at which the two gentlemen had been

A MOCKING BIRD.

sitting over their game, and came up to me slowly, with graceful gestures of his knees at every step, and brushing out

his whiskers a little as he advanced. It was his manner when he had something elaborately sarcastic to deliver. But he remarked, "What a singular man you are, Mr. Flemming! and what a singular man you have made of me! At the beginning of the month I took leave and came down to Heidelberg: you forced me to break off my cure of whey, to go and take it up again at Baden-Baden. Now you have got me back here, are you content with me?"

I wrung his hand: in my confusion it was the broadest acknowledgment I could make.

I tried to say something to Hohenfels: "There is a good moon on the ruins, old pal. I'd like to go up and sit there a while with you."

"You rheumatic infant!" said the baron, but he was touched too. "You must go to bed. The next chamber is engaged for you, you see. It is rather more comfortable than this: I have set the keys so that I can lock you up from the outside, and I am going to fasten you in. You are capable of running off from us again."

I slept as on swan's-down, and awakened to find myself in the shadow of the Myrtle Mountain, with Charles unrolling a napkin to wait on me in the breakfast-room, and my name on the inn-register next to the names of my oldest friends.

Sylvester awaited us in the adjoining room, where a little private table was laid. Charles relieved my wants with importunate compassion and waited on the others with much friendly interest.

Although I have long recorded my liking for public dinner-tables, where so many gentle things can be said without being overheard, yet I approved this time the confidential form of the meal. We had so much to say to each other! The private table, however, proved to be an arrangement of Berkley's. He did not choose to drink his whey along with the holiday clerk and the commercial gent.

The event of the repast was a letter from Josephine. It said, in so many words (addressed to Hohenfels), that Monsieur being certainly lost, she was going to look out for another situation; the solitude was unbearable; she was tired of acting as cook in the service of Argus and the two tabbies. I read the assurance of my loss in a loud voice to the others. For some reason or other, it gave me a fit of home-sickness. From the post-mark of Marly emanated a powerful influence over my spirits. I was conscious of an overwhelming desire to

DRUNK WITH REVENGE.

see my garden, with its pumpkin vines and Lima beans, its little rows of sweet Indian corn, and the other contrivances with which, in opposition to Laboulaye, I had created an *Amérique en Paris*. I wanted to fondle my dog, and I wanted to baste my cook. Of these desires I made a confidant of Hohenfels, proposing to him to fall into retreating order forthwith.

"Only last night you wanted to revisit the castle. You need not bring me so far to drive me straight back again. As for your cook, console yourself: I gave her news of your health in a letter mailed last night."

The baron, with his shackling, ungainly limbs, his enormous silken tassel of hair, has not improved in looks with age. A pair of deep crescent-shaped furrows have partially replaced his old smile, and his forehead is ruled like a country schoolmaster's copy-book for the inscriptions of Time. But the soft iris of his light-blue eye the years have not been able to wrinkle; and out of that mild azure, of a color eternally young, he gave me a look of exceeding friendliness as he cheered me up: it was not for my cook he consoled me.

"I am willing enough to see the ruins," I said, ashamed. "I only fear, if we go over the old spots again, that we shall take root here."

We beguiled Berkley by promising to drop him at the Molkenkur, his dairy of whey and buttermilk. It was in a grange so named, on the top of a hill, that Sylvester undertook to acquire the diplomatist's calmness by infusion and imbibition. From the plateau we lowered our eyes, and out of the midst of the lower part of the mountain, between Wolfsbrunnen and the Molkenkur, a magical apparition surged up before our sight in the dazzling morning sunshine.

A city of marble rests there as though it eternally heard the trump of a material resurrection. Columns and arches rise

THE GREAT TUN OF HEIDELBERG.

out of earthy graves. Men of stone, its only inhabitants—some of whom hold swords in their hands, while others are supine and vanquished in dusty moats—seem to keep up eternally some terrific battle. Immense piles of ruin deform the earth. Palaces rise around in majesty and seeming strength, but through their huge windows you see peeping the foliage of lusty trees. Ivies, like the snakes of Laocoön, roll up from the feet of the sturdy pillars, and bite again and again into the cracks and fissures of the stone. As Herculaneum lies fixed and mocked in its security of lava, so lie these buildings mocked with the cohesion of their own mortar and ironically cemented with their ruin.

"*Heidelberga deleta*," said Berkley the statesman in a low voice, repeating the sinister brace of words furnished by Boileau to serve as inscription on the medal struck in honor of Louis XIV., the destroyer of Heidelberg.

"Nay, I cannot think its life is completely trampled out," said Hohenfels.

"Some intelligence of its past purpose and splendor must remain, to give it a ghostly animation. Do you suppose these stones do not excite themselves, on quiet nights, by performing again the echoes of revel and pomp they knew of yore? Do you believe yonder stairs, plying up in spirals to the clouds, do not lead anywhere, or are not pressed by phantom feet? There is a voice in the Past, gentlemen, for him who can hear it:

Prophetic sounds and loud arise for ever
From this, and from all Ruin, to the wise!"

For my part, I recited one of Goethe's little poems, that one composed by him when sailing down the Rhine in company with Lavater and Basedow, and when, as we may fancy, he was suddenly

THE HERO.

struck by the contrast between some gray tower on the cliffs above and the floating life beneath:

He stands upon the turret high,
The Hero's noble wraith,
And to the skiff that passeth by,
"Fair speed the voyage!" he saith.

"Behold, *these* sinews were so strong,
This heart so stout and wild,
Such pith did to these bones belong,
So high the board was piled.

"One naif my life I stormed away,
One half in rest I drew—"

At that word of "rest" I looked at Hohenfels, and paused: he concluded the poem in his silver voice with a gentleness that turned its menace into a benison, and looking kindly straight at me:

"'And thou, thou mortal of a day,
Thy mortal path pursue!'"

Sylvester then, as his contribution to the literature of Heidelberg, furnished one of his neat and succinct little histories, resuming in a few words the past career of the stones that lay mute around us.

In the place now occupied by Heidelberg Castle the Romans had already constructed a fortress of a square plan. After the fall of the Empire the design was respected, so far as the form went, by the Franks in the first place, and then by Conrad of Hohenstaufen, who began to give it the appearance of a palace. Conrad's old mauer was reconstructed in the close of the fourteenth and beginning of the fifteenth centuries by Robert I. and Robert II., who added numerous parts to the building. The succeeding electors rivaled each other in adding graces and beauties to the building. Frederick I., called the Victorious, and Louis the Peaceful, ornamented it with towers and terraces; Frederick IV. erected a superb construction, whose remains prove its former grandeur; his son, Frederick V., king of Bohemia, built a second close by, calling it the English Palace, to recall the fact that his wife Elizabeth was daughter of James I. of England. In his unfortunate reign Heidelberg fell into the Bavarian hands, and its great Palatinate library was carried to Rome. Other palaces were added by successive princes, but the crowning glory was that marvel of architecture which was contributed by Otto Henry in the middle of the sixteenth century. The cluster of palaces had well earned its splendid name of the German Alhambra when, from 1674 to 1693, all the scourges of war fell upon the Palatinate. Of its palace there remained only that which the miner and sapper, the cannon and the torch, were unable to destroy.

But Louis XIV. did not sufficiently destroy the palace of Heidelberg. Its majesty has grown by what he did, and Versailles does not offer half the solemn beauty of this its murdered rival.

Sylvester continued his explanations as a resident and habitué. The castle in its present state has resident officers and guardians of both sexes. The Tower of Rupert, dating from the time of Louis the Débonnaire, is haunted by the devil, they say, since the doings in it of a certain Leonora of Lützelstein; but from this ill-omened edifice we heard the sounds of a piano: other habitable

THE JESTER.

portions are occupied by commonplace modern tenants. While Berkley was relating the history of Leonora, we observed a woman passing along an arched gallery with a plate of sauerkraut—surely an honest and healthy sign of life; another tower near by, half crumbled away, showed windows with good tight modern sashes; and while the screech-owl and adder were making the most of the ruined portion, a canary in a cage mocked the devastation with sublime impudence, singing as he swung over Heidelberg from a Gothic balcony.

We examined the buildings of the old castle in detail—the towers, rather, for in this ruin every separate portion is so called, and even the library is a tower. We inspected the terrace, with its fresh gardens in the pomp of spring-time, and we looked down on the roofs of the modern town. Wherever we went I fancied something was wanting.

Suddenly I asked myself if something was not *de trop?*

My eye fell upon Berkley, who was demonstrating a Roman coin in the museum with insufferable zeal and erudition. I glanced at my dear Hohenfels, and fancied that his thoughts were the like of mine. *This*, in fact, was not our Heidelberg, the Heidelberg of our Lang Syne, the Heidelberg of our memories and of our passion. How could we possibly fall into the old tone, how discuss

Hans Sachs or the Minnelays, before this frigid perfection, this person with opinions all made up and squared by rule, this perennial Prize Scholar fed on whey? We formed between ourselves a political party in opposition to Berkley. We spoke to each other with our eyes behind his back: we telegraphed over his shoulders or through his elbows. It is true that Sylvester bore the name of one of my best friends, a man who stood by me and cheered me nobly in a period of ridiculous trial; and the younger Berkley, for his own part, had overwhelmed me with civilities and obligations. I could not help it: the moment he presented himself, in complete armor of white kid gloves and insipid erudition, at the scene of my old fond confidences with Hohenfels, he became an enemy. I would not have offended him for the world, yet he was a mortal offence to me.

GUARDIAN OF THE CELLAR.

There was nothing for it but bravado. We must drain Berkley to the dregs. "I suppose we cannot escape from it," I said: "let us go and see the great tun. The guide-book will never forgive us if we don't."

"Yes," said Hohenfels, "let us beard the lion of Heidelberg. Let us see the great tun."

In this kind of desperation we paid homage to the coopers' marvel. We approached an angle formed by the palaces of Frederick IV. and Frederick V., and descended into the electoral cellars. I am not sure that in all our residence at Heidelberg, Hohenfels or I had ever visited the tun; but as a piece of acted derision to Berkley we both enthusiastically agreed to see the corpulent wonder.

In place of one astonishment, we had three.

Compared with the wine-tun of commerce, the smallest of the three tuns at Heidelberg is a giant, but by the side of the other two, it seems like a little anchovy-keg or mackerel-tub. The true monarch, the master-tun of Heidelberg, reposes in grand honor amongst the traditions of the German people. The vine-growers of the Palatinate, to fulfill their title, were obliged to fill it every year; but it had to submit to the fate of the castle: the castle was burnt up, the tun was drowned out. The revenge of all the enemies of Germany, the revenge of the French, the Bavarians, the Imperialists, Barbarossa, Turenne and Mélac, had to come by turns and slake its thirst at this symbolical, this eucharistic wine-vessel. They broke the vase after having let flow the contents. His enemies' backs once seen in retreat, the noble elector would cause the tun to be reconstructed, and always in augmented proportions. The astonishment of the world was increased, but so was the tax of the vine-growers. The curious may see accordingly, to-day, the most enormous cask which it has yet entered into the mind of a cooper to construct: if his ambition should increase by but one degree, he would be no longer a cooper, but a shipbuilder.

Indeed, the tun resembles nothing so much as a Dutch brig seated on the stocks. Reposing its majestic belly on a series of solid supports, it sits like an Ark of Jollity, its prow and poop, so to speak, both decorated with figure-heads and coats-of-arms, and a lusty Bacchus seeming to bestride the hoops in a bower of sculptured vines. A double stairway leads up on deck, where, in a lucky season, a ball has been given in honor of the vintage, and the elector has danced with the fairest women of his court.

This mastodon of the cellarage, built in 1751 by Engler, engineer-cooper, as he was proudly called, of the elector Charles Theodore, has been three times filled completely. If the crop were but middling, the good prince deigned to reduce the levy to the contents of his middle tun; if it failed entirely, he condescended to accept the fill of the smallest hogshead, called the Virgin's, which only held thirty thousand bottles.

In the same cellar, besides the three tuns, we saw the statue of Perkeo the jester, buried by desire with his mouth under the spigot of the largest cask. It is a kind of doll, or imitation, with a frame of wood, a coat of silk, with tow wig and short breeches, a wooden cane in the hand which is *not* an imitation.

Clement Perkeo, the buffoon of Charles Theodore, in addition to the ordinary habits of his kind, such as fishing off the general-in-chief's wig with hook and line, withdrawing the chair from the corpulent prime minister, and the like, had an enthusiastic addiction to wine. The finest building and eighth wonder of the world, he thought, was the tun, and he chose for his nearest friend Engler, the engineer-cooper. He brought in the most accurate news of the grape-harvests. "Is the yield large, Perkeo?" "Disgraceful: hardly the middle tun!" or, "Perfect ruin: only the Virgin this year!" By these symbols he announced to the elector the misfortunes of his peasantry, and to the greedy court-treasurer the prospects of his taxes. Lest the vicissitudes of the vineyards should affect his spirits (and the good spirits of a jester are his capital), he was allowanced with eighteen bottles of Markgrafter wine per day. His only wish on dying was to be buried with his lips under the grand faucet, doubtless hoping, even in death, to render the tun his tributary. The elector directed his

THE SHUTTLECOCK.

image to be prepared as guardian of the cellar: thus we see it, made of coopers' and caulkers' materials, wood and tow.

At the conclusion of our visit to the ruins we were resting, my dearest friend and I, in the largest chamber of our suite at the Prince Charles hotel. Berkley was off for his whey, and I thought the moment had come at last for Ulrich von Lichtenstein and Walther von der Vogelweide. But Hohenfels asked me for a full, methodical account of all my wanderings. I next tried to induce him to speak of his new acquaintance, Mr. Berkley, having myself a determined habit of discussing the last thing that has got into my head, and being willing to make common cause with the baron in execrating the diplomatist. But Hohenfels, whatever language his eyes might have spoken in allusion to Berkley, would not speak in his absence with any expression but a guarded chivalry and courtesy, protesting that he knew the gentleman too slightly to estimate his character, and again asked me for the full confession of my long error.

That history, which I had recounted to customs-officers and cab-drivers, to Francine and to Fortnoye, and which had rolled up like a snowball even as I was singing the cantos of my own Odyssey, I gave to Hohenfels in full: I did not omit the loss of an umbrella or the purchase of a hat.

Hohenfels made his comment: "It seems to me that if your friend Berkley has made himself a living churn for digesting buttermilk and whey, you have done even more to lose your independence as a man. You have lost your centre of gravity. You have become a mere shuttlecock between Accident and Caprice."

PART XII.

CONFLICTS AT HEIDELBERG.

THE TORTURES OF BÉRANGER.

THAT prince in the Arabian tale who, on pulling aside his robe, revealed his lower half turned to black marble, was doubtless very happy when the enchantment came to be canceled and the warm red current began to steal through his flesh of sculpture. So was I in recovering the baron at Heidelberg. Hohenfels again, and again Heidelberg! My thoughts began to knit, my stone age at Marly buried itself in flowers and became a forgotten loss, a dead period. I declared that, after all, a stay-at-home was a mere petrifaction, and that I only found life again when I found my legs.

For me an effort was necessary in renewing the old times: you cannot force the fine corpulent heart-throbs of fifty into the genteel waistcoat of nineteen. But for the baron no such transvasation was necessary: he became young, or he remained young, and fell into perspective with perfect ease. He was again my Hohenfels of the Carl Strasse, with the nature of a milky opal, always a little curdled and flawed. His long flaxen hair, flowing like the "curled clouds" on which an Ariel might ride, was hardly changed: Hohenfels' topknot, in fact, was of the colorless sort which eludes the approach of grayness, or conceals grayness when it comes; and I have often looked at the pale picture of his head, with its abundant fuzz and convolutions, and thought it the perfect image of his brain. My friend's long spine, his bent shoulders, his lank, aimless, companionable legs, which I loved with all my soul, were but the preserved features of his adolescence, and immortally beautiful for me. They gave him, to my notion, a lovable affinity with the portraits of that fairy enchanter born to us out of the Dark Ages, that undying boy, that sole possessor in our busy time of

IL TROVATORE.

the gift of legend—poor Hans Andersen. The discord in our exquisite union, the alkaline drop in our cup, was of course Mr. Berkley.

We essayed, however, to practice the old duet. We sought together those nooks and corners of the splendid ruin known, as we fancied, to us alone. We no longer regretted that the superb schloss was red, not gray. Youth demands for its poems the hue of ashes, but with the approach of age comes a love for any spot of color where the eye may warm itself. We sought our ancient haunt, the summit of the Rent Tower, where the lindens wave like plumes from a cloven helmet, and where Paul Flemming used to admire the Tree of Life brought from America two hundred years before, and standing like a kingly Louisiana slave in its iron bonds and fetters. Of all this beautiful devastation, Hohenfels was the voluntary bard and interpreter. "Sull' orrida torre" he perched, the troubadour. His ear had not forgotten its nicety: he could play as well as ever, and still preserved the remarkable gift of singing and smoking both at once.

The minstrel ought, perhaps, to have sung the War of the Palatinate ; or Louis XIV., who undertook it to reclaim the dowry of his sister-in-law, wife of Philippe d'Orléans; or Marshal Lorges, whose name is only remembered, like that of the aspiring boy who fired the Ephesian dome, because he laid in ashes the castle of Heidelberg. We ought, perhaps, I say, to have sung these flames of Troy. But we interpreted Heidelberg in another manner. Among these tufted walls, crumbling into melancholy beauty beneath the touches of Time and History, nothing seemed to us half so pathetic as the ruin of ourselves. It was here we had met and sauntered, dreaming young men, committed to lives of scholarship or art. It must be pardoned to us that what we looked at was the pageant of our own boyhood, lying in vision for us, bathed in sun, through any and all of these rugged arches. For this sort of sentiment there is just one perfect expression ; and we sang the "Grenier" of Béranger. We sang it through to its pensive close :

Quittons ce toit, où ma raison s'énivre;
Oh, qu'ils sont loin, ces jours si regrettés !
J'échangerais ce qu'il me reste à vivre
Contre un des jours qu'ici Dieu m'a comptés.

At each of the five repetitions of that refrain which closes Béranger's stanzas with a heavy sigh — at each turn of the "qu'on est bien à vingt ans !"—I fancied I heard a voice like a file. At the fifth refrain the sound was no longer doubtful: Berkley, whose existence we had forgotten, and on whom Nature had conferred the ability to tie a cravat, but not the gift of melody, was assisting behind us with the chorus.

"I see you both adhere to the poet of the First Consul," he observed with his most agreeable smile, "though his confirmed Bonapartism makes him an unwelcome exponent of feeling just now in most circles, and though his vaunt in the penultimate verse, that 'jamais les rois n'envahiront la France,' sounds nothing less than derisory when sung to-day by the Rhine."

"We were trying to capture another kind of kingdom," said Hohenfels. "You know, Berkley, that Tacitus describes the barbarians by the Rhine as not only lashing themselves to warlike deeds, but consoling their ills, with a song. We were only endeavoring to hit upon the old key, and with it, if you will allow me to say so, to enter the garret of Béranger."

But our talk was off the hinge, and we could but converse on indifferent subjects until dusk. We both love that placid hour of afterglow, that equipoise of day and night, which our language, with one of its most poetical suggestions, calls the *even-ing*. Berkley's endeavor to throw a slight upon Béranger had had the natural effect of fixing the minstrel firmly in our minds, and I supposed the baron and myself were equally possessed with a willful saturation of Béranger while we talked with Sylvester on politics or whey. At last, when a star shot, Hohenfels made a falling firework out of the sparks from his pipe, and hummed—

> Encore une étoile qui file,
> Qui file, file, et disparait!

Prompt as he began this couplet, a voice like Byron's "whetstone of the teeth, monotony in wire," began to "file, file" in unison, or rather in discord, with his own: it was Mr. Berkley, bent on being sympathetic, and contributing his mite to the entertainment.

"I am reminded," the latter continued, "of some rather interesting facts in the history of star-worship, of which a remnant is plainly found in the tradition that some one dies when a meteor falls. A long time before Zoroaster—"

"Don't go on with that, Sylvester," said the baron easily: "we had rather talk Béranger. You know he says he was made a poet by a thunderstorm: that storm made a swan out of the tailor's goose."

"All poets thrive on rain," I observed. "Burns was found by his biographer open-mouthed with enjoyment under a sort of waterspout, oblivious of the torrents that were filling out his galligaskins."

"Your pleasantry about the tailor's goose, baron," said Mr. Berkley, "re-

THE DISCIPLE OF STRAUSS.

minds me of the little poem 'Les Oies' which Béranger's translator, Prout, puts on the same page with his version of 'Shooting Stars.' Since you change your vein by means of a witticism, the satire of this little squib cannot be disagreeable. I will attempt a solo." And he chanted, with a measured smile:

> I hate to sing your hackneyed birds :
> So, doves and swans, a truce !
> Your nests have been too often stirred ;
> My hero shall be, in a word,
> A goose !
>
> Can roasted nightingale a liver
> Fit for a pie produce?—
> Fat pies that on the Rhine's sweet river
> Fair Strasburg bakes Pray, who's the giver ?
> A goose !

He interrupted himself to observe that as both his hearers had just passed through Strasburg, where they had doubtless paid the civic goose the compliment of at least one indigestion, the poem would be appreciated. We looked at each other, and hoped to get quit of the music by the acceptance of this impeachment. But in an instant another verse of the canticle was fluttering laboriously through Berkley's nostrils:

An ortolan is good to eat,
A partridge is of use,
But they are scarce; whereas you meet
At Paris, ay, in every street,
A goose!

There were six or seven verses, and he faithfully gave us them all, remarking occasionally that he had hardly ever sung before any one, and that his goose song was therefore a very callow gosling. Berkley scientific was supportable, but Berkley humorous was more than we could bear. We abruptly rose and went down the mountain into the city. During the descent I contrived to say interrogatively to the baron, "Fine fellow, Sylvester."

"Oh, a heart of gold!"

"And yet I got along with him admirably at Baden-Baden!"

"And yet I passed a capital time with him here until you came."

What did this *and yet* mean if Berkley was a fine fellow and a heart of gold? The fact is, like old friends as we were, we abused the laws of rhetoric in our talk and leaped to conclusions. We

THE GOSLINGS OF MELODY.

meant that Berkley was good, and even companionable in a strait, but no comrade for such a friendship and duality as ours. We both esteemed him, yet both would pay anything for an hour of freedom.

The baron thereupon had a bright idea: "Suggest to him to unstarch himself: invite him to a studenten-kneipe."

The stratagem was successful. The dissipations and, still worse, the philosophy, of a students' gathering were distasteful to our mediator between nations, who had knelt at the old crucifix of Baden-Baden. "My view may be a biased one," he said, "but it seems to me that, representing a country with a state religion, my place can hardly be among these disciples of Spinoza and Strauss."

So we went bird's-nesting like a pair of schoolboys, free and glad. We knew well the old lane where the tavern was, and entering by a garden we had a view into the hall without interruption, morally speaking: in reality, we could see nothing at the window where we had stationed ourselves, for the tobacco-smoke. The nearest head alone was recognizable, and to my surprise proved to be that of an acquaintance. It appertained to the hand that had thrown a shower of gold among the feasters of Allerheiligen—to my friend the student of pharmacy, as he had called himself, who tried to send me botanizing for chickweed. He sat in a circle of attentive listeners, who seemed to pay him a good deal of consideration, and it was easy to see that he was a bit of a hero among the students. Presently he turned his face from profile to full, and then it was the baron's turn to be surprised.

"Why, it is Fritz!" he exclaimed—

"the son, Flemming, of a man whom I have known like a brother, the Lithuanian baron Von Ramm!" And he tapped at the window.

A fat young man turned rather angrily and tottered slowly up to our casement. He raised the guillotine sash, stared at us blankly a moment, said "Death to the Philisters!" and let the glass fall with a noise. Then he retired into the cloud. Hohenfels tapped again, and this time it was the pharmacy-student who looked around: my comrade had taken out his card and held it against one of the small panes, where it was framed like a picture. The student quickly recognized the name, and we made an entry of considerable distinction, being drawn by the collars through the window itself into the den.

It was a page of my youth brought bodily before my eyes again: it seemed not a renewed crowd of callow students, but the same students, eternally young and kept from change by some enchantment. There were the Mossy-heads, the Old Ones, the Pomatum Stallions, the Princes of Twilight. They were discussing the laws of the Broad-Stone and the Gutter; they were screaming and whistling; some were in long yellow hair and braided coats, gorgeous and dirty; some had white woolly heads, and wore the schlafrock. It was a great throng, for there were Austrians, Saxons, Bavarians, Hessians, Hamburgers and Wurtemburgers present. They looked much alike, and the national differences were seen not in their faces, but in the patterns of the colossal pipes they carried. The tallest men seemed to wear the narrowest coats, those long, closely-buttoned, serious-looking garments: out of all proportion with the long pipes and the great-coats were the caps—the imperceptible caps, which, whatever wind may blow, rest fixed like a nail on the extreme summit of the head, thanks to the practiced skill with which the German student manœuvres his neck. On the table was a chair, on the chair was the dignitary known as Senior of a Landsmannschaft, and on the Senior a great pair of boots. "Silentium!" cried this functionary: "the chorus will recommence."

"I think a chorus is an odd sort of silentium," said Hohenfels; and the company began to sing a doggerel verse:

O Hans was Kost der Huat?
Der Huat der hat ein Thaler Kost,
Ein Thaler Kost,
Ein Thaler Kost,
Der Huat der hat ein Thaler Kost,
Und vier and fünfzig Groot!

As each student had his allowance of beer and butterbrod before him, of which he partook without minding the music, the words of this song were mostly uttered with the mouth full; nor did the consumption of butterbrod at all interfere with the smoking, for a German student will smoke and eat as easily as my friend the baron will smoke and sing.

We stayed late. Before leaving, Hohenfels said to his young acquaintance, "One thing is necessary to complete our joy in Heidelberg. How can we see a good duel?"

"How? Oh, anyhow," answered the Baron of the Golden Shower.

A FOX.

"But when will a duel take place, if you please?"

"When? Oh, any day."

"Duels are accommodating to tourists." With this remark Hohenfels relinquished a subject which he thought his friend seemed to surround with a certain obscurity. Conversing afterward among the students, however, he learned that a duel was really to happen in two days, and that Von Ramm was to be the hero. Hence his reticence. "It is with a young Fox from the University of Bonn, a foreigner. There will be several other matches, but they will be simply trials of skill. Fritz has the only affair of moment, good luck to him! The other man insulted our college." He was proceeding to answer our questions as to the hour and the place, when the round face of the fat young student interposed and emitted the following decree:

"Death to the Philisters! These are secrets of the college. Profane ears must not hear where the university defends its honor."

But we soon obtained an accurate direction from an old familiar acquaintance of mine. The ancient fire-tender and man of all work about the hotel was in reality none other than the postilion who had brought me into town at my first visit to Heidelberg: this worthy had a comrade, the wisest and best-informed

THE STUDENTS.

cab-driver in the dominion. The charioteer knew all about the honorable affairs of *die Herren Studenten*, and a duel with a baron in it was for him an open secret of his profession. At the appointed time we drove to the scene of action, where we found already two processions of carriages converging upon the spot from opposite directions. These were filled with students of the rival corps, their friends and their physicians: they carried almost enough lint, bandages and other surgical apparatus to dress the wounds of a regiment in action.

It was the baron's excursion rather than mine: I have never comprehended the duello. Its logic, for us moderns, appears to me incorrigibly faulty. In the Middle Ages it was different: then Heaven fought with the just man, as Heaven in Hebrew times presided over the drawing of lots. But now, in the nineteenth century, it is obvious that a good conscience does not give a man an experience of ten or a dozen years with small-swords. Technical skill may very probably lie with the side morally weakest. This mode of adjudication must therefore be rejected as spurious. I yielded, however, with a good grace, and went off with Hohenfels to the seat of war.

Some botanical specimens on the route attracted me, and the baron, best natured of men, conspired with me in my myrtle-chasing. When we arrived the friendly matches were all over, and the serious affair between Von Ramm and the foreigner was under engagement. The latter, whose back was toward me, smoked a pipe that out-Germaned Germany in its length and model, and he was lost in a pair of burlesque cavalry gloves from some theatre; his horseman's boots surprised me, for they were made of alligator's skin, and looked just fit to contain a bowie-knife or so; his pantaloons, too, were unlike anything Rhenish, for they were of a fine pin-striped jean, more familiar to the Mississippi than the Rhine. Except for a cuirass and fencing-mask he was unprotected. His adversary, however, whom it was difficult to recognize, was stuffed out into a state of de-

A PROFESSION WELL BOLSTERED.

fence that made him appear gigantic. The student-duels on the Rhine are literally a pillow-fight. This combatant had a mattress on his breast, wadding on his arms and cushions on his legs; for it is with wool pulled over his eyes, and, I doubt not, cotton in his ears, that the Renowner achieves his fame. A fine meerschaum issued from Von Ramm's wire-woven visor, like a lily from a flower-basket. A sufficiency of seconds and students, their tinsel locks lying on their shoulders like epaulettes, stood solemnly around and contemplated battle's magnificently stern array. These assistants are often so completely encased in leather and pads that they could be blown up with gunpowder without much injury. It is their duty to stand by with a sword, intercept any unfair strokes, and stop the fight if their principal is wounded. The scars of a college duelist are generally seen on his left cheek, and I understood this fact when I observed the play of Von Ramm, who seemed to be continually trying to cut over the guard of his opponent's sword-arm. He was an expert and graceful fencer, a hundred times lighter in all his stuffings than his unencumbered foe. The latter played very singularly: he kept entirely on his defence, with little or no exhibition of swordsmanship, until the spectators became tired of the monotony of his game. All were looking with interest at the expert motions of the brilliant Lithuanian, when finally, just as his second stepped out to announce that the fifteen minutes were up, the alligator-boots sprang forward, lunged at his neck, and delivered the point so strongly that the opposing sword only succeeded in beating it down

THE LINEN DUSTER.

a little toward the shoulder. Von Ramm staggered into the arms of his friends, where he bled quite profusely from a scrape over his collar-bone: seeing him so unexpectedly hurt, Hohenfels ran to his side. I prepared to re-enter our cab, very much disturbed and sickened, when the victor, who was examining the reddened point of his sword in an attitude of impartial interest, said, in a nasal inflection of my own language, "Guess I've euchred him with my little snickersnee!" The clumsy conqueror in alligator boots was then an American! I have never known a national victory to give me so little satisfaction. With a feeling of shame and self-condemnation I returned alone to the hotel. We had undertaken our escapade among the students for the purpose of avoiding the contact of a lower mind, as we fancied: we wished to get among German philosophy, romance and Bohemianism. The return, I felt, was the return of a blackguard. I was frustrated. I felt therefore repentant and civil toward Berkley, whom I found at supper when I had removed the dust and issued from my chamber. It was at the public table: Hohenfels was still absent. By two movements of the head the English statesman and I expressed, on the one hand deprecation, on the other pardon and pity. A new-comer was sitting near, and to my great surprise this stranger nodded too, without, however, betraying the least intention of disturbing his hat, which was a small wide-awake set rather back from the forehead.

"I saw you at the little unpleasantness:" this explanation he kindly added to his salute. He proceeded: "It is difficult to recognize folks through a wire basket, but my memory for faces is good: I am something of an artist."

The nasal accent revealed the man with alligator's legs. One of those sanguinary brutes of the battle-field was doing me the honor to claim me as an acquaintance, and to share my supper red-handed. His present appearance, at least, was pacific: he had come out of his alligator skin, and he wore that garment which the American tourist flutters like a victorious flag all round the world, and which, made variously of gray, white or yellow, is known as the linen duster. He was drinking coffee out of a larger cup than is usual for that beverage at a European dinner, but of a size familiar on most breakfast-tables in the United States.

"You are noticing my cup: I carry it around. They make this cup at Dresden very largely for the American trade: I am something of an importer. I cannot enjoy my coffee out of one of these poppycock thimbles they give you at a table-d'hôte, and I must have my coffee just so: I'm something of an epicure."

I judged it necessary to say a word to Berkley: "This gentleman, who appears to be my compatriot, has just pinked his man in an affair with a person I have met before—a musical pilgrim at Achern, in fact, who joked with me on botanical subjects in the character of a student of pharmacy."

"No more of a pharmacy-student than my cane: I'm something of an apothecary. He said our Western colleges were only primary schools, which it was a State disgrace to charter as universities. He totally denied the merit of Ann Arbor, asserting he had never heard of it. A college where they pick up a new asteroid every fine night! I've been at Ann Arbor: I'm something of an astronomer. I never fought before, but on that I asked him out for a walk, and I just waited for his jugular."

"You showed great coolness, certainly," I said in a kinder tone. I found something chivalresque in this young stranger, who had never fought a duel, coolly engaging an old hand in defence of his country's educational advantages.

"Yes, I am probably cool. I simply waited for his jugular. I had to wait for nearly all the quarter of an hour, but then he gave it me. You see, gentlemen, for a raw swordsman to engage an older one is an interesting, not to say a difficult, problem in the correlation of forces. My plan, which has succeeded, was, to go through the fight without trying to make any thrusts, and confine my attention to parrying: I thus got an advantage of fifty per cent. over my man, whose intellect was divided between the two schemes of parry and thrust. The watchfulness demanded in this exercise is simply the equal allotment of neurotic power through the nerve-branches of the whole body and limbs; this is harder than what is called presence of mind, which is only the concentration of force in a single organ, the brain. Thus, having put eyes, as it were, all over my arms and legs, I felt perfectly calm and sure he couldn't touch me. I had decided beforehand on this game, and to uncover my sally-ports only at the last. I was kept aware of the exact passage of time by my second, who made a signal every four minutes: that was the fellow who rigged me out, some theatrical fool from Munich. After the third four minutes, knowing my adversary was tired and unprepared, I cut just as his second was stepping forward to stop the fight. I had luck, and I reached his jugular or near it."

And calmly attentive to us, he poured down a draught of coffee.

"My order of sensations," he continued musingly, "was not dissimilar to what I have experienced at the Stock Exchange. There, too, we are obliged to combine ideas with rapidity, to be on continual guard, and to be ready with the nerve-force: I am something of a speculator."

FACTOTUM.

I looked anew at this surprising, unsurprisable American. I made sure that he was from West. His proportions were not quite harmonious: his legs and his duster were long and lean, but his trunk, hat and head were squat. It is generally said that the American race is approaching in physique the character of the native Indians, but it may be observed that if a certain class of my countrymen, led by temperament and predilection, are allying themselves with that branch of our barbarous population, there is a second class obviously assimilating with our other semi-civilized ingredient, the negro. Who has not seen, on American faces perfectly Saxon in their white-and-pink pigments, the negro's round nostril, blubber lips, curled eyelashes and depressed skull, together with the small, handsome, rudimentary ears, like the bruised ears you find on antique statues of Hercules? Our new acquaintance was of this type. His nose was fat, his lips large, his hair pale and bushy. There was something of the albino in his appearance.

As he sauntered out picking his teeth I called the man-of-all work. The old fellow came up, decorated with his trousseau of keys. I asked him familiarly if he knew my young countryman. "Is there anything peculiar about the habits or luggage of this Yankee?"

"Faith, sir, he took a little corner room in the garret, among the maids and kellners. He travels with nothing but a French horn, and a small bag which is all papered over with the labels of the express companies. One of the cards is marked New Orleans, Louisiana, ADAMS: the rest are distributed over Belgium and Germany, one of them reading Brussels, one Liverpool, and one Bonn. He is something of a Wandering Jew."

"That is quite enough," I said, ashamed to seem so inquisitive. "You understand your station, and have made good use of your eyes. Take this, and go off and drink your beer with my man Charles."

It was the custom of Sylvester Berkley to clamber up every morning to the Molkenkur, where he drenched himself liberally with whey. I once accompanied him and enjoyed the spectacle: the uncertain and testy character of the Berkleys was ameliorating sensibly under my eyes with repeated washes of the emollient liquor. Sylvester went so far as to bathe in it. With him, too, I chose to visit the most coquettish and artificial part of the ruined castle, the Rittersaal of Otho-Henry: its mixed Renaissance style gave occasion for a hundred lectures to so good an antiquarian as Berkley was, and I came away from his orations with an increased respect for bric-à-brac. On the lower part of its front are four statues —Hercules son of Jupiter, Samson the lieutenant of God, David the brave and prudent boy, and "Herzog Joshua, who killed thirty-one kings by the grace of the Lord." On the inside this tower offered a scene of lovely devastation: wild vines and flowers hung with insolent grace among the florid carved-work of the doors, through which used to pass high-stepping dames of the Palatinate in sables and feathers, but whose guests now are owls and crows, sometimes spotted or mantled with ermine of snow. Berkley, familiar with Heidelberg, was indeed the best of ciceroni. Visiting alone with him the Rent Tower — which under the reminiscences of Hohenfels had seemed more of a *grenier* than aught else — I comprehended its majesty as symbolizing the power of Frederick I., the Victorious, who beat Frederick IV. and the German princes at Seckenheim. It was eighty feet high, its walls on one side twenty feet thick: this monstrous shell was crushed by Louis XIV. like a filbert, while at present, as if to keep the warlike deed of the French nut-cracker for a show, the rent portion is restrained from crumbling in the mighty talons of the trees. My diplomate knew all these doughty Palatines like ancestors. After Frederick the Victorious, he elucidated

SERMONS IN STONES.

Ludwig V. and Frederick V.: their statues lean against the shadowy wall of what was built as the Great Tower. Frederick V., who married the granddaughter of Mary Queen of Scots, and died in exile, retains on his marble brow that crown of Bohemia which he accepted after its refusal by the powers of Austria, Saxony, Savoy and Denmark; but he has lost the two hands with which he grasped it. Ludwig V., whose figure stands near by, is not less gloomy: he seems to know that the Great Tower hangs in ruin behind him as he watches the ivy advance little by little over his stone face. The man of useful information had for each of these heroes a date and an anecdote: he gave a voice to all the petrified chiefs vainly standing in defence before their towers, from Charlemagne, who had lost his globe, to Otho of Hungary, who has but one leg, and Otho-Henry of the bric-à-brac tower, who has been bereft of his hand, and Frederick II., who is broken in half, and Frederick IV., who has dropped his sceptre, and Frederick the Victorious himself, among whose marble plumes the green leaves of ruin are playing. It is in such a spot and with such a guide that you learn how history may be better than legend. If I had had so wise a counselor here in my student days, I should perhaps have quoted less of Jean Paul and more of Clio. But at this period my Mentor was Hohenfels, then at his own cloudiest stage of development, who adored Goethe and insulted Tiedge, who knew the Niebelungen-Lied by heart, but could only ridicule the sketches, screech-owls, fallow-deer and straddle-bug figures of worthy Charles de Graimberg, the artist who for thirty years collected here in his chambers a museum of prints and books and pictures illustrating Heidelberg. I have not yet heard Sylvester ridicule a work of art: if the specimen be of a grand

SATIRE IN STONE.

master, he respects it; if it be art of the Décadence, somewhat low, poor, improper and profane, he adores it, and moves heaven and earth that he may buy it—the true spirit of the connoisseur. As we stood in the Rittersaal, the spectacle of the rosy Renaissance nymphs and nereids evoked from him his very best effort, an eloquence superior to the Neues Schloss and a piety beyond the stone Calvary. For my poor part, replete and saturated with historic lore, I would not have exchanged the trumpet of Fame herself against the flaring silvery rim, bright with starch, of that all-encircling cravat.

I would only have given a world populated with Berkleys for my dream-ridden poet, my friend, my baron, the accomplice of my student-life.

Heidelberg Castle is comparatively unhurt in front. The symmetrical profile of its long façade, with gables and pinnacles, the repose of St. Udalrich's chapel and the be-ribboned smartness of Otho-Henry's palace, speak little of decay: it is like a fair mask lying in an Egyptian coffin, and concealing a terrible heap of bones and broken jewels, and tufts of dry hair and shreds of rich clothing.

And then, what a satire it is that all this stately masonry should be but the

"ONE FISH-BALL."

complicated envelope of the biggest drinking-cask in the world!

I prolonged my walks with Berkley to the Schwalbennest (Swallow's Nest), the square tower which leans so directly over the Neckar from the heights of its mountain at Neckarsteinach. The inexhaustible cravat of the philosopher was still pouring out useful information from its polished lip, and I was listening to the tale of Bligger the Scourge, whose soldiers closed up this tower and left him to die when the pope excommunicated him, when of a sudden I heard the notes of a French horn from the river below. I borrowed the field-glass which hung eternally from Berkley's shoulder by a leathern baldrick, and there in a little boat I saw our Yankee, who was drifting past us on the river and relieving his soul with the soldiers' march from *Faust*. I watched with amusement this versatile pattern of my country's civilization. In a moment he had thrown down his instrument and had rowed himself carefully into the current. This necessity fulfilled, his mind seemed to be at peace

again, and he flung himself flat on his back in the bows. Another instant, and a fresh wave of melody came up to us in our watch-tower: this time it was vocal, and the virtuoso was pouring out with the full power of his lungs to the Vosges Mountains that classic morsel known as "One Fish-Ball." Directly he had exhausted this sensation too, but his resources were not yet at an end; unfolding a cast-net which lay beneath the thwarts, he flung it skillfully out into the broadest part of the stream; and I hope that the fishes of the Neckar, judiciously charmed by the noise of the horn and the song, made no delay in engaging their gills among the meshes of this energetic young sportsman. Berkley, in compliment to me, looked on at the vagaries of my countryman with a sad, forgiving politeness: I begged him to finish his story of Bligger the Scourge. It was now sunset, and when I looked again for the Yankee, he was vanishing like Hiawatha, high upon a sea of splendor, and teaching the echoes to repeat the adventures of Jeronimus Jobs, hero of that original epic the "Jobsiad." Ten minutes sufficed for my brilliant compatriot to prove that he was something of an oarsman, something of a fisherman, something of a vocalist, and something of a hornblower.

The linen duster was visible again at supper, twenty-four hours after our first meal with him. I sent him a mouthful of my Prince Metternich by the trusty Charles, and he grasped his hat and came over to touch glasses with Sylvester and myself.

"Your wine is not so bad, but in this confounded country I can get nothing but the superfluities—an intolerable deal of sack and not one ha'penn'orth of bread. At Bonn, and here, too, I had to dine without my crust."

"I have hardly noticed it," said I, "but here I believe it has always been so."

"I have seen the day when I would have given a dollar for a corn-cake or a bit of pone. They gave me at dinner with the soup a pretty cake, a sort of brioche. I just flung it at the man and asked for bread. Then he came up bringing a little biscuit stuck full of aniseed. Then I asked for bread again, and he brought me a turn-over full of plums and cherries, as if I had been Jack Horner, by Jingo! I stopped there, or he would have offered me every tart and pudding they turn out in the pastry-shops. I vow I don't like it: I am something of a Grahamite."

"It is just the same at our table," I said, applying myself to a kind of sausage or mince-meat which I was consuming, and which had prunes in it.

"The Repast without Bread," said Berkley, who saw the chance for an oration, "is an ancient tradition of the country, a legend enclosing the finest political rebuke ever made by the producing to the governing classes. The present observance, though, is probably an involuntary sequel to the old proverb."

"Oh! I thought likely," said the youth with a shrewd air, and indicating my sausage, "that they just didn't *give bread with one fish-ball*."

"Frederick the Victorious," pursued Sylvester, disdaining the interruption, "after conquering the robber-knights at Seckenheim, treated them famously, and had them all to a feast. Everything was magnificent, but when the guests called for bread, there was none to be had. 'My lords,' said Frederick, 'those whose life's trade it is to trample the grain, burn the mills and plant the fields with corpses must not ask for bread: that boon of industry is for other mouths than ours.' And he resumed his courteous talk as if nothing had happened. It was a fine Corn-Law speech of the date of 1461."

"Perhaps so," I agreed; "but it is unfortunate that the lesson is not learned yet in the country, and must be enforced at the expense of strangers. By the by, a pretty girl that," I said, willing to adopt a slightly rakish tone with my young

guest, and winking indulgently as a handsome laundress made her escape past the dining-room windows, a kind of Briareus of surreptitious stockings tossing multitudinously from out of her apron.

"Pretty girl! you must be fond of a

THE CAST-NET.

pretty girl!" sneered the stony-hearted student, with his first exhibition of temper. "If all the pretty girls of Europe were under the river in that seine of mine, it would not be I who should draw them out."

I felt surprised, and perhaps rebuked. I assumed a rather grand manner : "Your name must be Saint Anthony! Apropos, may we know how to call the guest with whom the custom of the place lets us share our cup, but not our loaf?"

"No objection," said the Yankee with a business-like air; and he opened his pocket-book, from which a card fell beside my plate. "Catch it! Not that," he said, and extracted another. I read them both without particular intention. On one was printed "*John Kran:ch*," on the other "*Jean Kraaniff.*" "Ah, now you have seen it," said the young man, in an easy, unembarrassed way, "and all the fat's in the fire. Well, we are a good way from New Orleans, and I may as well tell you all about it. You are a literary man, I judge, and perhaps you can help me to utilize my anagram."

"Your anagram?" I asked.

"The anagram of Jean Kraaniff, you observe, may be Jean K. Ffarina. I think that will do for New Orleans. I am known there as a wine and spirits merchant. From bay rum to cologne water is no great step. My game is to ally myself with the Farina family, represent in Louisiana the whole perfumery business of Cologne and Paris, and some day monopolize the Western States, South America and the Pacific Islands. How do you like the notion?"

"YOU ARE THE MAN OF THE TWO CHICKENS!"

"I am the last man to consult in a matter of trade," I replied: "your name seems to have a superfluous letter."

"Oh, that '*K*' will do for anything: *kind* means a child, *Koeln* means Cologne, you see—or I can drop the *K*. That is not what troubles me. Unhappily, plenty of people have seen my old card, the one you first read, and it will be tough to ask them to believe, as I mean to do, that I am a genuine Farina, who arranged his letters into Kraaniff because he was poor. Worse luck! my expectations come from the other name, from Kranich. Yes, aunty's name is Kranich, and be hanged to her!"

"I beg your pardon," said I, a sudden thought striking me, "but I have long known a lady of that name, and—"

"Have you? It is not so difficult, for she has lived in every capital of Europe. Now it is Brussels; a while back it was Paris; *my* christening-cup she forwarded from Frankfort. My ridiculous old uncle was somebody, my absurd old father was nobody, and so I was sent to exile with the grand duke of Mississippi. My poor uncle the banker was as crazy as a loon."

"I have seen him at a ball in a bed-gown."

"The ding-dong-deuce you have!" said the duelist, very slowly and mistrustfully.

"Frau Kranich was at Ems with him that season. He popped in to her ball and fainted, and the duke of Mississippi carried him to his chamber. But your aunt is a good soul. I cannot forget how she assisted me to the prettiest piece of work I have ever done. It was a bit of charity. Poor sweet little Francine! I hope she will make no bad investment of her dowry."

"Why, then," said the young man, rising and looking very black, "you infernal, oily, amorous old hypocrite! you are *the man of the two chickens!*"

People have different ways of meeting an outrage. I simply rose, conveyed my surprise and indignation in a look, and left the table and the room. Between a limb like this and a person of my age and phlegm no great insult was possible. The young man turned on his heel, grasped his hat again, and went to join his companion, a German who had served as second in his contest. It was a student of pinched and beery appearance, I remember, with fingers blazing with stones, ears hung with rings, and between them a round face bejeweled with gold eye-glasses.

Berkley would probably have gone out with me, but at that moment Hohenfels came rambling in to supper, cheery and star-gazing as usual, the duelist Von Ramm interlaced with him like double cherries moulded on one stem. I had rather repulsed my old friend while in this companionship, and now felt no appetite for duelists. "You'll have but ill *bred* to your supper," I said hastily in the door; and leaving him this choice pun, for which the baron would soundly have trounced me had he understood it, I went out with a little gesture of avoidance.

PART XIII.

ON WITH THE OLD LOVE.

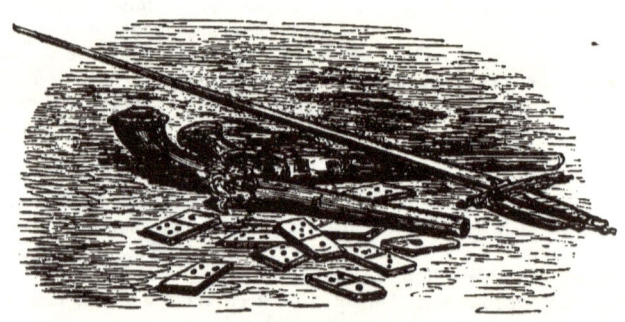

THE WEAPONS.

A GREAT walk that I took in the moonlight, a complete ascent of the Little Geissberg, cleaned out my ill-humor entirely. Besides, my conscience was clear. I slept like a log, and, was healthily confused in my senses when aroused by the opening of my chamber door in the morning.

"What game is afoot for to-day?" I asked, still entangled in my visions of the night.

"A chance unparalleled," said the diplomatist, who entered dressed, gloved, cravatted and enwreathed with smiles. "A diamond day—one of the few choice sunrises of this uncertain spot for the present season. The game, as you call it, is an excursion to Schwetzingen. The castle is immense—fountains, cascades, statues. If Heidelberg is Germany's Alhambra, Schwetzingen is her Versailles. You will be delighted, enchanted." (An unusual briskness was injected just now into Sylvester's periods: his style was growing *staccato;* but I took little notice.) "Come, here is your coat. Breakfast is over, but Charles has some sandwiches in your botany-box, and a flask of hot coffee. The driver is waiting."

And truly the faithful servitor appeared panting on the scene, his face striped with sweat, his hands filled with bags and valises, my sandwiches put to warm under his arm-pit. At the carriage-door, "Come, man, bundle up. Coachman, run like a greyhound to Schwetzingen!" said Sylvester. "Which seat do you like, Berkley?" said I, making room for him among my conveniences.

"Oh, *I* don't go," observed the statesman with his most diplomatic smile: "I have seen it a hundred times. You really must let me off."

"And Hohenfels?"

MY STIMULUS.

"Hohenfels has been up these two hours, and is over at the college. He has mixed himself in with drugs, chemicals and everything you detest. The pharmacy-student has put him up to it. If you could see him now it would be with a cowskin apron around him or in a glass mask and a smock-frock."

"But if the baron does not accompany me, you must."

"Let me off for this time, my dear sir. I am myself implicated in his experiments, and for once in your life you will be a good riddance. 'Tis something we discussed before you arrived, the direct creation of whey by macerating grass and turnips in the natural rennets. Goodbye. You can be back with us by dinner if you insist. Drive on, coachman."

"Drive on, coachman," echoed Charles, slipping a florin with vast secresy into the man's hand. "Drive on as though Saint Denis were throwing his head at you."

On the route, as I sat pretty passive, Charles kept feeding me assiduously out of the tin box, stopping my mouth with a croquette or a leathery egg whenever I showed signs of asking a question. He prolonged this exercise for nearly an hour, the wheels bowling smoothly and the landscape running softly behind us. At last, choking with tears and heroically sinking back in the cushions, he said, "Saved, thank all the saints! I can no more!"

"It is then, as I began to suspect, a plot," I exclaimed. "As you value your life and my service, let me hear all about it."

"It is only that I have saved the life of the dear *patron*," said Charles. "See, here in these bags are all your clothes, just as I brought them from Marly. Monsieur is self-supporting, self-escaping and self-acting, like a watch. Never, never need monsieur see these accursed stones and students more."

"But this is treason," I cried, growing excited. "In you, Charles, it is flat rebellion. I will not bear it."

"And an opera-hat in the large valise, and a small alarm wrapped up in his evening coat."

"Tell me the whole mystery, stupid,"

AMATEUR CHEMISTS.

I shouted; "but first— No! turn the horses immediately."

"Monsieur must condescend to hear my story first. It will be time enough to turn back when he knows the troubles we have saved him from." And with this my faithful idiot, after the manner of Sultana Scheherezade of old, plunged into a torrent of garrulity, with the pure object of making time.

"It seems, these Americans," said Charles, who never dreamed of including his employer under the designation, "are man-eaters and everything that is barbarous. Yonder Aztec from Bonn ought to be put in a cage at the Jardin des Plantes. I know whereof I talk, and that the savage, although he makes a feint of attending the lectures at Bonn, is no more a student than my shoe. He is a serpent out of a menagerie, who roves over Europe, and they say he has already exercised his vile fascinations on a poor young girl, whom he has slimed ready to devour." (Charles, not discontented with this careful metaphor, repeated it over again.) "Monsieur must know that his questions put to the serviceable man of the hotel awakened my ambition. With the assistance of that worthy person I have made inquiries among the university students. The stranger is known. His cold and calculating malice is incalculable, it is fatal. It is proper to rid the country of such a demon. Not a student but trembles at the thought of the bowie-knives which are concealed in the legs of this crocodile, and of the inexhaustible barrels of his revolvers of Colt."

Thus Charles, evidently sketching some hero whom he had relished at the Porte Saint-Martin Theatre. When brought round to a simple narrative of the scene at the supper-table, I found that matters of some moment had indeed taken place in my absence. Berkley the statesman, it appears, had been irresolute, unwilling to fly from the enemy, and hesitating between diplomacy and the underlying pugnacity of his temper, which the stranger's speech was well fitted to rouse. The arrival of Hohenfels and the American's late opponent had added fuel to the flame, and a wordy quarrel had arisen, the man in the linen duster quickly relapsing into the measured, cold, provoking style of banter. The dispute was raging when the late arrival of a pair of travelers at supper—

one a lady—had suppressed all demonstrations. Charles had noticed the cavalier, a handsome man in a gray overcoat. This person, it would appear, had some knowledge of the miscreant calling himself Jean Kraaniff. At any rate,

SOLICITUDE.

after supper, the quarrel was renewed in the billiard-room. Hohenfels (who, bless his heart! knew about as much about firearms as a nightingale) was for pistols and twenty paces; his *alter ego*, Von Ramm, preferred swords, without the usual mattresses; when the new arrival in the gray coat had begged to assume the whole combat. "I think M. Kraaniff knows me—we are both wine-sellers," he said (Charles had evidently been polishing a keyhole near the conference). "I have already been insulted by him, and I choose the weapons." He then, with a singular mixture of authority and lordly good-nature, dictated a novel sort of combat. Himself and the stranger were to play so many games of dominoes. ("As Monsieur Paul is a Latin scholar, I suppose I should say *domini*," said Charles proudly.) They were then to drink Rhine wine until one of them was lifeless. Mr. Berkley was to see fair play. The loser was to quit the country, drown himself in the river, or otherwise vanish from the terrestrial sphere. The fearful combat began, the games of dominoes were won about equally, but at the wine-match the American failed, and lost his stiffness joint by joint under the third bottle, while the other improved in wisdom and gravity. As he won the match, the conqueror made the American sign some paper, which he was just able to do, and which the English official witnessed. Charles of course knew nothing about the paper's contents. "But I can report the final speeches, which were made about sunrise this morning. 'If I can get Mr. Flemming quietly out of the way, it will be the triumph of a life's diplomacy.' Those were the words of Mr. Berkley, and I

GALLANTRY.

thought them most noble. 'This robber of women is harmless for the present,' said M. Fortnoye."

"M. Fortnoye?"

"Certainly—M. Fortnoye, the purveyor of wines for the hotel. The serviceable person had monsieur the purveyor's room all ready against his arrival. But he has never been seen before in company with a beautiful lady, as last night."

This recital gave me abundant food for thought. Berkley's spasm of gayety, and his whole ingenious manner of getting rid of me, were approved without much hesitation. But it gave me a pang to reflect that Hohenfels had been drawn into disputes for me, and that I had retreated without even wringing his hand: please Heaven, we should yet renew our twinship among the ruins of Heidelberg. The sudden apparition of Fortnoye gave me cause for jealous alarm—the familiarity with which he was escorting his fair companion, whom, as Francine, I could not mistake, was most disagreeable in every way to my feelings.

With all this on my mind the fairy show of Schwetzingen was lost upon me. Charles, I believe, found it an Elysium, and wandered through the clipped labyrinths with a delighted spirit; but for me the heart was wanting to admire the terraces and grottoes, the bandy-legged leaden statues, the fountains formed of spouting birds, the trim cataracts and little shaving-glass of a lake. I entered a convenient house, called, I believe, the "Imperial Baths," and tapped idly at a window. A couple passed before the panes, and were about vanishing through the shrubbery. The lady, handsomely dressed, showed me little but the ample rotundity of her back, disguised in the superfluous paniers and puffings with which stout females ever prefer to augment their personal majesty. The gentleman was gallantly shading her from the sun with an umbrella of white Chinese silk lined with azure. His gait, his hat and his overcoat of silver-gray seemed familiar. He caught a half glimpse of me, and quickly returned. He was now alone, but through a glass corridor I saw the lady enter the house where I was sheltered. She was decidedly stout, but did not lack the "grand air." Fortnoye, for he it was, was now running up to me.

"Dear Mr. Flemming," he cried with a hearty grasp of my hand, "I am enchanted to meet you—enchanted selfishly and unselfishly. I am in great haste: you will let me explain. I have just arrived hither with a lady, who must go this evening to Frankfort. I knew her late husband in circles connected with my business. She will arrive there at night—she cannot go alone. For my own part, an affair of real importance—real importance, or I would not ask you —recalls me to Heidelberg. You are doubtless on the way to Frankfort?"

I had certainly not said I was going to Frankfort. But it was not easy to confess how short my excursion was really intended to be, and thus give the impression that I had run away just for a morning from my enemy at Heidelberg. But who could be my proposed companion? Fortnoye's arrival with a fair comrade the night before had been explained by his acquaintance with Francine. A load was taken from my mind by the conjecture that, after all, it might not have been she; and certainly it was hard to imagine the natty Francine transformed by any freak or volume of crinoline into the opulent and noble figure I had glimpsed among the shrubbery. At any rate, my dream of immediately rejoining Hohenfels at Heidelberg was postponed.

But the lady had entered the building, and at this moment I both saw and heard her behind some screens of double glass. She was giving a fee to an aproned servitor of the place, old, owlish-looking and discreet, who quickly produced some towels. Her words, slow and measured, were, "I like them fine: I shall be visible in twenty minutes."

The contours I had not recognized. But the contralto's mellow music was what has rung in my ears from the first spring-time of my manhood; and I have often thought I should like to grow stone deaf, so as to have that voice, and nothing more vulgar, flowing perpetually to my brain. It was the voice I had last heard reading prayers in a bed-room of the hotel at Stuttgart.

I tapped the window still, in a reverie, as Fortnoye explained how my carriage could be re-engaged to conduct us to the railway, how Charles would relieve the lady and myself of all minor trouble, and how the preferable hotel at Frankfort had its frontage on the parade-ground. Presently the chandelier shook, and a faint perfume I knew floated on to me. I was being presented.

The well-known voice had struck again its bell-like music. I looked up from my conventional obeisance. An immeasurable pyramid of black silk and Cashmerean yellow stood before me; and at the summit of a broad, many-chinned face, drowned out in a waste of healthy, well-fed tissues, shone the eyes of Mary Ashburton!

The first excursion I ever took with Mary Ashburton was in that unlucky barouche to the Valley of Lauterbrunnen. *Then*, we were off for a picnic; *now*, I was flying with her to the city of the bankers, on a hot May day, in a railway-carriage softened to the feet with Brussels carpet and stuffed up to the eyes with

THE DISCREET SERVITOR.

drab cassimere and coach-lace. The bivouac wildness was missing which I used to describe when I would ask the reader if he knew the taste of cold meat under the shadows of trees. Colder than thy meats, O Vale of Fountains, were the hearts of thy lady-visitors! Wretched was the cheer I had from thee, land of the glacier and the goat, of chalets and of chamois, of poetry and of water-colors, of recitations and of students in green who wormed themselves into my path with their whispers of *Beware!* Cold meat, indeed! When I remarked to Miss Ashburton that I had never seen Chamouni, and she vivaciously said that *in my place she would not lose an hour in going thither*, the taste of the cold shoulder which she thus presented to me struck chills to my palate and rankled there for ten good years at least. I do not know why I recall those hard measures which were meted to me in Interlaken: I certainly did not think of them when I was privileged to ride with her again, and her presence, augmented to thrice as much as I had the thought or

LAND OF THE VALLEY, THE CHALET AND THE NANNY!

right of expecting, was palpably by my side.

My reception by Mary Ashburton (or Mrs. Ashburleigh, as she had christened herself) was a delight without the ghost of a complaint. For the Dark Ladye was no longer unapproachable. On the contrary, she received my homage very graciously, and indeed overbore me, flooded me and saturated me with a stream of hopes and wishes. Nothing that I had ever thought or felt before could stand for a moment in this grand, imperial influence: even the Mary Ashburton of 18— (when her weight could not have been over ninety pounds) did not constitute a vision of anything like the distinctness. I sat, like O'Shanter on his mare, enveloped in a whirling sphere of witchery and incantation: no previous impression had the least chance of remaining. Francine Joliet's capstrings in the mad storm drove away from my sight like white phantoms, level, helpless and confused in the hurlyburly. "Oh, madam!" I said in my corner, sitting with that rotary action of the thumbs which to my mind best expresses the rapt soul—"Oh, madam, why cannot I attach myself to you for ever?"

"You are on my skirts now, I think," she observed, just developing a kind of generalized marble smile from her noble chin.

Was there ever such a quick repartee? On her skirts!—like a purple bur or a fragrant brier, clinging with every tentacle of my nature as she traveled, and, what was better, admitted in her speech as such! Was it not a virtual invitation? It is only married ladies—perhaps only widows—who should permit themselves these chaste doubles-entendres; but the expression, as it stood, was perfect. This was only the first of the good things which Mrs. Ashburleigh uttered—gems of language which perhaps would have escaped a less keen listener than myself —felicities disguised in apparent commonplace and indicating the most adroit self-mastery of a creative talent—proverbial pith, fit to make Swift burn his *Bons-mots de Stella*, or Tupper publish the marvels in another volume of his philosophical writings.

Thus we traveled like a dream, passing Mannheim and Darmstadt. We sped from place to place without my giving a thought to the data of Progressive Geography. Equally obliterated from my brain was the compatriot who had insulted me at the hotel, the young son of commerce who had seemed so cold, so versatile, so truly American, until my mention of Francine had driven him into a fury perfectly worthy of the Latin nations. The young man and his impertinence slept undisturbed in my mind. It was all I could do to realize that Mary Ashburton or her double—perhaps, in truth, her quadruple—was traveling, not unkind, by my side.

"Don't you remember, Mr. Flemming, when I met you in Venice?—or was it at Brighton?—"

"Oh, my dear madam, surely you are jesting: we met first at Interlaken. Have you forgotten your sketch of the Lake of Thun — forgotten the Staubbach?"

"I really must confess that I have, or, at any rate, whatever happened there."

It was with this peculiar delicacy that she indicated how a veil was to be drawn over every circumstance of that Past so painful to me. Was it not kind? She continued: "Wherever it was, there was a large hotel, or a palazzo, or something of the sort, and outside it was always raining, and I used to let you read my diary. Would you like to repeat your lessons? I am something of a blue even now."

She fumbled in her little satchel. I waited as for the delivery of a Sibylline scroll. Every emanation from that rare intellect had a holiness for me. Extracting a book, and passing over a few printed pages containing, apparently, washing-accounts, my superb companion pointed out to me the following prose ballad. She remarked that she had written it out the evening before. "When I have finished one of my writings, and there is any kind of a literary person near, I am ready to die until I get it ex-

THE EARLY BIRD-CATCHER.

amined. That good creature Fortnoye would have received it if I had not met you. For mercy's sake, read it, and tell me if it is nonsense. We can relate our histories to each other any time."

It was the most exquisite manner of getting over a preliminary awkwardness that I had ever known. I took the sacred washing-book, which trembled in my hands. I could hardly say a word or read a line. If I had not afterward, during a more intimate relation with the

THE DISCOVERER OF THE FORD.

writer, got hold of the copy again, my reader would have but a lame account of the origin of the

"FRANKEN-FURTH.

"My poor mamma, who was a perfect toper at novel-reading, found this account in one of her romances. She told it me once, and suggested that if I ever had occasion to bank at Frankfort-on-the-Main (her own credits were always on Paris and Geneva), I might recall the story, which was pretty in itself, and might lend a new interest to the birthplace of those dear Rothschilds. I have been at Frankfort three or four times, and of course I forgot all about poor mamma and her old stories. Just now M. Fortnoye told me the very same rigmarole, with all sorts of French flourishes. Strange if I did not remember it, coming from *him!*

"It was a handsome young lad in trunk-hose and in the eighth century: he was only a shoemaker, but, like George Barnwell, or Eugene Aram or somebody in Bulwer's writings, his soul was above his profession. Having promised his blond lady-love that he would catch her a nightingale, he had come down at daybreak to the banks of the Main River with an abundance of birdlime, of glue, and perhaps of shoemaker's wax.

"Opposite to him stretched the great Hercynian Forest, which formerly was sixty days' journey across (am I not good to remember this out of my Cæsar's *Commentaries?*). Hidden behind a rock, the youth whistled and piped, imitating the notes of the birds whom he hoped to attract. To his chagrin, not a song-bird greeted the rising sun. But directly, as the morning-star vanished in the light of dawn, a frightful cloud swept tempestuously over the forest. He analyzed the storm: it was a storm of eagles. At the same time a throng of living creatures emerged from the woods and ran distractedly up and down the brink. He synthesized the throng: it was a barnyardful of neat cattle.

"Does and hares—the cows and sheep of the wilderness—were in fact herding on the farther shore of the Main. From the birds of prey in the sky, from the timid quadrupeds on the earth, ascended a coarse discord of bleating and barking. The boy grasped his nets, and fled with a hasty prayer to Odin: he had been converted but three years before to the faith of Rome, and must be pardoned if, in a moment of such perplexity, he forgot whether he was orthodox or heterodox.

"Arrived at the nearest hilltop, the youth's terror, which was strong, succumbed to his curiosity, which was stronger. He hid himself and watched. The extraordinary menagerie still roamed the river-bank, hesitating and distracted, now dashing back again into the thickets, now emerging to try once more the watery barrier which restrained them.

"The race of antelopes has been preserved on the earth on account of its superiority in powers of flight. This *élite* of cowardice was not unknown in the eighth century. The youthful spy saw a doe, guided by a keener fear than the rest, advance desperately into the water. 'Well done, pretty fool! You illustrate the survival of the fittest,' said this primitive Darwinian as the young deer, with frightened eyes and distended nostrils, stepped across the torrent, selecting a fordable passage in its extremity. The animal did not swim, but walked, and thus earned the honor of discovering a ford in the Main River.

"The path was quickly put to a more important use. From the hilltop where he crouched the little cobbler now saw a throng of figures, heroic and hideous, emerge from the Hercynian shades: they too paused at the brink, but, guided by the fawn, they strode tumultuously through the water, grim and bloody, carrying their wounded in their arms or on rough litters, and still clothed with the wolf-skins and bear-skins which they had assumed overnight with the laudable intention of frightening the enemy by their ugliness. I do not believe that the Franks were

CHARLEMAGNE IN RETREAT.

"FRANKEN-FURTH."

yet celebrated either for toilettes or manners. For the traversing army was the Frankish force, conquered overnight by the combined Saxons and Danes; and the general at their head was Charlemagne, generaled himself this time by a frightened doe.

"'Franken-furth!' said the grim leader, baptizing the shore, and thrusting his lance deep into the bank. And Frankfort is the name which the spot still keeps since the day when Charlemagne built a fortress around his spear as it stuck in the mud.

"The growth of a settlement about the fortress was rapid. Before the young bird-snarer and the blond beauty had named their second baby it was a city fit for them to live in. A cage hung always at the door as a sign of the shoemaker's abode, in which cage a starling sung perpetually 'I can't get out' a thousand years before Sterne; and Hans of the Starling, as he was called, became a noble in the land, the shoe being a sign of distinction at a time when most gentleman went without.

"Thus have I built in a night the city of Charlemagne upon my page, like to the mediæval monk, who constructed on the margin of his parchment a capital of his own device, with wondrous architecture and inhabitants in brilliant robes. When the clasps of his book were opened, like the turning of city gates, the populace awaked and stared at the reader with wide-open eyes: when they were shut, the figures all went to sleep and dreamed."

"You retain your poetic fancy, dear lady, and the habit of giving it vent in writing," I said, as I returned the manuscript, only half perused.

"Yes, it is my safety-valve," said Mrs. Ashburleigh. (How original her images were!) "Besides, the practice influenced the most important event of my youth—it almost procured me my husband."

"Do confide in me, dear madam," I exclaimed, deeply touched by this surprising confidence. "Are we not old acquaintance? Tell me all about it."

Mary Ashburleigh smiled. Talk of a chin with a dimple in it! There were a dozen in hers at the very least, developing themselves every time she playfully bridled her neck: in each dimple, for me, Love, in all decorum, sat playing. "Generals don't usually expatiate on their false moves," she said, "and my marriage was not what is usually regarded as a success. But I am a woman of the world, and you are grown up, Mr. Flemming, or ought to be. That episode, after all, was a short one. The document I refer to was a little essay in one of my old albums: it pictured the life of a painter from the North when he came to bask and bathe in the art of Italy."

"I know it by heart," I exclaimed, interrupting her: "I have committed it to memory this quarter of a century. It begins, 'I often reflect with delight upon the young artist'—"

"There, that will do," said my glorious companion: "you must have filched it from my sketch-book. Whatever the merit of the little *jeu d'esprit*, it was a study from a living model."

"Foolish Paul Flemming that I was," I broke in, "to think that a girl of twenty could write thus without a reason!"

"I will not tell you much, lest I should set you off sentimentalizing. Oblige me by fanning me a little with your *Galignani* as I talk to you. You must imagine, then, a young English gentleman-out-of-livery, perfectly gloomy and genteel, who had gone as cicerone for us into Italy. He had been dismissed for years and years, you know, when I saw him sketching in the Vatican. Suppose I found out afterward that he had taken a situation in one of those picture-factories where saints and altar-pieces are made for exhibition with stencils, pounce-bags and such things. No matter. I became interested in him, poor fellow! getting up at daybreak to work in the art-galleries. I wrote out his portrait, as I imagined it, in my album. He sent me a copy of a new poem, one that I had never seen, by young Tennyson: it was all about the maiden and the traveling lord disguised as a landscape-painter. At the head of this copy of verses was drawn a darling little illustration, with his own portrait in the part of the Lord of Burleigh. Of course then I knew that he

THE FATE OF HANNIBAL.

was a nobleman in disguise, and that love of me had brought him to Italy with us. My mother had trained me to high aspirations, but somehow I never imparted to Mrs. Ashburton my faith in Arthur's lofty birth, contenting myself with an impassioned correspondence until mamma's death, when we married. My husband's parentage, however, was not noble, his father being an innkeeper—a man from whom all his family had been obliged to flee on account of his shocking habits. My husband, with the pecuniary assistance I gave him, embarked in the spirit-trade— But why do I tell you this? Arthur was a kind and devoted husband, except sometimes when he had dined very heartily, on which occasions I was obliged to have recourse to great firmness with him. But all that is in the past, and I have become perfectly accustomed to my *veuvage*, certainly the lightest and most independent state in the world. If my darlings had only lived!"

"Dear madam! Your children are then lost to you?"

"Yes, four of them, poor dears! and laid to rest in different kingdoms. Hannibal, the first, who was born while we were crossing the Alps, was the brightest, and the only one who lived to be five years old. Poor love! he was so

THE JUDENGASSE, FRANKFORT.

logical! Having swallowed a lead-pencil, and being afraid to confess, he fancied that he ought to chew large quantities of India-rubber to obliterate the effects: the dear child was seized with cramps in the stomach before my eyes, as he played in the garden, a week after he had begun with that deleterious gum. He sleeps under a caoutchouc tree at Nice. Waterloo lies in Belgium, where he was born; so does another nameless little love; Lucia was born and died at sea, at two years' interval, and we carried her to Glasgow, where the spirit-trade is very good."

Mary Ashburleigh fell into a reverie. It was a privilege to see the plumed eyelids descend and sweep her cheek. The curved corners of her ripe mouth sank a little, carrying with them the faint moustache—down brushed from the wing of Night!—which goes with that style of beauty. Her breathing became more pronounced and rhythmic, and slightly stertorous. The book, which I had returned, fell from her hand. I had a hundred things to ask her, but I could not but respect an introversion so profound.

We had neared Frankfort when, after a long wool-gathering meditation on my part, I found the dark eyes of my companion fixed on me.

"Mr. Flemming," she said, "I understand that your affairs call you urgently to Paris, but I should be sorry to part before we shall have renewed our acquaintance fairly. Can you not spare two or three hours in the morning? I am acquainted with Frankfort, and should like you to employ me as cicerone."

I hastened to say that, notwithstanding the implacable importunity of my affairs, I should be happy to wait on her next day. For the life of me I could not summon courage to propose my companionship beyond that period, and in fact considered her speech a dismissal. "At what hour shall I bring the carriage?" I asked humbly.

"At nine. It is the number of the Muses, I believe."

This brilliant and elevated allusion captivated me afresh. I got little good of my pillow that night, and with early dawn I was out in the street. I went to the post-office, where a letter from Fortnoye was arranged to be sent me, and idly knocked at the closed doors as if there was any possibility of their unclosing for me at such an hour. I threaded the city. The Zeil, the finest street in Frankfort, showed me right and left a double range of magnificent buildings, giving me the most exalted idea of the old Free Cities of Germany. Over my head I had a magnificent emperor, intended for Charlemagne or Ludwig of Bavaria—I hardly know which, but assuredly unlike either. Tiring soon of these sculptural splendors, I sought the street of the oppressed, the Jews' Street of Frankfort, the Ghetto, the Judengasse.

At Frankfort there are genuine Jews and Christians, the polemists of the *Mer-*

chant of Venice — Christians who hate the Jews, and Jews who hate the Christians. Only some forty years back the Judengasse was closed by iron gates at either end, with bars, locks and sentinels. These precautions of the Christians against the Jews were amply reciprocated by the Jews against the Christians, for every son of Jacob fortified himself in his mouldy old house like a besieged captain. Evening arrived, the Jews stole into their quarter, with a fine if behind the hour. The iron gates closed. Then the Hebrews, being barred into their quarter like lepers in a quarantine, revenged themselves by fastening up their castles like garrisons in a siege. Now the street is broader and better ventilated, but the histories of persecution, of hate, of revenge, are written legibly over the narrow houses: many of them are decrepit and tottering, like the owl-faced old women who stare furtively through the thick window-panes. The improvements in the Judengasse are due to the ambition, and in still greater part to the affection, of the brothers Rothschild. Gudula Rothschild, *née* Schwapper, of the free city of Frankfort, and widow of honest Mayer Anselm Rothschild, was not to be bought off by any promises of splendor from the house — No. 153 — where her five sons and five daughters were born. Filthy and pestilential as it was, the Judengasse was the street of her preference. She never chose to visit any of the palaces built by her sons in Paris, London or Vienna. She never chose to get into a carriage, or to change in any wise her mysterious, Oriental rites of living. Unable to vanquish this humble and tenacious resolve, and not even daring to touch the crumbling wooden relic where she lived with all her pieties, her sons gave her the only boon that she could not refuse to receive — air and space. They bought a part of the street and tore down the buildings which overshadowed their mother's windows: thirty houses fell in this demolition, and enormous sums were spent to regale the old woman with a ray of sunshine.

Uneasy and preocccupied as I was, I forced myself to remember the singular foundation of the Rothschild fortunes It is as honorable as it is curious.

In the year 1795 the prince of Hesse-Cassel, forced to quit his dominions, and knowing of no one to whom he could well confide a sum of two millions, asked counsel of a trusty friend. The adviser pointed out the most honest man he knew, a Hebrew with whom he had had certain transactions. The prince sent for the Jew and remitted the sum to him. The Jew asked whether the money was a deposit or a sum entrusted for speculation. The prince was in a hurry. "Do what you like with it," said he; "only give me your receipt." On this the Hebrew shook his head, and begged the monarch to take back his money. "You may be captured or you may be killed," said this flatterer: "the receipt will be found on you, and I shall be persecuted."

Without a receipt the Jew would answer for the safety of the money: receipt given, he answered for nothing. The prince looked in the Jew's honest face, and put the money in his hands without guarantee.

The prince of Hesse-Cassel beat a retreat with all the other princes his confrères. At length, however, in 1814, the treaty of Paris restored to each prince about the value of his former realm; the earthquakes of empires, which had overthrown so many thrones between 1795 and 1814, had ceased; the prince of Hesse-Cassel re-entered his capital. One morning a Jew was announced. "If the Jews have any petition, let them apply to the ministers." His haughtiness did not affect the Hebrew in the least. His message was to the prince, and only the prince would he address. The Hebrew was introduced.

It was the Jew of 1795: it was the same coat, a little more threadbare; the same face, a little thinner; the same hair, a little grayer; the same beard, a little more white and long. "Ah, brave man," said His Highness, "it is you! I hardly expected that we should meet again. And what have you come to tell me? Has my money been discovered and stolen? It is a pity, but what may not happen in a score of years? I am not very poor, and I can afford to bid good-bye to my two millions."

"It is not so," said the son of Abraham, bowing at every word. "Thanks to the God of Israel, Your Highness's money is not stolen. But Your Highness allowed me to speculate."

"Ah, I see," said the prince: "you have speculated so cleverly that my money is at the bottom of the sea. Well, well, these unhappy times have been bad for commerce." :

"It is not that, Your Highness. The two millions are not sunk."

"How?" cried the prince. "You have brought my two millions back?"

"It is not that. I have not brought two millions: I have brought six. The money has bred."

"So much the better. But how do you propose to divide?"

"I reserve my commission of six per cent.; but that is not computed in the six millions. It would take too long to tell Your Highness all the little speculations, but they are explained in the accounts. Will Your Highness be pleased to look?"

"And you think I will take all that sum? I will receive my two millions, but I give you the rest. I do not speculate — I am a prince. If you say another word I will not take a florin."

"Ah, Your Highness, there are laws,

even for the poor Jews: I will force you to do it."

"What! to receive six where I gave but two? By all Olympus, you are exacting!"

"No," answered the Jew, after reflecting a moment—"no, I can't force Your Highness, since you might deny that you ever authorized me to speculate. There is no agreement."

"Just so, there is no agreement. I never gave you authority to cultivate the two millions, and if you say, another word I will prosecute you for violation of trust."

"There is no faith left in the world," said the Jew between his teeth.

"What are you saying there?" demanded the prince.

"Nothing, Your Highness. I say that you are a great lord and that I am a poor Jew. There are your two millions in good notes on the treasury of Vienna. As for the other four millions, since you positively refuse them" (the Hebrew sighed), "it is evident that I must take care of them."

And the Jew, who was Mayer Anselm von Rothschild, returned into Frankfort, carrying back the four millions, and understanding nothing of what this faithless world was coming to.

13

PART XIV.

AN AGREEABLE DUET AT FRANKFORT.

"AN ARYAN SUN-MYTH."

"FINE old generous spendthrifts, those Hessian princes!" I said to Mrs. Ashburleigh at the breakfast-table. I had arranged the story as neatly as I could, and presented it to her all rounded and compact, as an equivalent for her "Franken-furth:" then, continuing, "This is the proper spot," I observed, "for the greatest of modern fortunes to take its rise; for Frankfort was the last Protestant city to relinquish the odious mediæval custom of persecuting the Jews,

THE RESURRECTION-BELL.

and it is a proper compensation when Frankfort creates a Jewish plutocracy through the magnanimity of its prince."

"Yes," she said, "I certainly like better to picture to myself the prince cramming a Jew's hand full of banknotes than Schinderhannes insulting the Jews' feet. You remember the incident? He met a band of Hebrews while he was engaged in putting to fire and sword the valley of the Nahe: he made them take off their shoes, which he mixed irrecoverably, and then stood laughing while they shod themselves precipitately at his command, and limped away in each other's shoes to get out of shot from his pistol. Their gait must have resembled that of some of Mrs. Browning's verses. But were the old Hessian princes really so generous? Did they not spend on their pleasures the money they got by selling their subjects as soldiers to any government that had a war to make—an American Revolution to suppress, for instance?"

"The transaction with Rothschild happened after the independence of America. As for a mercenary soldiery, the stain of it attaches no more to those little patri-

archal German despotisms than to the freest of nations and the grandest of men. Othello, now, was a renegade, an artless hireling, whose sympathies ought to have been with the Ottomites he undertook to conquer for pay."

"No doubt; and this artless condottiere, if I remember right, caused the death of his wife, his father-in-law and his lieutenant, stabbed his ancient and made away with himself."

"True; but those methods of family correction were no reproach to him politically. His broils and battles, completely mercenary as they had been, were the admiration of the Venetian senator, you notice, and procured him a marriage of ducal rank. In recent times no nation has so largely engaged in the sale of soldiers as the model of my native republic—heroic Switzerland. Thorwaldsen's lion at Lucerne commemorates a few such poor Swiss idiots, who, being republicans, died because they thought they ought to keep republicanism out of the Tuileries. They were as much slaves to a routine and a fallacy as was Mayer Rothschild the First when he used to be chained in like a dog to his Ghetto at nightfall. How incredible, by the by, that this detestable bigotry should have been in force here within the lifetime of you and me!"

"Horrid! Then you have a contempt for the Swiss?"

"I? No: I adore them."

"Oh!"

"Dearest Mrs. Ashburleigh," I exclaimed, "I have the most violent taste for the Swiss. For a quarter of a century I have never seen a white, Alpine-looking cloud without asking, Does not Tell walk with Washington, Hyperion-like, on high? That was one of the finest phrases of my youth, dear madam, and I have never tired of repeating it. No, my friend, I have not lost my infatuation with heroes. For me, Washington still grandly flutters in the clouds and the stars and the stripes. Franklin, whose home at Passy I may be said to occupy, still teaches me, with admirable astuteness, that a man's first business is to save his country—his next, to leave it and live in Paris. Arnold von Winkelried leaps upon a point, Curtius leaps into a gulf—the one finding heroism in the form of a prominence, the other in that of a concavity: both are sweet to me. Those three fourteenth-century men of Rütli, Walther Fürst, Melchthal and Stauffacher, assure me that moonlight conjurations by a lake are as patriotic as they are operatic. Tell convinces me of the absurdity of worshiping a bonnet—"

"That is a lesson you would not always find it easy to teach me if you had me in Paris."

This archness conquered me afresh, and I had to close the subject: "I only desire the chance to try. As for Tell, you know he is really an Aryan sun-myth."

"Perhaps so, but Swiss heroism is not a myth: I shall never believe it while I can see a pair of peasants, in Lyons velvet tunics, embrace each other on the borders of a lake by the light of a vacillating moon, in the opera. But you spoke of Thorwaldsen's monument to the Swiss guards. Do you know there are fine works of Thorwaldsen's here?"

I confessed my ignorance.

"You must see them before you go. By the way, do you propose a long stay in Frankfort?"

I yearned to tell her that, as I should never have come but for her, so I would never go but at her side. I stammered that I believed I had visited everything worth seeing except the works of art she mentioned. "In fact, the Judengasse, as the last stronghold of Christianity un-Christianized, or Jewing of the Jews, seems to me the significant thing to see in Frankfort, and this I have seen."

"But you have seen nothing, then, absolutely nothing," she said, laughing deliciously at my shortcomings. "My guidance will be absolutely necessary to you."

I longed to accept, but I protested. I could not bear to trouble her, I said politely.

"You must not think of going until I have conducted you around the city," she insisted. "Listen to reason, dear Mr. Flemming. The taskwork laid on

THE GRIZZLY HEAD.

you by Monsieur Fortnoye—quite against my wish, it is true, but not the less worthy of my sincerest gratitude and friendship—is discharged. I have but an hour's journey to make from Frankfort, and I can make it in broad day; so I feel brave enough to dismiss my escort. It is now my turn to greet you as a free man, and propose my own services. Get a carriage."

Obedience was rapture. Mrs. Ashburleigh presented herself quickly at the porte-cochère, a little basket in her hand. "I will first show you my pet spot.—To the old graveyard," she continued to the driver, raising her deep contralto, so that it rang quite hollow under the arch of the porte-cochère and made the young coachman jump a little way from his seat.

"Two hours will suffice," she remarked, "and I will deliver you up again in time to take the train from Frankfort to Heidelberg, as I myself take that from Frankfort to Mayence."

I could not imagine why she led me to the cemetery, which was quite out of town, and my inquietude on this subject interfered with my conversation. I sat meditative. Presently, however, I remarked, "Doubtless it is the tomb of some relative that brings you to this old graveyard, and indeed to Frankfort. I cannot get over my surprise at meeting you here. I have fancied you in Italy always. In making this *rencontre* at such an unexpected time and in such a place, I am reminded of Petrarch's reproaches to Charles IV. for resting so short a time in Rome: 'What would the Cæsars say if they met you descending the farther side of the Alps, hanging your noble head and turning your back upon Italy?'"

"My residence among the Italians was not very long," she replied, "and I have lived in England and other places. My attraction to the old cemetery of Frankfort is simply artistic curiosity. It is there we shall find the works of Thorwaldsen. For Thorwaldsen, doubtless, you are willing to take a fifteen minutes' journey, are you not?"

I bowed.

"Besides, he is an American, of the most ancient lineage possible. He is the descendant of Snome, who was born somewhere in New England as early as the year 1007, son of the viking Thorfinne Karlsefne and his wife Gudrid. The historical band of Northmen who went to America in that year carried back their protégé, the Yankee Snome, of whose descendants was Thorwaldsen: the Historical Society of Rhode Island elected him honorary member in 1838 on this account, though you will hardly believe me. So much for Thorwaldsen as an American, if that attribute is a necessary conductor of your interest. But you must not be surprised at my choosing a churchyard as the point of departure for our discussion. There is nothing in God's Acre to displease either you, Paul Flemming, as I should fancy, or myself. Images of death have trodden on the heels of the most cherished thoughts of happiness for all who are as old as you and I. I know it is so with me. Let me confess it to you: the object of the journey I undertake this afternoon is a marriage-union that Heaven will bless, I trust and hope; and yet, still, the motive which attracts me with no less power toward the country whither I am going is a cemetery."

She bowed her head to think, looking at once monumental and Rubensesque, while I shrank back appalled to solve

CHANGE FOR TWELVE KREUTZERS.

this enigma. A journey undertaken for a marriage! Whose marriage? Her own? I had seen her yesterday on the arm of Fortnoye. Suppose for a moment that my suspicions of that ubiquitous personage had fallen short of their proper aim, and that the real object of his nomadic career was to rob me of my first love—to make me now the widower of her who had never been my wife! The mere conception and formulation of such an indictment against Fortnoye confused me. After all, I knew nothing. In sheer self-defence I put away the notion, and approached the sculptures with a partially-cleared mind.

The monument of Philip Bethmann Holweg at Frankfort exhibits a series of bas-reliefs in which Thorwaldsen has celebrated an act of courage which touched upon three cities in its effects and doom. The young Holweg had extinguished a conflagration at Vienna, died from his injuries at Florence, and been brought home to Frankfort for burial. In the principal design he is represented as expiring and handing his civic crown of valor to a brother—the brother who vainly nursed him in Italy: the Genius of Death already leans upon his shoulder, with the stupefying poppies in his hand. Beside, the mother and sisters are weeping; and in another compartment, near the river Arno and the Lion of Florence, is Nemesis—that fatal Nemesis which follows good actions as well as bad.

"It is characteristic, composite and eclectic," said Mrs. Ashburleigh with conviction, seating herself upon a neighboring tomb. The criticisms of this lady were always inimitable. She looked long at the monument, producing from her light basket a delicate contribution of refreshments, which we consumed as we gazed upon this elevating work. There were some little tarts, some slices of an admirable sausage, pumpernickel and a bottle of orgeat.

"I must jot down the main outlines," she observed. "I have in my sketch-books nearly four hundred designs of tombstones. That is my minor mania. I have a grand mania, which I will tell you of in a moment. I hope you foster a mania, Mr. Flemming. I should like to obtain squeezes of some of Thorwaldsen's details, but there will hardly be time. Have you a mania?" she asked, suddenly, calmly, imperiously, and with a penetrating melancholy. As she sat looking at me from her tomb, with the ruins of the lunch-basket, which she had accidentally crushed, just embossed beneath her paniers, she reminded me of Rachel sitting upon her teraphim, and I thought that ancient Rama itself had hardly seen a figure more superb, more mournful and more completely childless.

"I believe I have what you mean by the term, though Hohenfels calls it my *lubies*. It is geographical in its nature, and is the hope of my life."

"It is worthless. The progress of Art, upon which the higher welfare of the race depends, is not assisted by discovering the North-west Passage or the source of the Nile. My own collections are intimately associated with the arts and pieties. I collect wall-paper."

"Wall-paper! Mercy on me! So does old Mère Eulalie the ragpicker."

"So she may, and I would not discourage the germs of fancy and æsthetics among the lower orders. My own series of wall-papers will soon be the most complete in existence except that of a certain baroness in Munich, who is going blind, and whose taste, besides, is taking the direction of spiders. Other connoisseurs may easily exceed me in faïence, though I have a considerable cabinet of that. In lacquer, in Hindoo idols, in playbills, in beetles, in snuff-boxes, in etchings and postage-stamps, in Venice glass, in lace, or in empty relic-holders out of the monasteries, I do not compete; but I have distanced them completely in wall-papers, and, I am pretty sure, in tombstones.

"My portfolios, which are as large as window-shutters, fill three enormous coffers. You may see in them the designs of Louis XVI.—a balustrade and a cippus, a balustrade and a cippus, *ad infinitum:* a later pattern represents the king borne up by figures of Minerva and Fame, the upper part of his figure concealed by the repetition of the group, so as to dissemble the loss of his head—a constant succession of headless kings intended to go on thus up to the ceiling: it is a protest against his decapitation. There are the patterns of the Directory, with their narrow garlands of drapery,

THE VISITORS' BOOK.

intercrossing and pendent. There are the griffins and rosettes of the First Empire. There are the 'aurora'-colored papers of 1820, manufactured by Réveillon, accompanied by their velvet borders. There is the pattern of 1800, mentioned by About as probably unique, representing green roses on a yellow ground. There are the heroic designs in the style of David, in one tint—Andromache holding her boy, whose round cheeks are modeled with concentric circles of gray shadow. I have them all: it is a whole history."

"Dear me!" said I: "perhaps I could assist you. I remember an old garret in America papered with the *New York Mirror*, on which indigo stars have been stamped with a potato."

"If you could get me a square yard of it I should be eternally obliged. Nothing consoles the ills of life like a mania."

The sexton interrupted us: Would we like to see the Chamber of the Dead?

I shivered at this peculiar invitation. My lovely guide laughed at my fears: "It is one of the sights of Frankfort, and Murray will not forgive you unless you visit it. Besides, let me tell you, it is quite comfortable, homelike and hospitable. In winter they keep up a fire. Let me quote the good old guide-book: 'The Chamber of the Dead is arranged to prevent the danger of premature burial in cases of epilepsy and the like. It is a building composed of ten small cells, grouped around the office inhabited by a watchman. The dead are left in their burial-cases, but each of the ten fingers is placed in a sort of copper thimble, from which proceeds a wire communicating with a bell. The least movement rings the bell and attracts the guardian.' Come and see this strange utilization of thimbles."

I could but admire the comfortable smile with which she invited me to this awful sight. Mrs. Ashburleigh's nerves must have been indeed strong. Does one smile in entering such a ghastly morgue, where ten lifeless bodies, protected by one hundred copper thimbles, are awaiting the chance of stirring the bell-rope which summons them to a new lease of life?

The cells were empty, all but one, whose closed door was the only suggestive thing in the place. The watchman sat in the middle smoking a pipe and making a wreath of immortelles.

"How often are you aroused by the signal of this terrible bell?" I asked.

"Up to the present time, sir, I have never heard it."

"Indeed! Perhaps you have but recently taken charge here?"

"In forty years, sir, the bell has never been rung but once."

"Ah! once, at least!"

"Yes, sir: a bat had got in."

And Mary Ashburleigh smiled once more as we left the dreadful place. We drove back into the city. On passing the post I saw my man Charles, who was staring vacantly at the city sights, and whom I sent in with my card to ask for letters. One from Fortnoye awaited me:

"All has gone well at Heidelberg. Kranich is quiet, but apparently backing for a spring. He has asked after you, and without blushing. I am convinced that all the apparent malice of this cool young hand proceeds from calculation. If he could do you an injury he would, but I know how to prevent him. I will only add a word of thanks for your act of chivalry, so brusquely demanded and so obligingly performed. By your deed of courtesy, apparently so trifling, you have assured success to the most important action of my life."

This kindly message enraged me. "The most important action of his life!" Set this against the "wedding-journey" confessed by his magnificent companion! Their harmony of intentions was a drop of gall in my chalice. I could not conceal from myself that the match seemed eligible. Here were two hymeneal figures largely sculptured, with that breadth of style and simplicity of feature only found in Europe—without the tortured nerves and petty weaknesses so common in my own country, and of which I, unfortunately, showed a fatuous example. Where the American character seems cut up with anxious details and sensitive perceptions, the European character often seems stamped in one piece with a die. These two ample natures might pass a life of harmony and calm—she collecting her wall-papers from city to city, and he irrigating Europe with his wines. Either of them knew the world a thousand times better than I did. My interest in Mrs. Ashburleigh increased most poignantly as this root of jealousy began to pierce through my being.

I lost myself in a labyrinth of speculation. Mrs. Ashburleigh had not concealed her vast regard for Fortnoye, to assist whom, she declared, as Francine had declared in answer to a similar demand of mine, she would throw herself into the flames. This formidable fellow, then, had the secret of outmanœuvring all the men and charming all the women! Poor Francine! what was her part in the whole mystery? The part, maybe, of a sacrificed rival! She had been carried

THE SUMMONS.

off from Carlsruhe by a mysterious summons: perhaps, with the illogical conclusions of young girls, she had allowed some less worthy suitor to bear her away from her dreams of Fortnoye. This other—could it possibly be the repulsive young calculating-machine who called himself Kraaniff or Kranich? That would explain his quarrel with Fortnoye perhaps; but I had seen him at Heidelberg, apparently alone. In any case, poor Francine! And poor Flemming!

Under so lovely a surveillance I was guided till I was giddy. Dismissing the carriage, Mrs. Ashburleigh took me to the Stædel Museum, to the Bethmann Museum, to the Exchange. With her taste to aid me, I bought on the Zeil enough Bohemian glass to have furnished the basket of Cogia Hassan. The great caryatides (so common in the hotel-architecture of Frankfort) glared and grinned at me in a hundred bronze or marble grimaces as I panted along with my pockets full of toys, or with my hands oppressed under the bouquets and bon-

bons which she sweetly allowed me to purchase: scores of Vulcans and Atlases, leaning their enormous shoulders against the balconies, beheld me toiling without

THE SAGE AND THE SHADOW.

compassion or offers of assistance. At last my companion herself, taking pity on me, showed me how to have my treasures packed by the aid of a commissionnaire, and forwarded to my bankers at Paris.

"The bouquets are more personal," she said: "they cannot be despatched to a banker."

This charming sentiment, marked with all the amiable and considerate traits of this incomparable woman, melted my soul within me, and compensated a million times for the slight menaces of hernia and dislocation which assaulted my arms and the pit of my stomach. It was as a bower of bloom, an ambulant arbor or a processional Guy Fawkes, that I presented myself at the Kaisersaal with my adorable commander.

A public square with fine mediæval buildings, and with a couple of fountains, fronts the grand old triple-gabled hall. One of these fountains has a figure meant for Justice; only, as the scales are placed in its left hand, it is more commonly taken for Injustice. 'Twas in this square that the emperors were proclaimed—'twas in the hall that they were elected.

From 911 to 1556—that is to say, from Conrad to Ferdinand I.—the elections were had at Aix-la-Chapelle. Maximilian II. began in 1564 the series of emperors crowned at Frankfort. The ceremony at Aix I will not presume to explain, since the reader has a vivid if rather loose idea of it all from *Ernani*. Idle to go over again that immense Fourth Act, toward the close of which the king of Bohemia and the duke of Bavaria (in red baize with Canton-flannel facings) bring in a superb crown of bullion and pasteboard to the new emperor, who has been sitting in the tomb of Charlemagne like a ghoul.

The ceremony as removed to Frankfort appears to have been not a whit less dramatic. The hall, it seems, was by this time called the Römer, its usual appellation at present: the Italian merchants coming up from Lombardy and installing themselves in the Saal had caused it to take a Latinized designation. These mercers and money-changers had made niches around the walls to the number of forty-five, for the purpose of displaying their wares. The unknown architect who distributed those niches proved to be a better prophet than Nostradamus. Thus it was: in decorating the place for the imperial elections the forty-five niches were assigned to hold portraits of the emperors. Thirty-six had been elected at Aix. Their busts were introduced: an old woman said, "When the niches are all filled the German empire will be at an end." In 1765, when Joseph II. mounted the throne, he looked with apprehension at the fatal range of niches, for only one more place was left vacant for himself, and there was none for a successor. When Francis II. was elected the round of the hall had been made. There was a grand discussion raised as to the proper place for the new emperor's effigy, when, in 1806, Napoleon shattered the empire with the cannons of Wagram, and the courtiers were relieved of their difficulty.

But I was about to give a word to the electoral ceremony, comparing it with *Ernani*.

"You will fancy, dear madam," I said to Mrs. Ashburleigh, "the square here filled with a privileged crowd, among whom the big butchers and carvers have attained the best places by main strength. In the middle an ox roasts entire. One of yonder jets is replaced by a fountain of red and white wine, flowing respectively from the two heads of an enormous eagle. On another side is a mass of oats heaped three feet high. Near the hall is an urn of gold and silver money. The crowd waits with impatience the moment when the judges—the electoral archbishops of Mayence, Treves and Cologne, the representatives of Bohemia, Bavaria, Saxony and the rest—have announced the result, and the emperor appears, crowned, at the middle window. Then a trumpet sounds, and the arch-marshal forces his horse into the pile of oats up to the saddle-girth, fills a silver measure with the grain and gives it to the emperor—a sign that the stables are provisioned. And the arch-cupbearer, also on horseback, fills two silver cups at the eagle-fountain, and hands the red and white wassail to the emperor in token that his cellar is replete. It is now the people's turn, and when the arch-treasurer scatters abroad handfuls of the money, and the arch-steward flings out great slabs of beef, it is who can grasp the most, and who can win in the fight the ox's head, to be hung in the butchers' hall for a perpetual trophy."

"The lucky ones must have looked somewhat as you do at this moment under your burdens."

"A good omen! I accept the personation, and am ready to shout a million loyal *vivas*,' but it will be at the election of an empress, not an emperor."

On that we entered. Our application to see the Kaisersaal resulted in producing a shrill voice and a grizzly head, the latter looking out from an opening upon us as if we were contemptible enigmas, hardly worth to this Œdipus the trouble of a guess. The voice, which was a very high one, I really supposed to

THE FAMILIAR.

belong to this bearded head, until I perceived that the mouth was hermetically sealed with a thick clay pipe. "I am merely hunting for the key," said the voice, still appearing to come supernaturally from the sealed-up hermit. Presently a figure emerged—the figure of a female, a blowsed beauty, who was tying her apron and running pins into her hair, and who, I am convinced, had been occupied rather with research of coquetry than of keys. We penetrated a door inscribed "Kaisersaal" in great capital letters, and devoted ourselves with much concentration to the range of portraits, desiring to leave this lady a fair chance to arrange her hairpins according to whatever preconceived ideal she may have had. We ran the Cæsars down, from Conrad to Francis II., that fortunate father-in-law of Napoleon who died simply emperor of Austria by his adopted son's doing.

Our examination was done, though, before the janitress's toilet. Several unmated hooks remained to her dress, and I think several pins in her mouth, when at last she said, "Madam has doubtless seen finer halls, but she knows that a plain book sometimes has held great thoughts."

"True," said Mrs. Ashburleigh. "I hardly know where else one could be in a chamber with forty-five emperors."

"To see the archives, that is fine," added the woman. "They will show you the Golden Bull."

"The golden bull! Is it carved by the arch-steward?" I asked absently. I was wondering if this janitress, who only performed a toilet in the presence of visitors, was anxious to get back to her den merely to unpin herself.

Our little pecuniary acknowledgment to this guardian went into her mouth, mingling with the bodkins there collected. Six kreutzers more admitted us to the archives, and among them we examined the *bulla* of gold, named from the foil with which they cover the seal to preserve it from decay. This bull was given by Charles IV. in 1556, and became the fundamental law of the empire. For near three hundred years the great charter, written on forty-five skins of parchment, and beginning with the solemn words, *Omne regnum in se divisum desolabitur*, was the bulwark of imperial power. Napoleon one fine morning gave the city of Frankfort to the Prince Charles of Dalberg, under whom it became simply the capital of the grand duchy; the act of the Congress of Vienna in 1815 made Frankfort the seat of the Diet of the Germanic Confederation; finally, the other day, Bismarck swept the Golden Bull, with the Iron Crown and many other baubles, into the old portmanteau with which he has sent his master out carpet-bagging (as we Americans say) over the ingredient provinces of his great domain. The *bulla* was only shown to us through a glass sash, but the attendant had the gallantry to offer to my companion a neat engraving of the seal, underneath which was a note addressed rather to me than to her, perhaps, as it was upon me that it acted in the way of a fiscal aperient. The note was expressed thus: "12 kreutzers."

We came away from the Römer. "It affects me strangely," said Mrs. Ashburleigh. The remark was both subtle and touching—touching, in that she should have cared for all the dead emperors; and subtle, in that her emotion was ", strange," a word chosen well to express the profound depth and distance of feeling with which we contemplate that long

Augustan succession. We sought out Goethe's house; and here it was my turn to be touched, for I found in the old visitors' book my own name.

My reader may be a battered stager, callous to most of the emotions, but I defy him to forbid his heart to speak softly forth when he finds his name on some ancient tourists' register. Old schemes, old routes of pleasure, old friendships that were meant to be perpetual and are now dead enough,—how they start into the memory at sight of one's own pert autograph relieving itself there on the page, just as spirited as in that day when the hand was so lively and the foot so firm!

"You have, then, visited Frankfort before, Mr. Flemming?" said my companion.

"Yes, and so I have visited many other places in the New World and the Old. But it was before I had met you; and, in the words of Laertes, both the worlds I give to negligence, counting nothing noteworthy or remarkable that I do not behold by your side."

The house is in the Hirsch Graben, No. 74. Visitors are expected to enter and contemplate the modest chamber where, on the 28th of August, 1749, the little Wolfgang first saw daylight. We found out the house, and stood before the portal, where a page of white marble gives the fact and the date.

"I used to please myself by making out Goethe to be like our own Franklin," I observed—"a kind of rhymed Ben Franklin: many of his little maxims seem nothing more than versifications of Bonhomme Richard. His practical tendency and love of science were the same: in 1799, at the age of forty, he published his *Metamorphoses of Plants*, a work on which Auguste de Saint-Hilaire founded his *Vegetable Morphology*."

"Was that a specimen of your literary criticism when you were young?" asked Mrs. Ashburleigh, royally indifferent to Goethe's correspondence with Franklin. "I suppose you were a botanist even then. For my part, I have a strong objection to Goethe. It is not only for his views on love and friendship, which every woman is bound to find detestable from mere *esprit de corps*, but for another reason. I have always thought it contemptible in him to aid tradition in vilifying Faust, while he drew such vast profit from Faust's invention, and taxed it so heavily."

"But Faust—Faust is moral disease: Faust was specially tempted of the devil," I suggested.

"Not so," she said simply. "Every one has that personage at his shoulder if he will but turn his head."

I looked askance at this strange woman, to surprise in its flight her Socratic aphorism, so naturally and forcibly uttered: it was not one of her great *mots*, with their burden of poetry and sentiment, but its honesty gave it value. So, then, Faust, with his dark career, was but the terrible commonplace of humankind—of humankind, whether man or woman; and even our little Marguerites, pleasing themselves in the company of the men of wit, are a kind of Faust, signing away their souls because they love intellectual distinction; and Herr Wolfgang Goethe himself, coining as it were the heats and generosities of his heart into hard type, he is a Faust of more unpleasant aspect than any.

So do I interpret the chance axiom which Mrs. Ashburleigh, out of the wealth of her experience and her intellectuality, sowed upon me like seed by the wayside. We left the house of Goethe. As we emerged from the door a little ragged dwarf, who leaned like Asmodeus on a crutch, sprang up as if from the ground, and offered to translate the inscription of the entablature. "I know five languages, and therefore am as good as five men," he said, in fair English.

"You are somewhat less than one," I answered.

"*There* was a man!" said the dwarf, indicating the name of Goethe. "Those are the family arms of the Goethes," he continued, pointing with his crutch to three little lyres sculptured in the framework of the door.

"I imagined as much," I observed

ORIGIN OF THE LYRE.

coolly, not caring to accept the friendship of this chance interpreter. But it was not easy to abash him: he looked up at us with the sparkling points of two deep-set black eyes, haunched his shoulders like an oracular raven and continued: "Beware of the official guides and ciceroni! Beware of Murray and Baedeker! The idiots of Frankfort will tell you how Goethe's father, impressed with some miraculous foreknowledge that a great poet was to be born, adopted those three lyres for the family arms. Don't you believe a word of it. Grandfather Goethe had been a horse-farrier. He got rich and built this house. In gratitude to the trade which had augmented his comforts, he adopted three horseshoes for emblems. The father of Wolfgang, who was the blacksmith's grandson, was a lawyer. When he made an ambitious marriage with the daughter of Senator Textor, and brought the bride into his house, where the three horseshoes humbly swung from the lintel, he was seized with shame for those signs of plebeian origin. So he strung them with cords and they became harps. That was the way in which the poet's lyres had their origin at a time when the poet was but indistinctly dreamed of. There is the truth, sir, and a good joke it is."

And Asmodeus, shouldering himself away on his crutch, disappeared with sulphurous laughter. But not before he had deigned to accept two or three chance kreutzers.

PART XV.

EN ROUTE AGAIN.

"SORROWS OF WERTHER."

"IT fills me with strange thoughts, this bidding adieu to Frankfort. I recall, dear madam, my previous exit from the same city. I was a boy then, and I was with a young friend, Hohenfels. I recollect how we sat in the theatre after they had put out the lights, among the empty stalls and in the smoky twilight. We wanted to destroy the illusion, you know: boys can afford to destroy illusions, because they have a vast provision of them remaining to draw upon in the future, and so they are pitiless toward their own card-castles. And then we got up and shook off the dust of Frank- fort, and trudged on through Hochheim to the Rhine, and so to Schlangenbad and Langenschwalbach. Did you ever hear of the Stella, Mrs. Ashburleigh? The Stella was doing cachucas in the Frankfort theatre then. The lightest heel you ever saw. Stella might have said, like Beatrice, 'There was a star danced, and under that I was born.' We two lads sat in the pit, recovering from our illusions and enjoying some raisins and filberts; and then in the darkness we heard Stella's husband saying, just as if he had spoken of a horse, 'I shall run her six nights at Munich, and then take her on to Vienna.' We were greatly shocked, and I suppose felt complacent in being shocked; for we knew we were a pair of fine sentimental fellows."

"I think I remember Stella and Anatole," said Mrs. Ashburleigh. "Stella was as thin as a fiddle; and Anatole, who was her grandfather and very respectable, once danced his wreath off, with the hair it encircled."

"How little it takes to satisfy youth!" I pursued. "I know I thought Stella as beautiful as a bird, but it was before I met you at Interlaken."

The image of the theatrical goddess rose up for one moment beside the sublime actuality of the Dark Ladye who was deposited monumentally on a camp-stool. The triumph of the rich reality pleased me: for a single instant I just fancied the peerless Mrs. Ashburleigh curved across the footlights and raising her toe toward the boxes in the slow and measured style they practice in ballets. Her superiority was crushing: excelling as she did all women in everything, I need not say how instantaneously she finished the Stella. The poor chalky wraith of that performer sank beneath the weight of contrast like a stucco pedestal under a marble angel. Truly I had *not*, when I called Stella fair, encountered the peerless realism of British beauty.

"I have not danced, I think, since the death of Vestris," said my commander simply, and motioning for my field-glass with one imperial fore finger.

But where was this tagrag of conversation uttered? And why, if we were still at the sign of The Roman Emperor, was Mrs. Ashburleigh put upon so unusual a piece of hotel-furniture as a camp-stool? And why did I hand her the field-glass? And why did I recall a previous exit from Frankfort? *From* that city our paths were to lie far apart: she was going to Mayence, and I was returning toward Marly. Yet behold us still together, and evidently no longer amid the street-scenes or balcony-caryatides of Frankfort.

DANNECKER'S ARIADNE.

No. Frankfort is left behind, and I am on my route again. It is a naval edifice on whose unstable seats I am jotting down my notes. This fine river is broader than the Main. I am clear of Frankfort, and did the Fates encourage me I might go homeward. But here I am, pushing perversely forward instead of back, urged by another move on that chessboard of destiny which has already found me at many advancing posts of a fatal game—at Strasburg and Carlsruhe and Baden-Baden and Heidelberg.

I recalled to Mrs. Ashburleigh a previous exit from Frankfort. Let me recall this last to myself.

We left the house of Goethe, and the crippled Asmodeus slunk away with his stick as if he were vanishing into the ground.

"Goethe fatigues me," said Mrs. Ashburleigh. "His Werthers and Fausts are out of date: they hang on his shoulders like that eternal coat with the long skirts which we see in every window on the statuettes of Goethe. People may object to the modern spasmodic schools and their passions in tatters: passions in tatters are bad enough, but they are not so bad as passions from the ready-made clothing-shops—things that did not fit in the first place, and are long since old-fashioned."

It was perhaps a little tyrannical, for she had made me buy the statuette whose protracted garments she was now using for her satire; but woman's tyranny is in proportion to her loveliness. I agreed instantly with all she said, and quoted Titmarsh's lines to the effect that Charlotte "was a married lady" whose passions were in the nature of bread and butter:

> So he sighed and pined and ogled,
> And his passion boiled and bubbled,
> Till he blew his silly brains out,
> And no more was by it troubled.
> Charlotte, having seen his body
> Borne before her on a shutter,
> Like a well-conducted person
> Went on cutting bread and butter.

Yet I could not help wondering if her feelings had not changed a little. In the old days by the Staubbach, when I stole from her album the stories about students and painters, would she have relished a sarcastic allusion to Werther? Fatigued with this psychological inquiry, I had recourse to a bit of the pumpernickel and sausage which remained in brown paper at the bottom of my pocket. I offered some to her, and she accepted it simply, spreading her bread and sausage with that large tranquillity that goes with great natures. Charlotte was eclipsed. So we brought up at the Bethmann Museum.

It is there that we find the Ariadne of Dannecker. I did not forget how I had once greeted the sculptor in his old age, in his room at Stuttgart, where he used to pass hours in looking at engravings after Canova's statuary. Canova, too, is out of fashion at present, and perhaps Dannecker also; and indeed I do not know how many of my boyish idols have not been laid flat or corroded by the purism of the modern critics, the Neo-Grec revival of the Second Empire, and the æsthetics of ugliness taught by English pre-Raphaelites. But, at any rate, Dannecker was another of the good genii of my youth—one who had met me kindly and bidden me good-speed on my pilgrimage. He had praised my Flanders cognomen, reminding me that Paul Flemming was one of the old Minnesingers; and I made in return one of

VENUS OF MILO.

my best compliments, telling him that his head, with hair flowing to the shoulder and pale-blue eye, made him look like Franklin. Further than that I could not go as a connoisseur of heads or a connoisseur of Franklin.

But on reviewing the Ariadne at Frankfort in such company as it was permitted me to have, I hardly saw the technical merits of the work. I studied its symbol only. Immortal allegory of widowhood, eternal encouragement to second marriages, the myth of Ariadne in Naxos shines down through the centuries, casting a silver gleam of poetry on the very statistics of divorce-courts, and cheering, as with wine, whatever modern marriage-tables may chance to be furnished with funeral bakemeats. And I was looking on this figure with one whose claims, both to beauty and bereavement, were undeniable!

The Ariadne of Dannecker reposes upon one of the symbolic panthers which Bacchus brought over after his conquest of India, and turns forward and upward a soft forehead, from whence the new hope has just chased every lingering shadow of desolation. Even so, it seemed to me, did Mrs. Ashburleigh, imperfectly supported by the remains of the spirit-trade, turn a trustful front to the

HERR CUYPER'S INCOMPLETED TASK.

dawning future, and just hold a marble ear in a receptive posture for whatever promise might be in the wind from the wandering Hymen,

> whose usual trade is,
> Under pretence of taking air,
> To pick up sublunary ladies.

I have ever rejected, as coarse and unworthy, the specious explanation that the original Ariadne of Crete was an august but ill-advised princess who, after an unhappy love-affair, had rushed into habits of intoxication. Mary Ashburleigh, however, seemed to give some credit to this interpretation, or at least to have heard of it; for she said: "Do you think the sculptor has disposed her in a horizontal posture to indicate that she is not able to stand?"

I was relieved from replying to this conjecture, which I thought able but unlikely, by the assistant's putting the machinery in motion. The statue of Ariadne is occasionally turned round on its pedestal under a column of perpendicular light, which passes through a pink drapery, and gives to the revolving figure the hue and air of life. The pale nymph flushed, turned, looked s l o w l y around, and softly guided her panther away from our indiscreet gaze, while carnation hues and undulating reflections played fitfully over her soft limbs. And again Mrs. Ashburleigh obliged me with one of her penetrating criticisms: "Just like the ballet, is it not?"

And indeed the exhibition is too theatrical. My guide continued, piqued perhaps by a little becoming sense of rivalry: "Was the Stella as pretty as this?"

"I don't think she was quite so stagey," I said.

Near at hand was a cast of the beautiful puzzle found at Melos— the Venus, or Victory, or whatever divinity it may be, who, with the arms she lacks the possession of, has drawn all the world in admiration to her foot.

"It has been restored at Naples as fondling a Cupid; it has been restored at Paris as disarming Mars; it has been restored at Brescia with wings, and made to write with a pencil on a shield. That armless figure," I said, "has set all the archæologists to wrestling."

"I would restore it as a Diana," said Mrs. Ashburleigh, "and I would make her in the act of shooting an arrow at the entire race of impertinent young gentlemen. The Dianas, you are aware, know how to make themselves respected."

"No, no," I said: "Diana is no such bitter enemy of a whole sex as you represent her. I can give you an argument. You remember, in the same Louvre which enshrines yonder Venus is the Huntress

Diana, the *Diane à la Biche*. Well, the *biche*, modest little doe as she runs at the side of her goddess, is there represented with a pair of well-developed antlers—ornaments which in Nature belong only to the male. The symbol of Diana is thus the harmonizing of the two sexes, not their enmity."

"Since you are so analytical," said my commander, "I can tell you another of the public secrets of the Louvre. The Venus of Milo is not only separated at the waist, in the manner that has been discussed so widely, but the knot of hair is a separate piece of marble fastened on to her head. The Paris Venus is therefore very appropriately the inventress of the false chignon."

Rarely have I met so well-informed a critic. With a certain amount of tuition from her husband, joined to her taste for art and some taste for surgery, Mary Ashburleigh had become a matchless anatomist. It was while examining the little plaster Goethe that she alarmed me by suddenly making me throw my head back, and dissecting with a sharp crayon my sterno-hyoid, omoplat-hyoid and thyro-hyoid muscles, with the digastric, mylo-hyoid, and all that was visible of the sterno-cleido-mastoid above the necktie.

During this unusual *tête-à-tête*, "Unpermissible Fortnoye that you are," I cried to myself, "who would carry away so resplendent a creature! It will be the very shame of shames if you attach for the second time to the wine-trade this divine Ariadne!"

At the foot of Dannecker's statue she said suddenly, "And to think all this while a whole congress of dressmakers and hatters are awaiting me at Mayence! These antique belles are so superior to the needs of costume that they make us quite forget. Draw your watch, Mr. Flemming, and tell me if I have time to get to the station."

Instead of the hour, I told her the history of my repeater: she laughed musically, and we strolled to the Parade-ground.

The time of separation was come. I was preparing to arrange a system of correspondence, which I proposed to make very warm on my part, sure that I could in that way introduce a course of ideas which I found it impossible to conduct among the interruptions and hourly impertinences of travel. I was murmuring a few words, and she was glancing at the windows, eager and preoccupied. The porters from the hotel, marking their prey, gathered round us, and she and I were beating them off in two or three languages. I pressed my card upon her, with my hybernating address at Passy.

"I shall have you there next winter?" I importuned.

"*Je serais ravie!*" said she.

"Heaven forbid!" said I.

I stared after her retreating form. She disappeared in the hall, and the crowded Parade-ground with its throngs appeared to me the very desolation of the earth.

A figure from a shop close by attracted my notice by bouncing suddenly against me. It was my faithful assistant, Charles. He was admiring something in his hand, to the exclusion of all other claimants of attention: the object, no doubt intended for Josephine the cook, was a ball of wax-fuse, wound upon itself like twine, and painted externally with a wreath of forget-me-nots.

"Stupid!" said his employer. "Where are the trunks? Have you forgotten them in that tallow-chandler's shop?"

I had instructed him in the morning how to convey my trunks and botany-box, properly lettered and directed for the Frankfort-Heidelberg line.

"Monsieur will not be alarmed," said Charles with several bows, which under the circumstances looked as though addressed to the taper, still retained in his hand. "The baggages are safely at the railway. On my road I met the hotel-porter. He was wheeling off the trunk of the English lady in a large barrow, and, since monsieur is traveling with madam, I simply completed the load of the porter with the wardrobe of monsieur."

"Triple crétin!" I exclaimed, with an ardent impulse to strangle my good and affectionate prodigy. "Charles," I almost sobbed, "you have made me appear like an intriguer, a pursuer, a bore, a sticking-plaster, and I don't know what

CHARLES AS IDIOT.

else, in the eyes of a most critical and intelligent lady. She will never believe that I didn't tell you to lose those trunks at the wrong station. Run straight back and fetch them. No, stay! I cannot wait fuming here. I'll go with you."

As we descended from our carriage at the dépôt, Mary Ashburleigh got out of hers: "What! you here, Mr. Flemming?"

"Not at all," I said anxiously. "At least, it is only because you have got my clothes in your wheelbarrow."

"I have your clothes? What can you possibly mean?"

"Dear madam," said I, "allow me to explain. Charles is an idiot."

"I can hardly see how his idiocy impels you to travel so much farther in my direction than you said."

"Only hear and believe me, dearest madam, and I'll convince you that I am *not* going in your direction."

"Oh! then you are *not* going to Mayence?"

"By no means. Appearances are against me."

THE TRUNKS.

"Whither do you go then, Mr. Flemming?"

"Where I said—to Heidelberg, Strasburg and Épernay."

"I thought you had just been to those places."

"That is true; and I hope to see them again without loss of time. But Charles, by a blunder, has thrown me in a heap upon the tender mercies of your trunk."

"My trunk!" said Mary Ashburleigh in sincere alarm. "There are four uncut dresses in it. For the sake of old times, Paul Flemming, go and see if my trunk is marked for Castel."

I investigated. The baggage, my own included, was on the train, marked by the hotel-porter for Castel, opposite Mayence: I could extricate nothing.

"Then I am satisfied," said Mrs. Ashburleigh. A great relenting and heavenly charity now took possession of this loveliest of women. She said: "Your baggage is imprisoned. You had better get into prison too." And she pointed to the railway-coach.

In fact, I wondered that I had not determined to go home by way of Mayence and the choicest part of the Rhine, rather than by my old tiresome itinerary of errors. With my commander pointing that supreme fore finger of hers, to obey was to be happy.

The divinity, once assured that she was not bankrupt with her dressmaker, ameliorated like a summer morning. And thus once again I traveled by her side: our talk was sculpture, books and anatomy. In renewing our relations I could but growl once more, "Unbearable Fortnoye!"

In the course of an hour we arrived at Castel, where Mrs. Ashburleigh plunged into abstinence and retirement with her syndicate of dressmakers. It was a moral rather than a material separation which rose between us: physically, there was but the bridge between Castel and Mayence, in whose Hôtel d'Angleterre I established myself, but morally there was the gulf of Dress. I could get nothing uttered, yet I was not repulsed. My most ardent speeches were extinguished with woolens and silks, yet I was allowed to communicate day by day, bearing in my pockets across the bridge a telegraphy of buttons and sewing-silks—the Exchange quotations in those matters of the Castel and Mayence sides of the river.

And so I lay that lovely May night— while Hohenfels was fighting my battles in Heidelberg—under the moon-painted Dom of Mayence, whose outlines are clotted by builders' materials amassed by Herr Architect Cuypers.

Like the spire of my own life, which still shot ineffectually toward its Elysium when I last came hither, the cathedral of Mayence is a romance of the Middle Age—unfinished.

PART XVI.

EMBARKATION AND VOYAGE FROM MAYENCE.

THE HORRORS OF HYMEN.

HERE in Mayence, as in the city of Florence and in many a continental town, I have meditated on the strange slow gestation of a cathedral. Begotten when faith was strong, or at least when bishops were lively and temporally powerful in their judicial seats, your cathedral starts on a grand scale, and sucks up a principality's wealth in the pores of its great hulking body: its career continues through nine or ten centuries of unachieved intentions, oddly marked off to the beholder's eye by differences in the architecture. Probably some features essential to the original plan, as the *flèches* of Notre Dame in Paris or the *façade* of the Duomo in Florence, never get put on, and the poor abortion heals up, as it were, in an atmosphere that affords no more germs of growth, and desolately persuades itself that it looks better without. The crowning satire is when a cathedral front is elegantly and languidly completed, as a matter of æsthetics, by a government engaged in persecuting the Church which founded it.

I threaded the complicated interior of the Dom, where the episcopal monuments with their stone embroideries came back upon my sight like the tangled furniture of a dream. Long years before I had paced the same bowers and gardens of Gothic-work, but that was in my previous existence, before I had seen the Dark Ladye. In youth what I had demanded of the turkey-cock beadle was the tomb of Meissen the Frauenlob, who lies here, where the ladies of Mayence carried him, in his

CHAPEL AT MAYENCE.

tomb among the cloisters of St. Willigis. In maturity I sought the monument of Charlemagne's best-loved wife, Fastrada. Then, the young man's heart was wistful and curious, searching the future for the promised boon of love: now, the veteran's soul was crowded with undigested experience, and demanded some image of satisfied affection to rest its emotions upon.

The cathedral of Mayence, like some rich agglomerated crystal, consists of two or three churches grown together: this peculiarity gives it, instead of the single or double spire with which other churches are content, an opulent crown of towers, brimming over the lid-like roof and pushing from every corner up to heaven. The east choir and its entrance are of the tenth century, erected under Bishop Hatto; the west choir is of the twelfth; the nave, of the eleventh; and the chapels extending along the side-aisles are of the early part of the fourteenth century, or, as I should think from the style, as late as the sixteenth in some portions.

Schwanthaler's monument to Frauenlob, put up since my early pilgrimage in the most spasmodic taste of German romanticism, might have attracted my attention if I had still been the vaguely-yearning troubadour: it is on the south wall, and represents a lady putting a wreath on a coffin. But, as I say, I was now bent on finding images of love crowned and tested by matrimony; so I made my way, without any turkey-cock assistance, to where the tablet of Fastrada leans out from the wall, close to the "Beautiful Doorway." The stone which witnesses the queen's virtues and Charlemagne's devotion bears a Latin inscription, beginning, "*Fastradana pia Caroli conjunx vocitata.*" I made a sketch of it for Mrs. Ashburleigh, still busied with her milliners; and it was of Mrs. Ashburleigh I thought as I called upon the Carlovingian queen.

If Kaiser Karl loved no woman like Fastrada, it was not that he had not with three previous alliances pursued the hope of conjugal happiness, and after being for the third time inconsolable taken this clever princess to wife. Think of that, O widowed ringdove of my dreams! and see if the fable of Ariadne be not here repeated with improvements and appendices!

Fastrada was an astute princess. "Four affinities are enough for Charles," she observed: "a fifth would be ridiculous, and the idea disturbs me." Meantime, Carolus Magnus, disgracefully uxorious, spent all his time with the queen. The cabinet could get no sessions, the bishop no tithes, the courtiers no audience. "We must have recourse to the doctor," said they; and the doctor proved equal to the emergency. He came, prescribed and conquered. So Fastrada, when she felt herself about to die, concealed beneath her tongue the magic ring, the gift of the serpent, which secured to her, so long as she wore it, her lord's affection. The effect on Carolus was peculiar: he loved his wife even in the clay, and long after the poor thing had fallen to pieces he was found inseparable from her remains, caressing the bones and fondly winding the long hair around his fingers. These posthumous connubialities became embarrassing. Turpin, the archbishop of Rheims, and the courtiers, and the sexton, and the architect—who had received orders for a splendid tomb for Fastrada, but who could not bury Fastrada while she was still enjoying the coverture and protection of her husband—all were scandalized. At length, Turpin, with some white fiction about a message straight from Heaven, contrived to beguile the king away; and then the queenly skeleton was removed, and the ring found fast between the teeth. The affection, however, which Charlemagne had felt for Fastrada was transferred with magic promptness to the present holder of the talisman. This happened to be Bishop Turpin himself, who had thought no harm in slipping the bauble on his plump and white episcopal little finger. Charlemagne loved him with fulsome tenderness, overwhelming him with presents of wimples, coifs, Mechlin lace and stomachers. The pious ecclesiastic was so persecuted by the imperial love that he gathered up his gown and took to his heels. Arrived at Aix, he threw the ring into the lake which surrounds the castle of Frankenstein. The monarch thenceforth, and to the end of his life, loved Aix-la-Chapelle as a man loves his wife, and determined to be buried there.

This fantastic tale is better authenticated than many a plain one. Bishop Turpin himself is the chronicler of the fact, and Petrarch, when traveling in Germany, learned the history, and has repeated it. (*Epistolæ familiares*, lib. I., cap. iii.) As a persuasive toward repeated matrimony I know no legend so wholesome as that of Fastrada and her amulet. I copied the tombstone for Mrs. Ashburleigh's collection, though my artistic hand was badly out, and many a year is in its grave since the drawing-master smiled upon my album. Inside the design—in that spirit of perpetual half-courtship which I had now established, and which my noble inamorata seemed to permit—I wrote a sentiment. It was an improvement upon poor old Fastrada's eulogy, and I wrote it not in Latin, but in good plain French. "Look not *amèrement*," I said, "after the Past: he comes not again back. Go forth to meet *votre futur* without fear and with a trustful heart."

Every day, as I trudged over to Castel with my little sheaves of entertainment or of wisdom, I poured out my diurnal riches at those adorable feet, which did not trample on my poor offerings. Once she even received me in a wrapper. My homage she took with a careless familiarity, never choosing to see the point; and I, for my poor part, had no courage to risk our happy relations by an impertinence. Yet I wished that custom had permitted Mrs. Ashburleigh to manifest, by a kind of openness similar to that I used myself, the exact progress of her feelings day by day, instead of being so constantly bland, sunny and absorbent. I wished it were leap-year—I even wished it were that fatal year of 1780 which the men of Mayence still recall with terror.

In the year 1780—I have the story from a stout old gentleman of the hotel-table—an archbishop of Mayence, exercising the vestiges of judicial power that had come down with his seat from the days of Charlemagne, decreed that every promise of marriage should be binding, on the simple declaration of the female. The good archbishop reckoned without his host. In a month after the edict the mayor of the city was dragged to the altar by a fair and relentless governess, who, truly or not, made the proper declaration. The hapless mayor had evidently not had time to study the new law. From that day forth all the maids of Mayence—the portionless spinsters, the chits, the minxes, the old girls gone to seed, the large-nosed girls, the blue-spectacled girls, the clever little seamstresses—descended into the arena and gave battle. It was terrible to see the gentle creatures, armed with incredible quantities of ribbon, velvet, flowers, lockets, gloves, gaiter-boots and other seducers, engaged in set warfare with the male sex, and bent by all artifices on leading the enemy into ambush. A hunt or battue was organized against elder

THE REVENGE OF MARGUERITE.

sons and possessors of small vested competencies. Several honest citizens fell into the trap, and, nibbling at a rosebud or a dish of tea, gave the requisite promise. The ladies of marriageable age lost all reserve and all mercy: with eyes closed and elbows rigid they plunged precipitately into those gulfs of coquetry from which the traditions of a thousand years had warned them. The men were panic-stricken. Boaz, fearing lest Ruth should glean his fields like the locust, set a sentry at his tent and covered his feet with goloshes before going to rest.

Mephistopheles cursed the day when he provided the jewels, for here was retribution rising on every side, pale and implacable, before a thousand wretched Fausts: Marguerite was avenged. By an odd transition bashfulness and backwardness passed from the ranks of girls to those of young men. In all the crowds of Mayence there were but two or three awkward schoolmasters or discouraged bachelors, who did not curse the archbishop's law. It was suppressed, but not before most of the milliners and washerwomen had become bankrupt to the jewelers. In the fell purpose to become irresistible they had gone insolvent. So the marriage-law was replaced by a law of abstinence in matters of toilette, and the women of Mayence, except those of fixed income, wear a simple kerchief over their yellow braids.

"I thank you for your story," I said to my table-companion apropos of all this: "it is for many ears a tale of warning, doubtless; but I know a man who only wishes that he could go from here and shout out brutally a promise of marriage over a fair hand that should be legally bound by the declaration." I sighed. The burgher stared and left the company, tapping his forehead. The band in the dinner-room breathed out serenades from *Don Giovanni*, and the boy's wistful sadness of 18— throbbed back to me from horns of Elfland faintly blowing; for I remember the youthful days when those very instruments at those very tables had soothed my soul-thirst—days when I could think of Love simply as an unwritten poem, while I listened at Mayence to dinner-table lectures from the smooth-foreheaded gentleman on Jean Paul, the Only-One.

That night, after I had crossed the swinging boat-bridge and poured my day's gossip and a few yards of lace into the lap of Mary Ashburleigh, I said, "The Mayence men are lucky on leap-years sometimes."

"How so?" said the lady absently, counting the glass bugles on a belt she was embroidering.

"Oh, they may be betrayed to their good." And I recounted the case of the inveigled gentlemen of 1780. In my little tale it was the parures and ornaments of the feminine wooers that struck my listener. She raised up the belt— and a handsomer (and longer) bit of enamel and needlework need not be seen —and said as she examined it, "So, in 1780, women ruined themselves for dress and lay in wait for husbands in masquerade?"

"After a manner, yes."

"No doubt some of the men were equally good actors too, and made use of their fine figures or sported in borrowed titles before the rich widows or plain-faced heiresses of whom they wanted to be the victims."

"No doubt; though that may be done outside of leap-year."

"I am thinking of a legend of Frankfort; for you must allow me to go back for my illustrations to the place we last left, since you know I have only lived here like the lobster in the cave to which it goes to change its shell. I will tell you how a well-favored knave at Frankfort got a noble partner at a ball."

I placed myself at her feet on a stool, where she allowed me to string beads. She pursued the tale, weaving legend and embroidery together into the web of her fascination:

"At the Römer or Kaisersaal there was a grand festival for the coronation of Ludwig of Bavaria. Among the entertainments graced by the presence of the court was a grand masked ball. The costumes were very rich, but the most noticeable among the splendid dresses was that of one stately man, who had had the natural good taste and sense of distinction to come in plainest black. He moved gracefully through the gaudy throng all in velvet, and resembling a shadow detached from a moonlight turf and planted upright. The young empress remarked him, and was secretly anxious to dance with him, so that when he knelt at her throne and requested the favor of a waltz, there was no difficulty about granting it. Moving in his skillful arms was such a luxury that the one waltz became four. Meantime, as the black mask threaded in a lordly manner the figures of the waltz, another mask approached the ear of the emperor and asked him if he knew who was dancing with Her Majesty. 'No,' answered Ludwig. 'It is some sovereign prince, doubtless.'—' Not quite such a high rank as that,' said the incognito.—' He is some lord, then, some count or baron.'—' Lower than that,' said the mask.—'Can he be a simple chevalier?'—' Come down still farther.' —' Some bold equerry?'— ' Lower still.'—' Can it be that the empress would dance with a page?'—' You have not got it yet, sire.'—' With a servant, a hostler, a clown?' —' Ask the man himself,' said the confidant in his most sinister tones.

"'Who are you?' demanded the emperor sternly of the graceful chevalier in black.—' Sire,' said the unknown, ' I'm an author.'—' That, at least, is an honest

THE WORKS OF THE "AUTHOR IN BLACK."

OBJECTS OF INTEREST IN THE RHINE.

though beggarly employment,' said the emperor, 'and an author may be favorably known even to princes through his works.'—'Alas, sire!' said the stranger, 'mine have all fallen dead; yet there is a long list of them, enough to fill a church, and I contemplate the line of my works with pride—some in *éditions brochées*, some in boards, but all distinguished by the skillful suspension of the interest or the keen edge of the style.' The emperor took off the black mask, revealing the face of his hangman! 'Sire,' said the man, falling on his knees, 'though you were to kill me you could not abrogate the fact that the empress has danced with me four times. Do a better trick, sire. Give me your cross and knight me. Then, if any one attacks your glory, I will defend you with the same sword by whose means I execute your justice.' The emperor studied a minute and complied, the empress danced with the new knight for a fifth time, the Knave of Bergen became 'the last of nobles and the first of citizens, and still in ceremonial parades the executioner walks alone behind the peers and in front of the burghers. The original Knave of Bergen always kept the mask and the black velvet which had won him an imperial partner.

"I find myself dwelling unduly on costumes, masquerades, disguises, mantraps—I know not what," proceeded Mrs. Ashburleigh.

"And I on widows, Ariadnes, second marriages, Fastradas, fourth marriages, and leap-years," chimed in my own unuttered thought.

"I think I am unhinged by so much dressmaking," pursued my commander. "The idea of coming to a quiet little place like this where I could moult in secresy was good enough, from a strategic point of view, but it has affected my mind. To-morrow my things will be ready, and I shall proceed down the river. There will be a final trying-on, and you may come over and act as congregation, if you like. Then you may escort me over Mayence, which I have hardly seen; and then, after putting me on the boat, you may bid me good-bye—if you like."

I attended the trying-on. There was a little ecstatic German dressmaker, in a dress covered with ribbons, but made of a material so often dyed that its odors filled the room, and the expression of whose mouth was so altered by pins that she could never smile without dropping five or six of them. By this priestess I was placed in a dark corner, and Mrs. Ashburleigh, in a high light, was allowed to revolve upon me. There was a dress in the mediæval style, the skirt finished with embrasures and machicolations around the edge, corner turrets at either shoulder, cheveaux-de-frise about the neck, and a hanging wallet like a beggar's scrip. I forget most of them, but there was one painted over with garlands which I believed in my heart was made of wall-paper.

This exhibition, from which Mrs. Ashburleigh every minute derived new beauties, new roses and new volume, lasted until dinner, instead of merely through the morning hours, as intended. The morrow had been fixed for her departure. However, we snatched a flying view of Mayence, and saw the fine shops, and the Platz with the *Standbilder* of Goethe and Schiller and Gutenberg. The Gutenberg interested us, from our previous studies of Thorwaldsen: the twelve-feet-high giant, modeled in 1835 at Rome from the Danish sculptor's sketches, was cast in bronze in Paris. Dumas, who professes to find the statue ugly, relates how he was to some extent responsible for its erection.

He must reproach himself, he remarks, for having contributed his share to this bad business. When all the blandishments had been exhausted by which subscriptions are usually wrung from reluctant pockets, there was still a deficiency of eight thousand francs. The idea then occurred to give a benefit representation for the object, and the drama selected was Dumas's *Kean*, translated into German. This play, which Thackeray covered with his ridicule, succeeded so well in Germany from the patriotism or play-loving character of the Mayençais, that ten thousand francs were gained by the single representation. Walking afterward at Mayence in the shadow of the monument, Dumas took shame to himself for having been instrumental in its erection. For our own parts, though well enough content to find the figure of Gutenberg in his native city, we were scandalized to see no corresponding monuments to Faust and Schoeffer, and asked indignantly where were the privileges of collaboration.

In the antique part of the town, among the dark buildings around the Dom, Mary Ashburleigh succeeded in stripping away some quaint old patterns of wall-paper. Then we prepared to bid farewell to *das goldene Mainz*. One last time I crossed the fluctuating bridge of boats as I went to deposit my companion in her resting-place at Castel. Returning to my hotel, I rested long on the swaying causeway. The constellation of the Bear sank into the broad water as I looked over among the floating shoes and fish-baskets to

where the Rhene
Curves toward Mainz, a woody scene.

No young lover ever drew deeper sighs than I as I thought of my Dark Ladye sleeping with satisfied heart among her new dresses. Next day I had the honor of depositing (while Charles saw to the trunks) her satchels and shawls on the tables of the steamer bound for Cologne; and—I can hardly say how it was—my botany-box lay there also among them.

The hardy navigator who trusts his vessel to the Rhine must think often of those who have floated on it before him. The current is full of voices, echoes from

"SPIRITS TWAIN HAVE CROSSED WITH ME."

poets who have been impressed as *he* is now impressed; and he feels like the earlier Spanish sailors to America, who

SALUTATIONS OF SIMROCK.

peered through the sunsets of those dim golden seas for the Castilian flag, and ever hoped to catch on the spice-winds that shuddered with loneliness the echoes of the Spanish all-hail. Two literary sailors of the Rhine above all others have caught the ripple of its water upon their page and made it talk—Hugo, Dumas. As I boarded the steamer I said mentally to the gentleman at the ticket-office, "Take, O boatman! thrice thy fee: spirits twain have crossed with me;" imitating, as the reader knows, that song of Uhland's in which the thrifty bard proposes to acquit himself for a celestial revelation by paying triple fare. I have always found something deeply and comfortably German in the notion of meeting the apparition of departing souls with an equivalent of twenty-five cents.

But, Uhland apart, the world of romance into which I am now floating has already been conquered by a Victor and an Alexander—a Hugo and a Dumas. There is little room for such as I to say anything.

In the first place, I hear one author of the twain deliver himself of a kind of grand somnambulistic snore. It is he who contemplates the ocean, he who wrote *The Cultivators of the Sea:*

"What a precipice the Past! Descent lugubrious! Dante would hesitate at it. The Ego, the Hugo, does not. The Niagara flows from a Sea and falls into an Abyss. The Rhine flows from an Abyss and falls into a Flat. Paroxysmal paradox. The Lurlei sings at Saint Goar, and the bugpiper plays the bugpipe at the First of Fourth. The 14th July delivered; the 10th August thundered; the 21st September established. 1789, 1793, 1830. In 1690 a child was abandoned on the rocks of Portland, in 1800 the rocks of Portland were broken into Portland cement, and in 1845 the Portland Vase was cemented, after being broken by a young man named William Lloyd. John Brown, Montgolfier, Æschylus, Bug Jargal, Job. The facts appear, as connected with the Rhine, to the author, grave."

It is very impressive, and perhaps that is the reason that we like Alexander Dumas rather better. This jolly sailor does not know much about German history, but he can tell us a hundred facts about Rhine wine. His association with Mayence is of the tombstone in preparation for Lady S——, pending the completion of which he meets Lord S—— and a friend rolling promiscuously up and down the river and tearfully drinking fourteen bottles a night "to the memory of that dear lady." He knows on what rock, sun-baked under the "Prussian blue," the grapes of Prince Metternich are culled. He chuckles over the fruitful jest of Jules Janin, who, when Metternich asked his autograph, wrote: "Received of the prince one dozen of Johannisberger"—a receipt which the nobleman was in honor bound to vindicate with a hamper of the coveted nectar. Metternich, as a great vintner, and perhaps for other reasons, interests him; and he preserves the family legend— how, when the founder of the race, a simple bowman of the fifteenth century, held his ground alone against the foe, he was sent for by the emperor, and gave his name as *Metter*. The sovereign said, "My subjects retreated, but *Metter, nicht:* Metternicht shall he be called," and sealed the bargain by dubbing him a knight. Wherever Dumas goes, cheer and hospitality await him, and the land flows with Liebfrauenmilch and Ingelheim. At Bonn (whence he journeyed southward to Mayence) he was received as a guest of honor by Herr Simrock, a brother of the poet Karl Simrock, but himself a hotel-keeper. Dumas and the Amphitryon greeted each other on equal literary ground—that is to say, respectfully brushed the earth with their forelocks; and the novelist has particularly advertised the noble wines which Herr Simrock excavated for him from his own private cellar. He rewards the host's hospitality, notwithstanding, by an error, in forgetting the name of the house of which the poet's relative was proprietor, and calling it the Étoile d'Or. The Étoile d'Or has long been kept by one Joseph Schmitz — on principles of the strictest prose. The matter is a trifle, except as showing the overcoming effects of Rhenish wine upon the memory and intellect of a gifted writer. And, truly, Dumas seems to have seen the very color of the Rhine rubescent. Indeed, since Brennus first brought the vine into Gaul it can hardly have had a more ardent and corybantic priest than Dumas, who makes it a touchstone of virtue wherever he goes, estimates kings and princes according to their cellars,

And labels with the blessed sign The shaggy heathens of the Rhine.

THE LABEL.

There are passages, too, in his *Impressions de Voyage* where the red blood of the grape seems to have got into his pen, tinctured his style and given a rich unction to his descriptive powers. Apropos, accept this vivid little spot of color in which he paints the Rhine in its *via mirabilis*, its Appian Way, its Street of Wonders, marked with golden milestones of sunny castles—the famous distance from Mayence to Cologne:

"Here, vanquished, enclosed and as if fettered by its mountains, thanks to the granite cuirass against which it in-

THE PRETENTIOUS YET HOLLOW HERON.

effectually throbs, it twists itself about, it rolls, it doubles on itself like a fighting serpent, and, in its conscious powerless-ness, even while pressed to flight it menaces in flying."

But this gladiator aspect is not per-

FULL CROPS.

ceived at once on leaving Mayence. Until Bingen it is comical-pastoral, scene individable and poem unlimited. The sleepy banks stretch ignobly forth, undulating into graceful hills on the right shore, while on the left they are tattered away into boggy islands that gurgle and choke with all their bulrushes in the lapping waters. These islets, whoever might be their proprietors, presented to my own and my companion's gaze no more amusing or edifying rent-payers than the herons, moping motionless and stiff like that which guarded the water-lily for poet Hood. The heron, I suppose, has the prescriptive right to stand sentinel in front of mouldy castles, deserted Rhine-towers and haunted manors, but I find him, for my part, a very transparent and contemptible character. He is evidently longing to be drawn, arsenicked and stuffed. He regards that consummation as an alderman regards the glory of having his likeness painted; and until it can be attained he bloats and poses all day in a ridiculous portrait-of-a-gentleman attitude, carefully imitating the stilted look of the preparation, and so glares at himself eternally in the water, a padded Narcissus.

I was better pleased with the storks I had observed at Strasburg. Humanity expects two didactic services from the stork: in the first place, to build in your chimney without being disturbed by pedantic theories of draught either on its own or your account; second, to carry its parents pickaback. The sacred ibis of Strasburg does not appear to fail in these particulars. We have tasted so many smoked Strasburg pies that the civic chimneys must evidently be well stuffed up. As for the filial part, I saw, when rattling away from Kehl, groups of elderly, rheumatic, stoop-shouldered storks picking up worms for their young; and evidently this assiduity would not have been practiced unless the stripling storks had been satisfactory in their part of the contract, and had been in the habit of loading on the old folks as luggage in most of their excursion-trains. And is there not a touching story of the stork at the time of the late German bombardment of Strasburg?—how the birds, frightened at the din, resolved to leave the city, though it was long before the usual date of migration, and held a town-council on the eaves of the cathedral, where they talked and fluttered a huge while, and finally spread their white wings above the gunpowder-smoke and sailed away? In this intelligent movement Fancy cannot doubt but that the storks acted up to all the requirements of literary tradition: she perceives each ornithological hero taking his little one in his claws, getting the broad of his back well under the old Anchises, with instructions to hold on grimly yet without prejudice to respiration, and so flying through the scorched sky from the flames of the Ilium. Only, as the retreat was at night-time, the manner of it could not well be verified.

Among the white villages which punctuate the flowing hills of the dexter bank we saw now and then a pretty sight—geese, queenly waddlers, coming down to the river like creeping threads of waterfall, or cattle, or quaint row-boats. One exhibition, more in the style of Dumas, was pointed out to us by Charles, who, as usual, revenged himself for an unmerited scolding of mine by being uncommonly attentive. It is hereabouts that on the rocky hills some of the most famous wines are made. The soil retains the sun's warmth, and the grapes manage to extract from them a delicious juice. Near by are found the glorious vineyards of the Rüdesheim, the Geisenheim, the Markobrunner, the Steinberg, the Johannisberg brands. In certain hamlets on the left bank, along by Ingelheim, the wine is made and the plants tended by women alone: the men drink the result, and are reported well content with this division of labor. Farther down, near Andernach, where the basaltic rocks are quite black and absorb a tropical heat from the sky, the vines grow in baskets of earth, which nestle over a hundred and fifty acres of the crag: an exquisite nectar proceeds from this giddy hanging-garden.

The discovery I speak of on the part of Charles was announced in his own fashion by the abrupt cry: "Well, if I am ever believed again! A blackbird cultivating wall-fruit!"

And we saw a little white church at the edge of a sparkling village completely encircled with a cornice of blooming vines. On a ladder against the wall, in the strongest possible relief, was the silhouette of the sacristan, who was occupied in training the grapes. Snipping and peering, now crushing an insect, now decimating a faulty cluster of buds, now tying up his turbulent garlands with bulrushes from the river, and all the while ticklishly afraid of falling, he presented a cheerful picture of bustling old-maid's labor.

"He makes a good *pendant* to Dannecker's Ariadne," I suggested; and add-

WORKING IN THE ECCLESIASTICAL VINEYARD.

ed: "Let us hope those consecrated grapes all go to the altar's use, and never leak out into the profane wine-trade."

A little shocked to have called the wine-trade profane in the hearing of Mrs. Ashburleigh, I settled her in her shawls and turned to promenade the deck for a few minutes. The scenery so far required but slight attention, and I was not sorry. I paced the boat in a meditative, Napoleon-like attitude, somewhat surprised to find how difficult it was to fold my arms over my doubt-racked heart. The journey had evidently agreed with me, and I was getting better than ever. Ah me! how easily I crossed these arms when first I journeyed up the Rhine in the youthful years that were for ever gone!

I could not but remember that the stretch of travel now before me was the same by which I had begun my earliest journey—the journey which had led me to Mary Ashburton and all the ashen orchards of Sodom. Behind was Mayence, whose Walhalla-like table-d'hôte of a forty-pound sirloin in a Mediterranean Sea of brewis I shall never forget so long as I have a palate or gastric apparatus. Before me was Bingen, where in the White Horse tavern I had taken a slate roof and chimneys for ruins on the Rhine. Beyond that, Andernach, where I had emptied to my own health a bottle that looked like a church spire.

And now, as I crossed the arms of melancholy over the waistcoat of well-being, I could but ask myself if I were the same Paul Flemming. And the river, reflecting my roseate gills, appeared really to doubt the assumption. Was it wise for me to go telling again the stations by which I had marked in boyish years my Hyperion-like ecliptic over the earth? Had I not abjured the Rhine, the enchanted serpent-river whose wisdom and lore have power to charm all the charmers, and which had now tempted me into its coils once more? It was a moment to review the past. Of all my loves, which remained to bless me? Of all my friends, which was at my side?

"Mr. Flemming! Mr. Flemming!" my commander appealed in a voice like a golden bell as I passed her on my beat, "you don't show me the ruins. Where are the ruins?"

The ruins! The ruins, Mrs. Ashburleigh, are here. If you want a Palmyra, if you wish for a Karnak, if you desire to be accommodated with a Herculaneum, here, in this heart, madam, is the lava and the desolation. And you, you too, are a sojourner and a pilgrim. Yet in this desert shall ever be an oasis, a spring, a softened shadow for you. Rest your regal form a while, tired q u e e n, upon my granite!

STABBED WITH THE COMPASSES.

She was resting it a little too trustfully on an artist's stool left inadvertently by a Swiss painter who had gone to sketch over the railing at the stern. As I picked up the fragments and assisted her to a stouter seat, "The ruins, madam, are coming," I said, "but for you and me they are obsolete. They begin with the Rheinstein yonder, which is not a ruin: it is a residence. Yon towers are fitted up with stained glass and baubles, and the owner shows them like a kaleidoscope for a groschen or two. The rest are on their way to us, and you will soon have them importunate enough. The heights down yonder are much alike, and afford, in the first place, a brand of wine which connoisseur-travelers must be able to discriminate and talk about with supernal wisdom; secondly, a girl who at some epoch has jumped into the river; and thirdly, a thief who built a stronghold and stole from all the caravans that passed his side of the river. One of them, wiser in his generation, built his castle, the Pfalz, in the middle, and took his toll from both banks."

"Drink, death and thieves!" said Mrs. Ashburleigh, estimating the charms of the Rhine. "But where, then, shall we find romance? where is poetry?"

"Ah, madam, have you not heard the news? Poetry is dead, killed by rule and line."

And I read to my commander the little poem testifying to the fact by that very Simrock whose brother was Dumas's host at Bonn.

But Mrs. Ashburleigh, I thought, looked

hurt at the brusque way in which her favorite Muses were treated. So I gave her another story, more appropriate to the place, and pretended to read from an old book in my hand

THE TRUE RECORD OF LORLEI.

In nomine Patris, et Filii, et Spiritus Sancti: Before me, Johan de Haga, ecclesiastical judge and grand penitentiary, committed to this inquisition by my lords of the Chapter of Saint Ewald, in the presence of our lord Conrad of Hochsteden, archbishop, on the plaints and quarrels of many good and worshipful brothers of the Church, have been heard the ensuing testimonies as to the behaviors of a demon vehemently suspected to have taken the form of a woman, at present in the gaol of the chapter. And to arrive at the verity of said quarrels and griefs have I opened this hearing, after mass duly performed, to this end to record the witnessings of one and all as to the said demon; the same to be thereupon put to the question and judged according to the laws provided against devils, whether demon, incubus, succubus, undine, or warlock's familiar. In this inquest hath assisted me, that all may be written and established, Gulielmus Geestmund, rubricator of the chapter, a clerk skilled and learned.

In the first place, hath come before us my lord the palsgrave of Bacharach, who, by me reverentially besought to enlighten the religion of the Church, hath responded that he hath great willingness thereunto, and engageth his faith of loyal knight to say nothing but what he hath seen or believed. Hath thereupon declared that his eldest son, after his first sojourn and siege in the lands of infidels, had brought back in guise of bride-betrothed a white wife of Venice, or female appearance thereunto resembling. That the young count had wellnigh immediately departed for his second crusade, being so incited by two special and mov-

THE JUDGE OF THE COURT ECCLESIASTIC.

ing reasons—first, because he would win fame and great dower for his lady, the said Venetian; and second, because he, the palsgrave now speaking, having engaged the hand of the young man to the dowager-widow of Rheinstein, had despatched him about his affairs with much personal correction and with many sacred promises and oaths of further chastisement; the which oaths, being measurably repeated in court, have not been recorded in these minutes by the rubricator.

That about twenty months thereafter the said wife of Venice had, to his knowledge, emerged from the convent whereunto she had been committed, and had been by agents to him unknown set up in state within the castle of Saint Goar. That the common report of the vulgar had been to the effect that the living body of his son, or otherwise his wraith and apparition, had marvelously her installed in Saint Goar, having appeared boat-carried on the river to that end in the second quarter of the moon. That this rumor was openly incorrect, because the young man had never manifested himself unto him his father, though he had published many offers of paternal correction and discipline, and offered

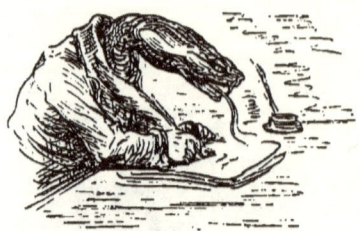

A CLERK SKILLED AND LEARNED.

large reward for the body of his son, alive or dead. That the said offers having been wholly ineffectual, evident it was that his son was no more. That having at all times avoided the castle of Saint Goar, abominating its lights and its music, its glamour and its melancholious seclusion, he had no direct witnessing to proffer on the diabolical character of the said white wife or widow, having heard but her harp from the river.

Being asked whether it had been borne in unto his mind to have masses performed for the perilous state of his son's soul, he devoted twelve thousand crowns to that use, and departed in all honor.

Secondly hath appeared, on the privilege extended by us not to be required to kiss the cross, and on the promise of liberty to retire in all freedom for the resumption of his traffic, a Jew named Shiloh al Rathschild, who hath by us been heard, maugre the infamy of his person and his faith, with the single end of enlightenment on the behavior of the said demon. Accordingly, hath been absolved from all oaths the said Shiloh, seeing that he is beyond the pale of the Church, and to us hath said that to the said sorceress or female appearance, who had come from the southern countries with intent to establish herself in these lands, he had leased, with records of bail, the castle of Saint Goar, fallen within his hands through bankrupture. That, as sureties, had given themselves up divers lords, squires and gentlemen drawn to the assistance of said sorceress by virtue of the charms, philtres and enchantments to her belonging. That the gathering of the rents agreed upon had ever filled him with amazement, seeing that when led into her presence by one her servitor, a strange Moor half clothed, black and with white eyeballs, he had found the said female in rooms of purple, vested in mourning weeds and blazing with jewels, clothed in her Venetian locks of gold, evermore singing dirges of heavy dole in a voice whose sweetness could not be portrayed. That from time to time, in the way of his traffic, he had bargained unto the said female many things of cost, as plates of silver-gilt, chandeliers, Persian carpets, birds, stuffs, clavecins and other instruments of music curiously adorned, and diamonds. Had likewise sent to her, on the behalf of neighboring lords, more than a thousand rare gifts. That the said female to the external eye presented no appearance of diabolical arts, but wore the guise of a comely woman mourning for her liege in all innocency. The said Shiloh al Rathschild, his castle of Saint Goar being confiscated to the Church for the vile and unholy usage to which he had put the same, was permitted to withdraw without being tortured. To the said Jew, before his departure, was shown the Moor or African, whom he recognized as the page of said demon.

Thirdly, the aforesaid Moorish man (who, black from head to foot, hath been found to be deprived of the beard with which all Christian men are habitually furnished), having persevered in uttering no word after various torments and rackings, during which he hath complained in a high voice, is convicted of not speaking Christian language.

Fourthly, hath come before us the most high, noble and puissant princess of Schwartz, and hath declared to us with tears, on the faith of the Evangels, to have laid in the earth her only son, dead by the deeds of the said female demon. The which noble youth, aged twenty years, having frequented the residence of said demon, in the manner of all the young lords of fifty leagues' vicinage, who had every one the habitude of visiting the sorceress with intent to make her change her widowhood, had in great despair thrown himself from the rock, rashly and blameworthily. And the said dame hath in addition said: "Alas, my lord! this priceless treasure hath been taken from me and dropped into the pit by the demon. My poor boy, his hopes and his inheritance, his life and his eternal welfare, all of himself, and more than himself, saw I dashed on the rocks like a grain of corn in the teeth of a dragon. Therefore have I no other expectation of joy than to see in flames this sorceress nourished with blood and gold. Burn and torment the vampire who destroys souls. See, my lord judge, to the tormenting of this devil who has made me an orphan in my old days: she has all the flames of the fiery lake in her eyes, the strength of Samson in her locks, and instruments of unearthly music in her voice. She charms that she may kill body and soul in one blow. Oh, my son! my son!" And the said princess of Schwartz, having purchased the burial of her son's body in consecrated ground for fifty thousand crowns, and bought two annual masses for his soul, hath retired in great dole, followed by a body of men-at-arms to her palace, at the command of the archbishop.

Then fifthly hath appeared Hugo von Engelheim, aged twenty-and-one, brought into court by the sompnour and guarded by twelve pikemen, under accusation of having conspired with divers lawless youths to lay siege to the gaol of the archbishopric and chapter, with intent to deliver the said sorceress. Notwithstanding his evil design, we have commanded Hugo von Engelheim to testify truly what he knew of the demoniac in question; who to our great outrage hath said: "I swear the woman accused of sorcery to be an angel, a perfect woman, and more worshipful of soul than of body—nowise evil, but generous, greatly given to aid the poor and suffering. And this beloved wife of Venice, having sworn never to replace her knight of Bacharach, and thrown into despair many nobles, hath in pity granted me the worship of her chaste heart, of which she has made me the suzerain. There-

upon, electing the wife of Venice to be evermore my lady, admitted to breathe her air and to hear her voice, I find myself happier than the lords of paradise.

THE PALSGRAVE.

Making it my task day by day to become the worthier of her patronage, I receive from her a thousand good advices; as, to acquire the fame of a bold chevalier; to become a strong knight, fearing naught but Heaven; to honor the ladies, serving only one, and loving them all for her memory; then, after many dangers and stout deeds, if her heart be still pleasing to mine, to hope that she might be my own in heaven, for assuredly she would give herself to none other than her dead crusader." Many further things hath said the young knight with a speed and vociferousness little considerate toward the secretary, and also with tendency to show clearly the abominable, unheard-of, fraudulent and damnable powers of the said female demon over the souls of youth. And hath been borne guarded to his father, with the intention to define the extent and tenure of his estates, and to know what might be the fine in his power to pay as the penalty for his disturbance of the force of justice.

Sixthly, hath been drawn from gaol and brought before us the said woman presumed to be a manifestation of the devil; who, much broken by torture and the salutary effects of the rack, hath remained back-bowed and head-buried during all the reading of the testimonies precedent. And, asked if she had practiced many sorceries and melodies, charms and witch-crafts on divers knights of the Palatinate, made answer: "My knight lies deep in Rhine: let me join him." And asked if she had caused the death of the hereditary prince of Schwartz, had replied: "My knight lies deep in Rhine: let me leap into his bed." And questioned on the spells and glamours of her house, on the tapers, and requiems, and mourning weeds, and palls, and spice-burnings, and rich harness, and intolerably sweet sounds reported thence to the court, had replied likewise: "My knight lies deep in Rhine: let me join him."

Whereupon by us hath been required that she acknowledge herself to be a demon and redivest her body for the tormentor; when suddenly hath she risen upright and dropped her mantle, crying, "I am a woman, and mortal. Kill me!" Upon the sight of her face and throat, and the dropping of her hair, maliciously revealed of a sudden for the perversion of justice, and resembling the drawing of the curtain from the Italian altar-picture in the cathedral, have I the judge been swiftly overclouded in the brain, unable to clearly see in the presence of those carnal beauties, which exercise over the will of man a supernatural co-ercion. Master Geestmund the clerk hath, by force of Nature, dropped the quill and retired from court, declaring that he could not, without incredible agitations which harrow the brains, be witness to the torture. Thus concludeth the session and end these memoirs, finished by the hand of me, Johan de Haga, the judge.

THE ARTICLE OF DEATH.

This is from the act of extreme confession made in his last hour and within the article of death by Johan de Haga, penitentiary of Saint Ewald:

After trial had and performed, I visited the gaol of the wife of Venice, or female demon. When I was within the closure of the gates I saw no more any appearance of a prison, because that evil spirits under authority of witchcraft had filled the place with wines and meats, with flowers and perfumes. There saw I the wife of Venice, in form of a damsel white and little, on a carpet of Persia, wrapped in the hairs of her head and weeping; the chief gaoler and torsionary at her feet, which he rubbed with ointment after the torment. The damsel looked up and asked me why I would needs hurt her. Then, having been drawn by the remembrance of her aspect in court, and by the special cords of diabolical temptation, into the focus of her sorcery, my strength departed from me. On questioning the demon I was bewildered with such terms of answer that it appeared to me in all firmness of persuasion that I should do a crime in punishing a poor soft maid, the which sobbed like a little infant. Then fell I further into the toil, my head being filled with warm light, my heart with young and leaping blood, and my bewitched body falling prostrate before her. I asked her to be my daughter, my joy, my treasure, my châtelaine, my wife. And she answered: "My knight lies deep in Rhine: let me go to him."

Thereupon got I home in fever, of which now I fail, and desire the unction of the Church.

This is a parcel from out the private chronicles of the Geestmund family, and, written in very clerkly style, appeareth to be in the hand of Gulielmus Geestmund, in guise of his last testament and will:

MY ONLY AND WELL-BELOVED SON: Before thou canst read this I shall be in the tomb, imploring thy prayers. Govern well the family after that I am gone, for I have written these counsels from a sharp sense of the injustice and topping willfulness of men. In my youth, seeing the Church before me as mine alone way of promotion, I learned not only to read, but to write; and by the aidance of Master Johan, the penitentiary, did assume the quill and inkhorn for the chapter of Saint Ewald in my thirtieth year. It was then that the process arose up against the demon of the Lorlei; which, until the production of the culprit in court, was heard by Johan with wisdom and discretion; but at the view of her face was Johan suddenly and shamefully persuaded of the said nymph's innocence, and died soon after dishonorably, much mourned for his apostasy, of fevers in which he saw many idle visions and splendors. Then Rufus of Fulda, a rigid and holy man, succeeded him as judge, and quickly brought the embroilment to an end; for, perceiving that the only proceeding needful for the condemnation of said nymph, and the acquisition of her rich gems and moneys to the Church, was the retraction of the verdict of said Johan, he persuaded him into such a confession as deprived his first ruling of all credit and force. Thus confessed Johan the judge to her magics and the rich state she still kept up in her gaol, being persuaded thereto by threats of the deprivation of extreme unction in his death-bed. In that time all believed the sorceress to be so abundantly provided with gold that she could, if so minded, buy the whole Palatinate; yet did not the gold, when weighed and melted, suffice for more 'han the overlaying of the high altar, to

THE LEAP OF LORLEI.

the niggardly cheating and cheapening of the Church's revenue. Now, I, Geestmund, in visiting the gaol after the nymph's second torture, had found a chain of diamonds hidden in her hair, with some of which she had bought the gaoler to her, and, prudently possessing myself of said jewels without words spoken, was immediately (on the gaoler's word, though I offered him a share) deprived of mine office, and forced to feign illness and privily forsake the land: they are the gems which hang about the neck of Saint Ludmilla in the north chapel. The clout being now wrung dry, the widow's possessions sequestered to holy use, her residence confiscated, and the souls of her victims solaced with many and costly masses, nothing further remained but to bury her out of sight, the formality of execution first being had and observed upon her body. She was tortured, led up to penance; tortured, let out to confession; tortured, let go; tortured, and released to the soldiers.

Of all which had I small care, being now in Flanders, and disgraced by those whom for prudence I do not name. Yet did the circumstance of her death reach unto mine ears, having caused huge talk in the country, and is still recited in ballads after vespers, secretly, with vain additions of them called poets. For when led to the stake this sorceress did overcome the men-at-arms with her supplications and with the remanent enchantments of her beauty. So that they let her go on before, being likewise awed by the throng of youthful nobles and of beggars, her friends, who closed about them. Also were some present of the House of Bacharach, who deemed their kinsman insulted in the person of his widow; for it seemeth that verily the palsgrave's son had returned from the infidel wars, and had lived certain months in bridal with her, until drowned a-fishing; but this the Church ever denied. Now, she, being got nigh Saint Goar, asked grace to go up for one more season unto the rock whence she had always thrown her dirges and musics athwart the stream; and breaking away, the soldiers also making small resistance, she fled forth, much admired by all, and clomb from pinnacle to pinnacle of the rock, going very lightly on her feet, bruised from the torment; and when mounted and all alone she flung nimbly out into the abyss; for they lie who say she first sang a dirge, but she went forth silently, falling like snow, only since hath she been heard to rise and sing. Thus was she undone, and I disgraced, who went into the butchering business, and am become a rich flesher. And now being in age, yet clear of head, I put certain thoughts into writing, my son, for thy guidance. In the first place, to live happy needs is it to abide far from those of the Church and from the nobles. Secondly, always remain in the condition of butchery — marry thy daughters to good butchers, and nourish them in honor of flesh. So shall not any get hold of the Geestmunds, neither the State, nor the Church, nor the nobles, to whom, as it may fall out, and they being the stronger, it will be necessary to lend certain crowns without ever indulging the hope of seeing them again. Thus shall every one, at all seasons, love and despise the Geestmunds, the poor Geestmunds; and they shall not be burned or quartered for the advantage of Church or king.

PART XVII.

THE CURRENT OF FATE.

LATTER-DAY REFORMERS.

I FINISHED my screed of Lorlei, and pocketed the old Tauchnitz edition of *Ingoldsby* out of which I had feigned to read it. "These antique records," I observed, "shed a curious light on the realities of church history." And I glanced at Mary Ashburleigh, who had heard the recital not unconcernedly.

"True," she said; "but was the Church ever so grasping and so cruel?"—Adding, with an indescribable smile, "Those were tiresome times for vagabond widows."

I gave Mrs. Asburleigh a little bolus of wisdom: "You must remember what is remarked by Lea, the authority in church history: 'Almost everything is to be forgiven to the mediæval clergy, who represented an idea in times when physical force was the only power respected.' The Dark Ages are, you must remember, past the virgin days of Christianity: she is now rather a widow grasping for her thirds among the close-fisted and niggardly executors. Her lucky day is over

—the day in which Charlemagne lent all the power of the State to the Church, which he used as an instrument in constructing his evanescent civilization."

"How impure, even in the greatest times of the Church, were the sources of

THE BATTLE OF THE CREEDS.

its power!" said my commander with her pretty sententiousness.

"Millenniums are treacherous affairs," I answered. "Men usually get tired, and yawn them out of the way. Just hereabouts, you know, they claim that Christianity, as a worldly empire, took its rise. It was over Andernach, the Germans will tell you, that Constantine saw the cross in the sky."

"What a thought," said Mrs. Ashburleigh, kindling and letting fall her Baedeker, "that combination and fusion of the Roman empire with Christianity! The force that swayed the whole world made one with eternal Truth! No dreams could have seemed too wild and beautiful for the faithful then. How I should like to have been some saint or holy woman of the time, just to have seen the emperor bow his helmet, and to catch the last shadows of the fading Cross as it rose out of the Rhine to embrace the world with its shadowy arms of air!"

"There were such saints and holy monks, and their dreams were as bright as you can possibly imagine. With Rome converted, it seemed to them that the earth would become identical with heaven. Lactantius, rejoicing after Constantine's adhesion, boasted, 'How blessed would be that golden age among men when love and kindness and peace and innocence and justice and temperance and faith should spread throughout the world, and neither prisons nor the sword of the judge would be wanted!' But the world wearied of its millennium, and for the sword of the judge Christianity soon became a most keen and persevering aspirant."

"Using it on helpless wretches like poor Lorlei," put in Mrs. Ashburleigh.

"The fact is," I went on, "the ideal of the mediæval Church was too unnatural to last. When the clergyman can make humanity a strong worker in the state and in society, lending his religion to the purging of politics and to the pleasantness of his own breakfast-table, then comes the statelier Eden back to men—not when they make their saint a stagnant solitary in a cell."

"The statelier Eden will never come back to men," said Mrs. Ashburleigh archly, "without a woman in it."

"Why, that is just the conclusion—don't you see?—that Christianity was forced to come to. And so at length you have the monk that married Catharine Bora."

"You mean—" asked Mary Ashburleigh, whose attention, a little overtaxed, was wandering.

"I mean Luther, of course. Germany may well be proud, for when Luther arrived, and stretched out his dark-robed arms in the attitude everybody knows from Kaulbach's Reformation-picture, then Constantine's cross came and stood a second time in the German sky."

"What a rich country in prodigies!"

"Precisely. And Germany, more than any other nation, has got accustomed to them and impatient of them. Never was there such a people for yawning away its millenniums. As for its Luthers, in these latter times they have become a mere drug. They call themselves Kant and Fichte and Herbart and Schelling and Hegel, and they appear with a new German millennium in their right hand and a new German Bible in their left."

"And how many reformers have there been, then, for mercy's sake?"

"Oh, the first was the serpent, as Heine will assure you. That footless blue-stocking, he says, that lithe lecturer, that private expounder who addressed his class from a tree in the garden of Eden, explained the whole of Hegel's system six thousand years before Hegel was born. This professor, to use Heine's words, 'clearly showed how the absolute consists in the identity of being and knowing;' or, in more familiar terms, 'Ye

THE DRAGOMAN.

shall not die, but shall know good from evil as gods.'"

"Then reform," said my commander, "is one of the oldest of earthly privileges?"

"Evidently. Did not the wisest of men, the prize pupil of the serpent, declare that there was nothing new under the sun, and no end of rewriting the *biblos?*"

We were on one of the "reformed" steamers, the American boats as they call them—handsomely making Americanism a synonym for improvement in fluvial navigation. Most of the little comforts to which the Yankee is accustomed on his Sound steamers or Mississippi triremes were around us. At first the voyage was quiet enough: there had been but few passengers from Mayence. Until Bingen nothing in particular attracted our attention, and Mrs. Ashburleigh's sketch-book lay in her lap ominously gaping, like a voracious lion waiting to be fed. For me the flat transit was a grateful, dreamy period. I thought the river paused to hear my story of poor Lorlei: I thought the gentle banks rolled and fawned at the feet of me and my adored.

But at Bingen our calm was violently interrupted. A precipitous invasion of tourists took place. Not only were there Bavarian opera-singers, Prussian officers, homeward-bound Leyden clerks and rattling Viennese, but there was at least one company from whose midst I could hear my own mother-tongue. I did not clearly distinguish the individuality of this party at first. The tourists rolled down the companion-way to deposit their bags and shawls. The stout porters of Bingen were handling immense trunks as tenderly as egg-baskets. A confusion of boxes, crates and hampers rattled into the boat. A Swiss youth brought on a velocipede; a governess appeared with a spaniel and a consumptive monkey; there was a corpulent English mother in a wheeled chair; and a photographer,

OBERWESEL.

fresh from the slaughter of unnumbered tourists beside the river Nahe, jumped red-handed among us, his camera in the arms of a servant, and ready to transfix us in groups at every pause of the voyage. The porters trampled each other, couriers shouted, the monkey swore, and from the wheeled chair Boadicea, standing loftily charioted, raved and shrieked between her daughters in her fierce volubility. It was at the height of the tumult, just before pushing off from Bingen, that I was aware of a calm voice proceeding from the English-tongued company I speak of, and controlling the turmoil like an orchestral bâton when everybody is tuning: "The next coupon wanted will be the green one: if each lady will select her green coupon and stuff it into her left glove, it will be ready for the dinner. By our arrangement, ladies, you dine at precisely two shillings instead of three; the knowledge of which need spoil no one's appetite."

I looked at the group in question. A circle of British spinsters had by some magic obtained possession of the bows. They were unencumbered; their knapsacks were stacked and ticketed down below with military precision; their sketching-albums were ready on their laps; their faces were calmly receptive, shaded by ample hats and gig-tops of sensible patterns. In the midst of them stood a gentleman with mutton-chop whiskers, his body diagonally bisected by the straps of his opera-glass, a little Mercury's hat on his head. Correctness and reliability shone all over his person like a varnish. He wore a white cravat, and looked much like Berkley in a tourist suit. He was now addressing the whole dovecote with a studied oration in which could by turns be heard the names of Rolandseck and Drachenfels, the Seven Mountains, Andernach, Linz, Stolzenfels, Marksburg, Ehrenbreitstein, Herzenach and Oberwesel. By a slight attention to his discourse I found that it was a judicious mosaic of paragraphs from Murray, Baedeker and Joanne.

I listened to this Homer chanting the Odyssey of the Rhine. It was very complete: the proper stories were introduced, the suitable quotations from Byron, and the mild jokes appropriate to the locality. I waited to hear what the minstrel would say about the cliffs this side of St. Goar, from whose top the Lorlei leaped.

It was not long in coming: "The rocks fancifully assigned to the Lorlei are four hundred and forty-seven feet in height. A man at the cottage will blow a horn and discharge a gun, to afford a test of the echo: the expense of the powder is borne by the steamboat company. The particular rock from which the nymph leaped is now penetrated by the railway tunnel."

All the spinsters put down the figures 447 in their albums. "Your sketch-books, ladies, will not be strictly necessary before Oberwesel. The surroundings of Oberwesel seem to have been arranged expressly for artistic purposes: nothing is wanting there for the picturesque, whether woods, waters, ruins, rocks, rustic belvederes and *aussichten*, or cascades. The late mayor of Oberwesel, an artist of some repute, has published a drawing-book in which all the beauties are taken from his own surroundings. This is the origin of the famous jest, that when you ask the echo for a definition of the burgomaster of Oberwesel, you are answered—"

"Oh, I know," said one of the ladies, the oldest.

"What?" asked the gentleman with the opera-glass.

"*Easel!* Don't you see, girls?—an artist's *easel*." And the fair tourist collected her tribute of little laughs, better satisfied with her answer than if it had been the right one.

THE MOUSE.

The Mentor did not correct her. He continued: "Just beyond St. Goar we shall find the Neu-Katzenelnbogen and the Thurnberg. The first-named castle, known to English travelers as the *Cat*, is interesting as showing the obvious origin of Perrault's story of 'Puss-in-Boots.' This fastness, putting on at first the humble airs of a lowly hermitage, hardly lifted its walls from the level of the earth, and watched softly from behind a simple palisade of wood. It seemed less occupied with attack than self-defence. But all the while puss-in-sabots was not idle, but, like many seeming cowards, amassed a quantity of secret spoils from the wealthy merchant-trains that came up the Rhine; so well that, by a judicious alternation of force and strategy, it made of its master one of the richest robbers on the river—a true marquis of Carabas. His end was that of all who in those days measured themselves with the Church. The owner of the Cat aroused the jealousy of Bishop Hatto, surnamed 'The heart of the king.' A strong castle was built opposite, not on the hillside, but on the summit of the mountain, and Hatto called it the Mouse, declaring that this time the mouse should eat the cat. This was easily done, and the bishop made no bones of the powerful robber opposite, whose spoils and gold soon went to enrich the great church at Mayence. But Hatto went a little too far with his holy zeal, and, having speculated in corn, was eaten up in his fastness by an army of mice, who devoured first his tabbies and then himself."

And the guide, as a matter of course, recited Southey's poem, with sufficiently good accent and discretion:

The cat sat screaming, mad with fear
At the army of rats that were drawing near.
They have whetted their teeth against the stones,
And now they pick the bishop's bones.

"Who can he be?" I asked of Mrs. Ashburleigh. "Some kind of a courier, I suppose?"

"He does not look to me at all like a courier," said my leader in a tone of rebuke, her eyes fixed approvingly on the fluent cicerone.

When I next listened he had got still farther down the stream : he was evidently keeping his party posted well ahead. He described a town which was not without old and tender associations for me :

"Andernach is largely built of black basalt taken from the neighboring hills. Some of you may have heard a curious but unsupported tradition of the Christ on the wayside cross of Andernach bowing its head: this legend is unconfirmed, and the citizens, unable to vouch for it, have carried the wooden figure inside the church. The anecdote doubtless came from the fact that the head of the principal figure was one day found broken and lying at the foot of the calvary in the churchyard, a renaissance structure erected in the Greek taste."

CALVARY OF ANDERNACH.

"Do you know, I fancy," said I confidentially to Mrs. Ashburleigh, "that this must be the honest man who makes the guide-books for Murray? I never imagined before that the person had any particular existence in the flesh, but he must be somebody or other of corporeal substance."

"He is a mysterious but not unfascinating person," said the Dark Ladye: "he reminds me— But no matter. Who can the ladies be?"

"I can hardly guess. Probably they are his short-hand writers to take down his notes. They all have albums."

"Rolandseck, ladies," said the inexorable voice, "is celebrated as having been built by Roland after he had been killed at Roncesvalles. From this remarkable specimen of posthumous construction we get the best view of the 'castled crag of Drachenfels,' opposite. This latter is one of the heights of the Siebengebirge, or Seven Mountains, so named because there are eleven of them. The village of Königswinter will afford us a dozen donkeys, housed with a dozen scarlet saddle-cloths, by which to make the ascent of ten hundred and sixty-six and a half feet. In climbing this hill you will enjoy another benefit from our system : the usual fee for the ascent is twelve and a half silbergroschen for each donkey, and a little less, or ten groschen, for the guide. Our arrangement affords this trip at six silbergroschen apiece, all around, for men and animals; which, besides its economy for ourselves, avoids the drawing of invidious and disparaging distinctions between the donkeys and the drivers. For this enterprise, ladies, the blue tickets will please be in readiness."

But the most copious of wells may pump itself dry, and there came a moment when the eloquence of the man in the spyglass-strap came to a stop. At a signal from himself each lady extracted from a square tin box, made to resemble a Murray, a little thong of Australian meat and a few ounces of bread. Soon, instead of the steady voice of their entertainer, I could hear nothing from that quarter but the little mandibles of those fair beings. The man himself seemed to have no appetite except for his own mutton-chops, which he was fingering and chewing over the rail as I approached him.

"I beg pardon," I said, "but it is so pleasant to hear my native language—and one is so glad to meet a man of information—and I can hardly be mistaken in thinking you in some sort a public character."

The man bowed, left his whisker alone, and plunged for a card-case. I was as quick as he.

"My name is— My card," I observed.

"Certainly, certainly," he answered with equal civility: "my own is, as you will perceive— This is my card. My name is

COOKSON & JENKINSON."

I acquiesced with another bow, though the gentleman's plurality of name left me considerable choice, and his "card" was a pamphlet of fifty pages.

"I have no disposition to conceal my name, which represents perhaps the foremost enterprise of the nineteenth century. I surmise that you are a fellow-countryman of mine?"

"That I can hardly say," I replied with a smile, "until I know your own nationality. But even then I should be shy of claiming you as a compatriot, for I haven't the faintest idea what country I belong to myself. I have long been a renegade from my own nation, without attaching myself to any other. In fact, I am a Progressive Geographer in search of his home."

"The very thing!" said the traveler: "we will find it for you. It is quite in our line. Our Tours include every country on the face of the earth. We will establish you in little more than no time on the most advanced principles of ethnographical distribution. We already cover the globe with our Advertised Routes. Our terms" (and he took out a

DRACHENFELS.

THE SERVILE WAR.

long zigzag ticket resembling an accordeon) "are arranged with an advantage to the purchaser of from twenty-five to fifty per cent. We ensure satisfaction, avoid extortion and guarantee sound sleep, for we fine landlords for all hard or unclean beds. In a few years traveling will be unknown except through us —in fact, impossible but by our assistance. We are arranging objects of interest along all routes that are a little deficient in incident. Wherever a deficiency of ruins exists we supply the need. The Rhine will be quite another

SERVILE RECONCILIATION.

thing when you next pass, my dear sir: the proprietors have done a little hereabouts in the way of artificial ruins, but nothing to what we contemplate."

My Ariadne had now approached, and was listening to the details of this new Bacchic conquest of India. Her face wore a look of great interest and sympathy. "May I ask whom you have with you?" she inquired.

"They are governesses and schoolteachers, madame, doing the Rhine under my auspices. The party is small, but most intelligent."

"But how did you manage to collect so many ladies of similar age and condition?"

"Not the least trouble in the world, madame. I combed them from the advertising columns of the *Times* in three days."

Mrs. Ashburleigh took me aside. "That is the image of the man I have dreamed of," she said hastily. "I perceive that for the present my destiny is cast with his. Do not ask me further: I feel all you would say. I confess to you that my heart has been touched. We shall meet again. But for this time I shall enter the company of that gentleman. It only remains for you to seek, at the next stopping-place, the best excuse for leaving me."

This mysterious advertisement quite overcame my courage. What did she mean—rejection, encouragement or general mystery? As for the pretext of which she spoke, accident furnished it, most unfortunately for me, at Coblenz.

PART XVIII.

THE DIFFICULTY OF CATCHING UP.

TOMB OF HOCHE AT WEISSENTHURM.

"WHAT are these cruel words?" I cried to Mrs. Ashburleigh, "and why, after so faithful an attendance, am I overslaughed in a moment by a courier?"

"I never saw him before. He is a link, Mr. Flemming—a link. As for my cruel words, though we have not time for many speeches, I will repeat them. I confess freely that my present journey, if it has found my heart sleeping, has not left it untouched. Now seek your pretext and abandon me: yonder is Coblenz."

And now my factotum Charles, working in dark collusion with Fate, proceeded to give the pretext in question. It was his chance, and he magnified it—so successfully that the great sunstroke suffered by Charles at Coblenz has become an historical epoch among my friends.

237

Some of the English schoolmistresses, whose occupations were of a noisier nature and indisposed them for listening to the traveling-agent's lectures, had found a nook on the deck toward the stern. From this group a cry of female shriekers roused me. The schoolmistress who was declaiming the part of Thekla in *Wallenstein* broke off abruptly; the two schoolmistresses who were going over the German declensions broke up their mutual quizzing-class; the hoarse schoolmistress with a talent, who was running up the vocal scales of an absolute prima donna, and who learnt in suffering what to teach in song, left her exercises: they all screamed, the vocalist embracing the opportunity to discharge her highest head-note, finished with a shake. The elder lady-grammarian approached me, saying, "Don't distress yourself, sir, but I fear your man's overpowered—"

THE COLPORTEUSE.

"My man overboard? Can I believe my ears?"

"You can't believe your ears, and the man's *not* overboard. I said *overpowered*, as plainly as lips could utter the compound."

And she deserted me, flouncingly. Through the aperture left by her person I perceived a marble group, consisting of Charles, insensible, and the traveling-agent, rigid as a sculptured Charity: the latter sustained the former with one hand, and with the other inundated him with hartshorn.

"Help me down with him into the saloon. I have a battery among my baggage which has recuperated whole regiments of fainting females," said this man of resources.

We got him down the stairs. Mrs. Ashburleigh, never *de trop*, was now particularly useful, for she stood in an attitude of astonishment in the gangway, which she completely blocked, preventing the mass of ladies from precipitating themselves upon us.

"I shall continue the hartshorn, with cupping and galvanism. The lower orders like an abundance of physicking. Leave Cookson & Jenkinson alone for dealing with the servile classes!" continued the excellent man, while I, over come with sorrow for my poor friend, was indisposed to pay much attention. "The management of domestics is one of our specialties. At first we counted against us every Swiss chambermaid and Alpine guide. I have had them pointing after me as a man accursed, but now they follow me like little dogs; and it is all owing to our happy idea of a matrimonial agency."

"You marry people, too?"

"We began with the lower orders. But we are working upward. We distributed the servant-girls among the guides that go up the mountains—the shrillest wench to the guide of greatest altitude. We had our circular printed on red cotton handkerchiefs and given away at fairs, until the remotest Black Forester knows us, and every washerwoman is a matrimonial colporteuse. You will find the wedding-card the last coupon." (And the man actually showed me the formula,

GALIGNANI.

in pink, at the end of his zigzag pasteboard.) "I believe the lady in your company is one of our patrons: I am sure she corresponded with us from Heidelberg."

"Let us attend to our patient," said I, not exactly liking the last allusion, but unable to think much of anything but my unlucky Charles: "he is opening his eyes."

The poor fellow revived enough to turn a dark purple and to grasp my hand. While his brow was burning to the touch he complained of cold and his teeth chattered. The impromptu physician shook his head. "It is a more serious case than I like to undertake," said he: "you had better give him rest and a good doctor. Get him on land the first time we stop."

As he spoke the steamer was coming to a pause at Coblenz. And so, with my big great baby half in my arms, my trunks forgotten, and only my tin box strapped to me—denuded as when I started on my walk to Marly—I found myself staggering to the shore.

Mrs. Ashburleigh found time to console me as I left the boat stunned and heartbroken. "Never fear," she said. "I am in experienced hands, and shall do extremely well. If you discover any curious wall-papers in Coblenz, do not forget that in me you have always a true and grateful friend."

The representative of Cookson & Jenkinson grasped my fingers, in which he left a little printed matrimonial scheme. In the confusion of our disembarking, the admirable woman I adored, whose very bewilderments had an inspiration in them, lost her balance in such a way as to set her weight on Charles's instep,

EXTINGUISHED.

and I am certain that nothing that had been done for him was of so stimulating an effect as this primitive application.

I had the pain of seeing the travelers' agent assume Mrs. Ashburleigh, whom he seated among his clients with a protecting manner very hard for me to bear.

THE SYMPOSIUM.

As I had parted with Francine at Carlsruhe, as I had parted with Berkley and Hohenfels at Heidelberg, as I had parted at Wildbad with the revelers of Épernay, so I now saw my Ariadne drifting away on the tide of destiny. My Ariadne, do I say? Nay, rather was *I* the Ariadne, and Coblenz my Naxos!

On our route to the nearest hotel Charles's complaint took a pronounced form of menengitis. His brain seemed to wander, for he asked in a low, thick voice for his "young master." The people at the Traube inn received us with positive rudeness, the landlord declaring that he had no room for maniacs and gentlemen without baggage. I was unable to see that want of baggage would tax his room more heavily than the presence of it, but I readily agreed with him to leave his premises as soon as possible. I asked for the address of some sanitary establishment away from the noise of the town, and the eager host poured out the names of a whole college of doctors. A happy accident led me to choose the thermal establishment of Herr Elssasser in the village of Capellen, beneath the castle of Stolzenfels, a league or so from the city. Blessed be the chance that led us to this Samaritan! He keeps remedies for the mind as well as for the body. Up to the second day my humble friend's hallucinations increased, while his proprietor poured out a stream of letters to Mary Ashburleigh, with the direction left

BLITZ.   HUYOT

blank upon the envelopes, because neither she nor I had attended to that important little specification. On the fifth day Charles took his first soup, and I was able to water the poignant recollection of the Dark Ladye with a gentle thought or two directed to Francine: on the same day I applied myself, not without difficulty, to some letters for my male acquaintance. In ten days my patient was lustily calling for kidneys and coffee, and my own sombre spirit had recovered so much of its natural versatility as to notice that Charles's nurse, a maiden from Saverne of the name of Gredel, was a model for grace and as handsome as the "beautiful chocolatière."

On the twelfth morning, as Charles was trifling with a jelly in his easy-chair, and his master—or servant rather, as the case then stood—was translating news for him out of the broad page of *Galignani*, a footstep resounded through the corridor.

"It is Gredel," said Charles: "she has new shoes on."

But I called him an idiot, resuming with his recovery my usual endearments. The step was the step of Hohenfels, as I knew very well. I rose from my seat quite guilty and troubled. I turned toward the door: the latch rattled, and the baron appeared, a volume of poetry in his hand. He shambled up to me, and after his dear immemorial custom kissed my cheeks and wished me well.

"Am I not to be scolded?" I asked.

"For the sickness of your aide-de-camp? I am hardly so unreasonable. I wish to interest you in my chemical experiments. Was it not here you formerly learned the tale of the archbishop who lived in the Stolzenfels and practised alchemy according to the Hermetic philosophy?"

"It is true, my friend, that I abode here in Capellen for a season when very young, and gave my mind a great deal to the old archbishop who tried to make unto himself a child in the manner taught by Paracelsus—a foolish homunculus in a glass bottle. But I told all the story in a book written long ago, and Herr Elssasser informs me that I told a fib, for that the Stolzenfels was a ruin long before 1541, the year in which Eremita Paracelsus died in Salzburg."

And the baron plunged with me into chemistry as if we had only parted since breakfast. As the science became, in his descriptions, seriously mixed up with the Schiller he had been reading, and as my own enthusiasm for chemistry is entirely mediæval and scholastic, we did not add much to what is known of the subject. But Hohenfels and Berkley, with the assistance of young Von Ramm, had invented an artificial whey out of substances entirely mineral, which Berkley was coming to explain to Doctor Elssasser.

Before the baron of Hohenfels would take a seat he drew from his pocket-book a couple of notes and handed them to me. They both presented the view of a broken or unlatched seal, and a superscription addressed to my friend. "Read," he said: "they concern you rather than myself."

The first, signed "Fortnoye," recalled to monsieur the baron's recollection the pleasant friendship mutually formed at Heidelberg, and desired news of Mr. Paul Flemming. It begged to know whether I was actually residing at Paris or at Marly, or was on the route of my German peregrinations. The writer's intended wife, who kept me "in the very kindest remembrance," desired to have me for groomsman at the wedding.

"And who is this vintner's noble landlady?" asked the baron with the very faintest possible interest; "and how comes it that she has kept you so very kindly in her memory?"

I turned and stared. "Don't you know?" I asked.

"H'm! Not in the least," said Hohenfels, who was carefully setting his watch.

"H'm," said I myself. "The proposed bride of M. Fortnoye is an enchanting little fairy in an artisanne cap— No, no, not at all! I mean to say, the object of M. Fortnoye's attentions is a superb Englishwoman of the most brilliant accomplishments and highest distinction— No, that is not right, either. When I come to think of it, I have not the remotest idea whom that insupportable, meddling marplot of an odious Fortnoye *is* going to marry. Hohenfels, I don't know what he is going to do. That person has sealed the wretchedness of my existence."

"How has he done that, if you don't know what he is doing?"

"The fact is, Hohenfels, I am but trying to deceive myself. I do know his intended: I have the fact from her own lips."

"And who is the fair object?"

"She says," I answered, now fairly intrenched behind my handkerchief, "that she would pass through fire to save him. I have myself been the accomplice of my own destruction, for I have escorted her on what she confessed to be a wedding-journey—a wedding that Heaven will bless, she hopes. Fortnoye had some romantic association with her at a grave in Laaken; besides, the lady's previous husband was in the spirit-trade. Her name is Ashburleigh, and she is the most graceful authoress in Europe."

HOW MUCHE CROSSED THE RHINE.

"As you like," said Hohenfels, looking narrowly at me. "Have you settled on a wife for the wine-agent? I only want you to make up your mind. Have you quite decided? Whatever contents you will suit me perfectly."

"My friend, I cannot deny it. I am in the lady's confidence: I have but just left her on the river yonder. I brought her from Schwetzingen to Frankfort, from Frankfort to Castel, and from Castel to Coblenz."

"Very well," said the baron. "If you have decided, you may as well read the second letter. But I fear it conflicts fatally with your theory. The lady in question, this distinguished authoress and accomplished widow, at the moment when she is going to marry another seems to have become an unresisting prey to your enchantments. For the proof, read!"

It was a note from my cook. She poured upon Hohenfels a deluge of confidences, blamed him for not taking better care of Monsieur Flemming, protested that she was palsied from idleness, and promised to leave the key in the door and instantly seek other service. She knew, by the most positive information, that I was paying my addresses to a traveling adventuress of the watering-places, a self-styled widow, a great *brune*—a Mrs. Asburlais, or some such name.

Then renewed lamentations: she was not accustomed to having a lady in the kitchen, she was about to suit herself elsewhere, etc.

I knew my good servitor, and I made

TAKING EXERCISE.

little of her threats. But who could have been the tale-bearer? who could have been the sender of the "positive information"? As I looked around inquiringly, with the letter in my hand, my eye met the eye of Charles. My valet twisted himself uneasily in his easy-chair. The author was confessed.

"Do you know," said Hohenfels, "you are getting to be a hard horse to bridle? I have given you your head long enough. I supposed you already at Marly, and had prepared to follow you thither. As I was strapping my trunk I got a letter, undated, as usual, but with the postmark of Coblenz: a day or two after your good cook writes me that you are marrying a soldier of fortune. You need not try to protest. I was alarmed. You are neither young nor beautiful, but you are cut out for the victim of an adventuress. I interrupted my chemicals, left Berkley in a bath of artificial whey, and rushed to Coblenz. Thence to Stolzenfels, where I was prepared to meet the Lorlei and dispute the prey with her. Happily, I learn from Dr. Elssasser that your skirts are clean, or rather that you brought no skirts into Capellen. The defendants are acquitted, the house is pure, but I have no confidence in you for the future. To make things sure, you must accoutre yourself with your botany-box once more, and come along with me."

"What are you thinking of?" I cried. "Charles is the doctor's most beautiful case: I cannot break up Dr. Elssasser's clinic. Besides, as a minor annoyance, the thing would be fatal to Charles."

"Nonsense! We shall leave Charles here. Berkley is coming immediately to this establishment, which he has known for years, and where he has drunk oceans of whey."

I deliberated a minute: "The fact is, I cannot support the effort. It may seem, Hohenfels, but a slight service to attend the wedding of this fatal Épernay wine-agent, for whom I have had a sort of fascinated attachment ever since I saw him in a white beard befogging that Scotch quack, but the marriage will tear my heartstrings, and it is asking too much—asking too much."

"I care but little for your Épernay vinegar-man in a beard. All I want is to set you in motion again. You need not return by way of Épernay, where your doings, as I have heard, were rather discreditable. We will go quite around by the north, taking Cologne and Brussels. Next Sunday you may be at home among your geography-books."

All I could obtain was a furlough till the next morning. Hohenfels wished to see Ehrenbreitstein. We took a carriage, rolled into Coblenz, and thence over the Rhine, crossing the bridge, to the mountain on which, in its new, bare strength, sits the stark fortress. Like the serpents in the cradle of a just-born Hercules, the Moselle and the Rhine wind in from the distance. Then we drove down again into the town, winding round and round the mountain as in the ascent, and so losing foot by foot the broad panorama of palace-studded plain. And then across the bridge once more, through the fashionable quarters of commonplace Coblenz, and back to our nest under Stolzenfels. Through the twinkling twilight-lamps of Capellen I now began to look out for Charles, at such an hour usually to be found, since his convalescence, supporting a street-corner, communing with his soul and staring at the donkeys. But not in street or doorway lurked Charles at this final hour of a final day. I found him, when I went to order his early attendance for the next morning, enthroned in the kitchen amid a symposium of maids and male nurses, freely distributing the sparkling Moselle that he had purchased himself, and absorbing gustily a good marrowy soup that Gredel had made in special honor of his departure.

"Call me at six, Charles," said I, "that we may get bright and early into Coblenz."

"Certainly, monsieur," replied the invalid, a monarch here in his own country. "What wine may I offer monsieur, that he may toast the ladies?"

The next morning, as a matter of course, it was I who woke up Charles, whom I found extinguished under his nightcap in his hospital-cot, dreaming the sweet dreams of innocence and Moselle. We took a sunrise review of good Doctor Elssasser and his agreeable family. The physician, his perpetually head-kerchiefed wife, Gredel (who had accepted my toast with piquant bashfulness), the honest gymnasts and acrobats who nursed the patients, had all aided me in one way or another, and gave me a pleasant hand-shake at departure. Even Blitz, the great bull-dog that kept the cabbage-garden and had looked on me at first as a natural enemy, relented and gave his paw.

We left Coblenz just as the morning-mists were rolling off the Broad Stone of Honor and the dewy lights and shadows chased each other along the Rhine-shores. There was a heavenly girl in the principal English party on deck, with a sweet veiled hat and admirably short skirts. But why do I mention her? Why mention Gredel? Hohenfels was beside me, guarding me with his motherly blue eye; and besides, had I not an enemy who made it a point to intercept me whenever a chance acquaintanceship with some lovely woman arrived at the point where it became interesting? Was there no Fortnoye in the air, hovering fatally between me and female beauty? Fortnoye would affront me had I the

THE AMATEUR BOAT-STEWARD.

mind to wive as abundantly as the Grand Turk. By reason of Fortnoye I shall die a bachelor, henpecked by my cook, and with constant threats of divorce even from her.

The last thing I noticed at Coblenz was the famous Russian pleasantry, which, as the only Russian joke I ever happened to meet with, has stuck in my mind. While Napoleon's army was on its way to conquer the kingdom of the Czars, the French mayor in occupation wrote on the fountain here a little braggart epigram, to the effect that this was a mere milestone on the way to the French province of Russia: after the Corsican's fall it was the turn of Russia to make epigrams, and the Czar's commandant in the city inscribed his name just beneath, like the *visé* on a passport, only biting it in deeply with the indelible pen of the stonecutter: "*Seen and approved by us*, Russian commandant in Coblenz." It was the eloquence of events that made the jest tell.

But just below lies the body of Hoche, whose audacious crossing of the Rhine under the very swords of the Austrians gives a real dignity to the French name hereabout. It is a little difficult to see the lustre of his reputation across the intolerable sulphurous splendor of Napoleon's, which obscures, as by the explosion of a volcano, the glories that

MUTUAL ESTEEM.

came immediately before him in date. Hoche, Marceau, Desaix, Kleber formed a worthy and noble group of standard-bearers who gave consideration and dignity to the first French republic. Of all their names, that of Hoche is perhaps the loftiest. It seems to make higher, by some hundreds of feet, the little truncated pyramid at whose base it is carved on the circular tumulus at Weissenthurm. The generals of the First Revolution were brave and devoted. But from out that earlier constellation one planet, at first unnoticed, rose and swelled and brightened so terribly, and cast such long-darted shadows on the earth below, and cut such chasms in heaven when it burst, that the cluster beyond it looked pale and poor, and thus hardly anybody conjures by or honors this bold young dawn-star lying where it fell beside the Rhine.

As we passed Weissenthurm I uncovered to the tomb of Hoche, as I felt that my exemplar, Franklin, would have done. Any one of those brave heroes would have been, with only opportunity given, a La Fayette, and his name been sung to glorious rest, night after night, by sweet lips all over the American continent. As I uncapped to the pyramid, Hohenfels chanted Becker's popular ode as a sort of challenge: "It never shall be France's, the free, the German Rhine!" I could not help muttering for my own part, upon that, the keen, taunting reply to Becker by Alfred de Musset, I have heard it rise from so many studios and cabarets, with the magnificent snarl in its chorus: "*Nous l'avons eu votre Rhin Allemand!*"

But we did not carry this conflict of national predilections too far. The lavish beauties of the route were constantly interposing themselves as harmonizing objects, and my own soul was busy strewing regrets and memories, like wreaths of immortelle, on every jutting corner of the way. At Andernach, as at Capellen and Coblenz and Salzig, I had precious reminiscences to cook and to serve, hot and hot, for the baron: "A century's rounded quarter lies between these scenes and my earliest familiarity with them, Hohenfels: it makes me feel, somehow, as if I were looking at everything at an angle of forty-five degrees. These places I saw in boyhood, as I was journeying to meet you in Heidelberg: their images lie for me, distinct and precious, at the

THE SLUMBER OF HEALTH.

end of all that swelling arc of time. Resuscitating them thus is like digging up the fabled treasures that lie at the bottom of the rainbow. From Salzig a fair boatwoman rowed me away down to Kamp, telling me the while a legend of Geraldine of the Liebenstein. At Cob- lenz I remember how I called to my servant, a fellow as universally and reliably ignorant as Charles, for the meaning of

COLOGNE: THE HOTEL DE VILLE.

the Man in the Kaufhaus. At Andernach I wondered over quaint stories of the wooden Christ that mended the leak in the roof of pious Frau Martha, and of the tower-keeper's daughter. Which are the true images, baron—the pictures of that olden time or those I enjoy with you to-day? The early ones almost seem the more real, for besides the fact that they were seen with the clearness of youth, they were crystallized and made tangible by being put into a book."

And I remembered, what I did not recall to my companion, that these first wanderings were undertaken in the horrible restlessness of having lost a dear friend, in the exile of a shattered home, and because, to use the old words, Paul Flemming "could no longer live alone where he had lived with her." Were the fair faces more lately encountered lost as irrevocably? To say nothing of pretty Gredel, was I to bid farewell also to Mary Ashburleigh and Francine?

So we made Bonn. Charles, in view of his sunstroke, was not allowed to show his nose above-decks. Hohenfels and I were about equally concerned for this burly invalid. Immediately on boarding the boat at Coblenz the baron had taken Charles firmly by the elbow and marched him down stairs into the mysterious region which in a steamer is divided off into saloons and baggage-bins: here, as the patient must not lack exercise, Hohenfels marched him conscientiously up and down. It was not the least droll of spectacles to see the baron achieving this sanitary duty, the natural aimlessness of his long legs increased by obstacles and by the throbbing of the engine — leading Charles blindly over mounds of baggage, plumping him up against dozens of waiters, cutting him with the edges of tables and delivering him upon plush divans. After thirty minutes of these delights he left the sick man to his devices and came up on deck to read poetry to me. A few minutes afterward, uneasy for Charles in my turn, I went down to see what had become of him. Knowing his modest instincts, I was hardly surprised to find that he was in neither saloon nor in among the baggage. But when the passages and byways of the boat had been searched without effect, down to the oily and coaly recesses oc-

THE ETERNAL RUBENS.

cupied by the engines and the fires, I began to be alarmed, and really feared that another delirium had sent my poor man over the ship's side. There was, however, a little lean-to chamber excavated under the stairs for the use of the chief cook, and here my master was discovered at last, perspiring and humming for contentment like a warm tea-kettle, occupied in scraping saucepans and rinsing dishes for the use of the stewards. He could not stand still doing nothing below-decks, he explained: he was not used to it.

I marched up stairs satisfied. Hohenfels was looking for me about the deck. "Apropos of Fortnoye, whom I scarcely know," said he, "have you written to him about this wedding? He appears to be a good fellow, and to appreciate my playing on the accordeon."

"You know I have not: I don't know his address in Épernay."

"You might have written in care of any of the champagne-merchants."

"I shall write when we three are snug at Marly. It is hardly worth while to try and establish a communication with him, when to avoid him we have taken all this détour. There is always plenty of time to write when it is a refusal you are sending."

"So you shall refuse?"

"I refuse absolutely. I would not delay my return to Marly by two hours to see your own wedding, my mediæval baron."

"You may be right, Flemming. At your age it is best not to frequent either weddings or interments: a spectator is so often persuaded by the force of example."

"My age? You know it: I am forty-eight."

"At least."

Arriving at Bonn, I haled Charles from his well, whence he came up glowing and candid, like Truth. His adieux with the cook were touching: never had he had such piles of plates to wipe, and his spirits rose with the occasion. He was brisk and active, mending visibly beneath our eyes. He took on himself, for the first time since his attack, the functions of service, and terribly incommoded the baron and myself by incessant and needless changes of our books, newspapers, glasses, etc. Finally, at Cologne, in the Hôtel de Hollande, I had the pleasure of seeing him sink into a cherubic, natural sleep in broad daylight—the sleep of utter weariness, content and health.

The Hollande is a convenient house, because it is just over the principal pier of the great bridge, and most of the life of the city comes pouring beneath your window like a stage-pageant. Crowds rush constantly to and fro, even as the allegorical beings who poured across the bridge of Mirza. Like Mirza's bridge, too, this causeway of fourteen hundred feet breaks open now and then with a sudden pitfall, into which no doubt an unwary passenger may tumble occasionally: the drawbridge is opened, that is to say, the driving crowds collect in desperation, and are often detained half an hour or more before the vessel passes and the lid is shut. But I cannot describe bridges and architecture. Let another try to get up a joke on the eleven thousand virgins who grin at St. Ursula from their shelves above the faces of the little school-girls kneeling there at confessional. I saw them, but I heeded not. The commissionnaire, who had been a

THE FIRST YOUNG MAN.

valet of Chevalier Bunsen's, remarked to me in English that Attila "put she's all in a carrt and meurrtrred she's." And I replied, "It would take an uncommon cart to hold her." The honest fellow bowed, not knowing that I meant Mary Ashburleigh. I dreamed of nothing but her, my own, my old, original best half. My love for her was ancient and gray, while her eidolon in my eyes was the achieved image of perfect youth. Could I ever have given Fortnoye reason to believe that I would be the groomsman of him and this paragon? Had she spoken of him to me as her intended husband, or extinguished in my breast by her behavior the fluttering hope that I might yet conquer a place in her regard?

I only remember how I was wearied with the eternal Rubens. That inexhaustible man was baptized though not born here, and, taking the names of St. Peter and St. Paul, devoted a great part of his life to celebrating their histories. He has endowed the church of St. Peter's with one of his acrobatic *chefs-d'œuvre*, and Hohenfels actually wanted me—me, a man with not only an Ashburleigh but a Francine upon my bosom!—to admire the impasto and appreciate the brio and befog myself in the chiaroscuro! Let no lover travel in Germany to soothe his heart-pain. The churches—which are exactly like the galleries—all offer you the same distractions: a Rubens, always, in my opinion, hung upside down — the martyrdom of St. Peter certainly is; and certain Dürers and Holbeins, esteemed more sacred in feeling than the Rubenses, simply because they are stiff and formal, but with no better glimpse of holy or any other sentiment than a signboard. In each of these places, when you have visited all the apparent curiosities, and paid your toll to the young man who has accom-

THE SECOND YOUNG MAN.

panied you, another young man, exactly like the first, springs fuming out of the ground, shakes some keys, and shows you a still more sacred Dürer or Holbein.

The second young man charges twice as much as the first young man. You now believe in the *doppelgänger*.

"Do you know," said I dreamily to Hohenfels, "that Agrippina was born here; that the ruins date from Claudius; that the cathedral was built by Satan, and that the Christians have never succeeded in finishing it; that the town-hall is a pompous Renaissance structure in

CHURCH OF THE HOLY APOSTLES AT COLOGNE.

which you see the busts of the Hanseatic commissioners all cast in iron; that Cologne provides breathing-places for its population to the extent of thirty-seven public squares—"

"I suppose, to nullify the seventy-two well-defined and several stinks; but even that gives us about two smells to a square, with only a couple of perfumes wanting. They ought to blow up the Farina establishments once a week, all the thirty of them, and flood the city with cosmetic water. But I, for my part," continued Hohenfels, "have been more exercised with the 'pavements fanged with murderous stones.' I have seen all the sights while you were watching the slumbers of Charles. I have seen St. Cunibert's, St. Pantaleon's, and the Holy Apostles'. I have seen the tablet on the birthplace of Rubens, who, it happens, was really born in Siegen. His patroness, Marie de Medicis, who gave him the biggest order he ever had in his life at the time

she was adorning the Luxembourg, came hither to die—in a garret, they say. I have been looking up the scene of her death, and I went to the cathedral to see the slab under which lies that stiff and self-asserting heart which sustained the widow so long in a perpetual duel with Richelieu."

"I admire a stout-hearted widow of all things. You may go on, Hohenfels."

"Marie de Medicis," pursued the baron, "was rather hard-hearted than stout-hearted, I fancy—like one of the mothers-in-law you find in Thackeray. On the French coins of her regency she has thin lips, and a pinched nose that looks as if it were red. However, the unfortunate soul had her troubles, and crept about through England and Holland telling the rulers that she was a widow who had seen better days."

"Poor queen!" said I—"poor Ariadne! Go on, my dear Hohenfels. Did they not find her a Dionysos and an apotheosis?"

"It appears they only found her a garret. Her apotheosis had been painted by Rubens. And I *will* go on, an it please you. If you recollect, Flemming, when we were lads and you wrote a book about us, you gave yourself all the eloquent speeches. Now that we are grown, and are simply talking for conversation, I mean to take my fling."

"It was only because you were such a pump, Hohenfels. Where I talked pages you talked oceans. If I had undertaken to report you, I should have written a library instead of a book."

"I went to see the slab that covers her heart, F l e m m i n g. While I looked a poor match-girl entered the cathedral, set down her sulphurous b a s k e t on the heart of Marie de Medicis, said a prayer or two, and went out a b s o l v e d. The interior was thronged with C h r i s t's poor. The scene was a rare one, Paul. I looked around me in the golden altar-lights. I thought I was in a forest — a forest at sunset. The choir was almost filled with rising incense, touched with the yellow flare of the tapers, and it seemed through the columns like a vista into the clouds. The grand stems of the arcades rose thickly crowded, only they fell into a natural order and alignment like the trunks of pines: overhead they rolled to meet each other, breaking out everywhere into stiff, thick-set needles and tufts of Gothic - work. Vast patches and shields of prismatic hues lay rounded against their mighty cylinders. But this forest was not a solitude: it was crowded with speechless figures, thick as thoughts. And it was not silent, or simply whisper-haunted, like the real woods. It was all inflated and swelled and dazzled and broken with pomps of organ-music that almost overcame the heart, and made the pillars seem to reel and the painted windows to rock in the Jove-like storm. The beauty of the cathedral is that it is not finished.

INCOMPLETE GREATNESS.

A Gothic church ought to be ever growing, like the branching laces of the forest. If a day should come when we could say, It is done, why, then we would seem to say, It is dead. And that is just the difference between the cathedral and the basilica. The Northern architecture has in it the forest's life and its voice. The Italian basilica, an immense cube with a triangular pediment, is fixed like a crystal, and if it is not finished it is unmeaning. Your basilica, founded on the old Roman law-court, is something arrested and positive. Your cathedral, founded on old primitive woodland rites, I suppose—what *is* the Gothic founded on, Paul?—is full of aspiration and unachieved desires. The former is Authority—the latter, Love."

This lecture of the baron's, which I cannot be accused of cheapening in the recital, occupied us till dusk, and I felt it incumbent on myself, as Charles's body-servant, to return and see how that worthy was getting on. He was found at a window overlooking the bridge, a bowl on his knee containing his second supper, and his eyes fixed on a cart that was going across to Deutz filled with lambs tied together—the poor little involuntary criminals! The observation made by Charles was that the nourishment in this hotel was very good, and that he feared he should not be able to leave before morning.

I was burning to attain Marly, where I meant, in the security of home, to make a full confidant and fellow-plotter of Hohenfels, as yet very imperfectly acquainted with my heart-history in relation to the Dark Ladye. We filled in the evening with a concert, where the involutions of Wagner's compositions allowed me to dream undisturbed, as you may beneath a headless and tailless sermon. The most comprehensible *morceau* was the *Adelaïde*, grandly sung by an eminent tenor, but I spoiled it in the hearing, for into its noble polysyllabic continuity I was ever trying to fit the two soft accents of "Mary."

PART XIX.

TYING UP THE CLEWS.

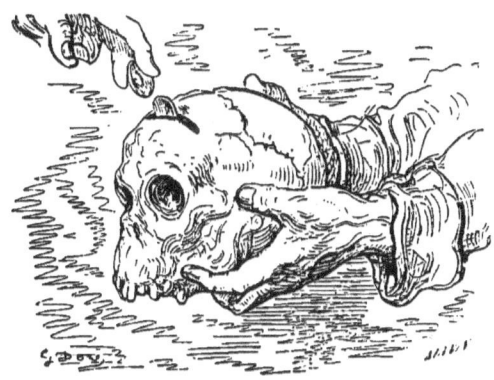

CÆSAR'S PENNY.

IN leaving Cologne for Aix-la-Chapelle you turn your back to the river—a particular which suited my mood well enough. The railway bore us away from the Rhine-shore at an abrupt angle, and in my notion the noble Germanic goddess or image seemed at this point to recede with grand theatric strides, like a divinity of the stage backing away from her admirers over the billowy whirlpool of her own skirts. As I dreamed we penetrated the tunnel of Königsdorf, which is fifteen hundred yards long, and which seemed to me sufficiently protracted to contain the slumber of Barbarossa. The thought gave me a useful hint, and I fell into a light sleep, while Charles and Hohenfels pervaded the darkness merely by their perfumes — the former with whiffs at a concealed bottle of Farina, the latter with a pastille counterfeiting the incense of the cathedral. In a couple of hours from the Hôtel de Hollande we reached Aachen, as the fond natives call the burgh so dear to Charlemagne. Deprived of that mag-

251

nificent mirror, the Rhine, the pretty towns throughout this part of Germany seem but like country belles. We should hardly have paused at Aix but for the sake of affording a rest to Charles, who grew worse whenever lunch-time competed with railway-time. As for the dull little city, for us it was a wilderness, with the blank cleanliness of the desert, except in so far as it was informed and populated by the memory of Charlemagne.

Here he died, and entered his tomb in the church himself had founded. Into this sepulchre the emperor Otho III. dared to penetrate in the year 997, impelled by a motive of vile and varlet-like curiosity. They say the dead monarch confronted his living visitor in the great marble chair in which he had been seated at his own command, haughty and inflexible as in life, the ivory sceptre in his ivory fingers, his white skull crowned with the diadem of gold. The peeping emperor looked upon him with awe, half afraid of the mysterious and penetrating shadows that reached forth out of his rayless eyes. Before he left, however, he peered about, touched the sceptre and the throne, fingered this and that, and having, as it were, trimmed the nails and combed the beard of the great spectre, retired with a valet's bow. Observing that Charlemagne had lost most of his nose, he caused it to be replaced in gold very delicately chiseled and enchased. The sacrilege was repeated by Frederick Barbarossa in 1165, who went farther and forced Charlemagne to get up from his chair before him. The corpse, in rising, fell in pieces, which have been dispersed through Europe as relics. We saw such of them as remain here at the Chapelle. I was allowed, for about the equivalent of an American dollar, to measure the Occidental emperor's leg—they call it his arm. And then, as a makeweight in the bargain, the venal sacristan placed in my hands the head of Charlemagne.

I thought Hohenfels would have sunk to the ground with disgust. He colored deeply and dragged me into the air. "I am ashamed of every drop of German blood in my veins," he cried. "What are we to think of the commerce of these wretches, for whom the very wounds of Cæsar are the lips of a money-box?"

I had given back the skull, as Hamlet returns the skull of Yorick to the gravedigger, and was dusting my fingers with a handkerchief, as hundreds of Hamlets have dusted theirs. I said, "'Thrift, thrift, Horatio.'"

"At Kreutzberg there are twenty monks on the counter! This morning, at St. Ursula's, it was the eleven thousand virgins, their skulls ranged like Dutch cheeses above our heads or in rows around the walls, with a battery-full of them in the neighboring apartment, like a cheesemonger's reserved magazine.

THE THRONED CORPSE.

Here, the very leader of modern ideas, the creator of our form of civilization, is shown for so many pennies to any grocer who wants to weigh the head of a king! Profanation! Barbarians! Philistines!"

I turned rather hastily, while my hands were yet clammy with the skull, thinking that this accusation of Philistinism was aimed at me. But Hohenfels thought of nothing less than of a personality, being in his cloudiest mood of generalization. So I only concealed the handkerchief, while I said, as easily as I might, "You need not accuse your German blood, for I have lived long enough in my American's Paradise to know that civilized Paris is considerably worse in this particular respect, with the addition of a certain goblin levity particularly French. How often have I seen babies frightened by the skulls in the dentists' windows, with their cynical chewing action! It is said that a child sat next a dentist's apprentice once in an omnibus, and was observed to turn rigid, fixed and white, but unable to speak: he had sat on one of these skulls, and it had bitten him. Silver-mounted skulls set as goblets, in imitation of Byron, are to be seen at any of the china-shops rubbing against the chaste cheeks of the old maid's teacup. Skeletons are sold, bleached and with gilded hinges, to the medical students, who buy the pale horrors as openly as meerschaum pipes. Have I not often found young Grandstone supping among his doctors' apprentices of the Ober restaurant after theatre-hours, a skeleton in the corner filled with umbrellas like a hall-rack, and crowned with the triple or quintuple tiara of the girls' best bonnets? Ay, Mimi Pinson's cap has known what it is to perch on the bony head of Death. The juxtaposition is but an emblem. The sewing-girl, like Hood's shirtmaker, scarcely fears the 'phantom of grisly bone.' Poor Francine! where have you

THE SKELETON IN ARMOR.

taken *your* artisanne's cap to, I wonder? Are you left alone, all alone again, and thinking of the pretty solitude you have left behind you at Carlsruhe? Who uses those polished keys now?"

Hohenfels interrupted me, complaining that my monologue was uninteresting and diffuse, and was interfering with the railway time-table. But I finished it in the car: "And the railway! What has a person of fixed and independent habits to do with railways but to growl at them? Before I was tempted upon the railway by that impertinent engineer at Noisy, I got up and sat down when I liked, ate wholesome food at my own hours, and was contented at home. Confusion to him who made me the victim of his engineering calculations! Confusion to Grandstone and his nest of serpents at Épernay! Did they not introduce me to Fortnoye, who has doubly destroyed my peace? Where are the conspirators, that I may pulverize them with my maledictions?"

This question—which Hohenfels called peevish as he buried himself in his book

BRUSSELS.

—was not answered until we had passed Verviers, Chaudfontaine and Liège. I was aroused from a sulky slumber in the station at Brussels by Hohenfels, who said, in his musical scolding way, like the busy wheeze of a clicking music-box, "You may say what you like, with your left-handed flatteries, in regard to Fortnoye, and you may praise Ariadnes and widows to the end of the chapter. You are sorry at this moment not to be at Épernay to see the destroyer of your peace married: you had rather assist at the making of a wife than at the making of a widow."

I was just sending Fortnoye to the gloomiest shades of Acheron when a strong hand entered the carriage-door, helped me handsomely down the steps, and then began warmly to shake my own. Fortnoye!—Fortnoye in flesh and blood was before me. While my mouth was yet filled with maledictions he began to pour out a storm of thanks with all his own particular warmth, expressing the most effusive gratitude for the trouble I had taken in forsaking my route to be his wife's bridesmaid. That is what he called it. "She has but one other," said Fortnoye. At the same time I began to recognize other faces not unknown to me, crudely illuminated by the raw colors of the railway-lights. They all had black wedding-suits and enormous buttonhole nosegays of orange-flowers. I picked them out, with a particular recognition for each: 'twas the civil engineer of Noisy; the short gentleman named Somerard; James Athanasius Grandstone, with his saintly aureole upon him in the shape of a Yankee wide-awake; the nameless mutes, or rather chorus, of the champagne-crypt; in short, my nest of serpents in all its integrity. Still entangled with my slumbers, I hesitated to respond to the friendly hands that were everywhere thrust centripetally toward me.

I looked blackly at Hohenfels. He was chuckling.

At Heidelberg, making the acquaintance of M. Fortnoye contemporaneously with my departure, he had become more enthralled than he ever confessed to this radiant traveler — whom he called a packman, but regarded as a Mercury—and his pretty scheme of matrimony in motion. Even now, if I can believe my eyes, he goes up to the "vintner" and "peddler" of his objurgations, and meekly whispers into his ear with the air of a conspirator reporting a plot to his chief. Having engaged to produce me at the wedding of Fortnoye, and finding me unexpectedly recusant, he had adopted a little stratagem for bringing me to the scene while thinking to escape from it.

"Thou too, Brutus!" I said, and gave it up. It only remained for me to return all round, after five minutes of petrified stupidity, the hand-grasps that had been offered from every quarter of the compass-box.

Next morning, at an early hour, I was interrupted by a knock, just as Charles had buttoned my gaiters and the young man from the perruquier's (who had stolen in with that air of delicacy and of almost literary refinement which belongs to his gentle profession) had lathered me. A nick he gave my chin at the shock made my countenance all argent and gules, and the visitor entering saw me thus emblazoned, while the barber and Charles, "like two wild men supporters of a shield," could only stare at the untimely apparition.

"Do you know him, Charles?" I asked, not recognizing my guest, and putting over my painted face a mask of wet toweling.

"I know him intimately," replied my jester-in-ordinary: "I would thank Monsieur Paul just to tell me his name. Do you remember, monsieur, a sort of beggar, with a wagon and a stylish horse and a pretty wife, who limped a bit with his right hand, or perhaps his left hand? Does monsieur know what I mean? He used to come and see us at Passy; and monsieur even had some traffic with him in a little matter of two chickens."

"Father Joliet!" I cried.

"Present!" shouted the personage thus designated at my appeal to his name. I turned round, toweled, and he grasped my hands. The unusual hour, appropriate as I supposed only to some porter or other stipendiary visitor of my hotel, caused to shine out with startling refulgence the morning splendors in which Papa Joliet had arrayed himself. He wore a courtly dress, appropriate to the

PERRUQUIER.

most formal possible ceremony; his black suit was glossy; his hat was glossy; his varnished pumps were more than glossy —they were phosphorescent. Gloves only were wanting to his honest hands.

Soaped, napkined and generally extinguished, I could only stammer, "You here in Brussels? What a droll meeting!"

"Wherefore droll?" asked Joliet, with a huge surprise, which lasted him all through his next sentence. "I come here to marry my daughter. Everything is ready; we count on your presence at the wedding; the lawyer has drawn up the contract; and the breakfast is now cooking at the best restaurant in the place."

"Francine's wedding, my dear Joliet!" I exclaimed. And, going back to my apprehensions at her furtive disappearance from Carlsruhe, and to my conjectures of some amorous mystery between her and her Yankee traducer, Kraaniff, I added gravely, " It is very creditable!"

"How, creditable—and droll?" repeated the honest man, evidently much surprised at my own accumulating surprises. "Did not you hear?"

"Not the faintest word," I said, "but I am none the less gratified to find this

FATHER JOLIET.

affair ending, as it should, in the presence of a lawyer. As for your wedding-invitation, my good friend, you are a little tardy in delivering it, for it is exactly to-day that I am obliged to attend at the marriage of one of my friends, M. Fortnoye."

"Ah, that is a good joke!" cried Joliet, breaking into an explosion of laughter and clapping me pleasantly on the shoulder—an action which caused a slight frown on the part of Charles. "You always would have your jest, Monsieur the American! Tease me and scare me as much as you like: I like these hoaxes better before a wedding than after. Hold that," he added, extending his hand as if it were a piece of merchandise.

I "held" it, and he went on, dwelling slowly on his words: "If you are at Henri Fortnoye's wedding you will be at Francine Joliet's also, for both of these persons are to be married at one church."

"Impossible!" I exclaimed, dropping the hand and stepping back.

"What! again?" said Joliet, his manly face visibly darkening. "Droll! and creditable! and impossible! Why impossible?" Then he dropped his head and looked angrily at the floor. "Ah, yes, even you," he said, his eyes still fixed on the boards, "believed that a French girl, trained as French girls are trained, would flirt and expose herself to remark; and all on account of such a man as your compatriot, the other American! Well! well! you ought to know your countrymen best."

"I know of no harm," I interposed hastily. "I should always have thought Kraaniff hard to swallow as a mere matter of taste. I can but recollect, Father Joliet," I went on more seriously, "that the last time I met you you begged me not to talk of Francine if I would not break your heart. I have to add to this the news brought me from Heidelberg, that this Kraaniff was a serpent who had fascinated some young girl for an approaching meal. — How dare you, Charles," I cried suddenly, recalled to the consciousness of his presence by this souvenir of his oratory, "stand here staring? Show the young man out directly, and pay him."

I will not answer for Charles's having got much farther away than the door. Joliet continued: "But his aunt knows him now for what he is. Kraaniff, say you? I call him Kranich, though he had better change his baptismal record

THE CATECHISM.

than disgrace one of the best names in Brussels."

"Frau Kranich, then, my old friend, is really his aunt?"

"Madame Kranich, whom I have

known in your parlor, is really Francine's godmother. Did you never know of all her secret kindness? That rigid lady would commit a perjury to deny one of her own good actions. Young Kranich has written her a letter confessing his lies. Don't you know? The very same day when you were determined to fight him in a duel—"

"Certainly, certainly," I said, a little confused. "We will change the subject and leave my ferocity alone. Let us understand one another. In regard to Fortnoye's marriage, was there not some talk of a Madame Ashburleigh?"

"I believe you. Madame Ashburleigh is the very key of the manœuvre. Madame Ashburleigh—don't you perceive?—lost a child."

"For that matter, she has lost four. I know the lady confidentially, and she told me their histories and present address. Lucia lies in Glasgow, Hannibal at Nice, and Waterloo sleeps somewhere hereabout, as well as another nameless little dear."

"She is a good woman. She has collected all her proofs, and has come hither with them voluntarily—has perhaps already arrived. Brussels, where two of her marmots rest, is one of her most frequent stations. That censorious Madame Kranich made a scene, but she had to yield to conviction."

"A censorious Madame Kranich! Is the young duelist married?"

"What? No, no! It is Francine's guardian I speak of. Of late years she has become a sort of Puritan abbess, seeking the Protestant society which abounds in Belgium, and lamenting her husband, whom they say she used to drug with opium."

"Then is she not Kranich's aunt?"

"Oh yes, an aunt by marriage; but he is not her nephew: I will die before I call him so."

"Listen," said I, "Father Joliet. You are as full of information as an oracle, but you are not coherent. This month past I have been hunting down a chimæra, a hydra with a dozen heads: each head shows me by turn the portrait of Fortnoye, or Francine, or yourself, or Kranich, or Mrs. Ashburleigh. Ever since Noisy I have been meandering through the folds of a mystery. My

FRAU KRANICH.

head is turning with it. If you want to save me from distraction, sit down in this chair and answer me a long catechism, without saying a word but in reply to my questions."

"I am sure I talk as plain as a professor. Look! You frightened me at first with your doubts and your impossibilities. You have only to make Kranich's aunt agree with Francine's guardian, and at the same time forgive Francine's husband for having assumed the undertaker's bill for Madame Ashburleigh's baby."

"Yes, yes, my dear Joliet, you are clearer than Euclid." And I administered a category of questions. Joliet, with his fatherly joy bursting out of him in the longest of parentheses, kept quiet in his refulgent shoes and answered as well as he could.

Francine, he protested, had never beer

a flirt (I have met no Frenchmen who were ignorant of that one English word, to which they give a new value by pronouncing it in a very orotund manner, as *flort*). When she came to be ten

"TO MY ARMS."

or twelve, Frau Kranich—until then a well-preserved lioness with an appetite for society—ceased to give her dolls and promised to give her an education. At the same time, the banker's widow left Paris, and repaired with her charge to Brussels, where the little girl received some good half-Jesuitical, half-English schooling, of the kind suggested in the Brontë novels. Her diploma attained, Francine begged to accompany her English teacher back to London: she wished to become a *meess*, she said, and be competent to teach like a new Hypatia. She had hardly bidden her kind protectress adieu when Frau Kranich's nephew arrived at Brussels, exceedingly dissatisfied with his American business in the barrooms of the grand duke of Mississippi. A sordid jealousy of Mademoiselle Joliet's claims upon his aunt took possession of this prudent spirit. He took up a watch-post at a university town on the Rhine. He began to whisper vague exaggerations of her coquetries and liveliness, which the Protestant circle that revolved about Madame Kranich did not fail to bear in to her. This lady admired her nephew, sure that his want of manners was the sign of a noble frankness. She wrote to Francine, bidding her come immediately from London. The girl not replying, the hopeful nephew was put upon her track. He went away. His letters from England reported that Francine was no longer in that country, but was probably come back to Belgium. "I know not in what suburb of Brussels our very independent miss may this instant be hiding," he wrote.

About the same time, in the circle of French exiles at Brussels, a young *romantique* named Fortnoye was reported as weeping and lavishing statues over the grave of an unknown infant in the churchyard at Laaken. It was a delicious mystery. Kind meddlers approached the sexton, who said that all he knew of the babe's mother was that she was a beautiful lady from London. Kranich carried the story dutifully to his aunt, adding his own ingenious surmise: "Can Francine have become sufficiently Anglicised to contract secret marriages with roving revolutionists, and scamper about the country with ardent young Frenchmen in the style of Gretna Green?" In fact, it was really from London that Mrs. Ashburleigh was proceeding, for the purpose of taking care, in the Rhenish city where he was dying, of her handsome, dissipated, worthless husband. Taken suddenly ill at Brussels, she left her infant to the unequaled chill of a strange, unknown cemetery, hastening thence with tears and despair to the bedside where duty called her.

Has my reader forgotten the dim, tear-swollen story which I heard—not at all improved in the telling—from my generous young friend Grandstone—how an impulsive Frenchman had laid to rest, in flowers and evergreens, the unnamed baby of a woman he had never seen? Jealous as I was of Fortnoye, I never could think without tenderness of this singular action. To make the tomb of this helpless Innocence the young man braved the curiosity of his comrades—despised the rumor, the obloquy, and, hardest of all, the jests. Well has the wise dramatist decided that Ophelia must needs be laid in Yorick's bed!

Poor Francine, gay, frivolous, innocently vain of her little travesty of English behavior, found her accomplishments and graces received by her guardian's circle with incomprehensible coldness. Hurt and humiliated, she asked to pay a visit to her father. The honest rustic received her with a miserable confusion of doubt and severity, for her escapade to England had never pleased him, and her return from her godmother's home wore to him the air of a repudiation. At her father's house, however, she was discovered by Fortnoye, who had never heard the ingenious Kranich's theory of his own private wedding with Francine, and who thought to find in her the veiled unknown of the cemetery. He saw for the first time, in the flowery home at Noisy, that fresh ingenuous beauty, a little overcast with disappointment. His generous nature was touched; and, with his talent for administration and planning, he conceived the idea of establishing Francine in the pretty bird's nest at Carlsruhe, distant alike from the strongholds of her calumniators, Belgium and France.

Fortnoye now had an object in life. "There is a very young person in the cemetery of Laaken who is much in need of a chaperone," he said. The frank proofs of his own relations with this churchyard would not only do credit to his own reputation, but would gratify the best friends of Mademoiselle Joliet and at least one other lady. To attain these proofs he had to step over the coiling, writhing bodies of a whole nest of rumors. When he seized by the throat the especial slander that he himself was the husband of the babe's mother, he found written on its crest the signature of John Kranich. He sought the aunt. This lady gave him several interviews, the Lutheran prayer-book for ever in her hand. "Why does the dear girl not come to me?" she would say, weeping, but she refused to hear a word against her precious nephew, the personification of bluff frankness. As if to make crushing him impossible, young Kranich had now withdrawn to America, leaving his reputation in that best possible protection,

THE FUTURE OF FFARINA.

the chivalry that is extended toward the absent. Fortnoye was baffled. "I will ask the baby at its tomb for its mother's and father's name," he cried. In the pretty God's Acre he found a fresh harvest of flowers and a new statue over the well-known grave. It was a pretty miniature of Thorwaldsen's Psyche, on which the proud copyist had inscribed his name. A respectful correspondence with Mrs. Ashburleigh, to whom he was guided by the sculptor, and who was now taking the waters at Wildbad, soon put the whole tangled story to rights. Fortnoye had the happiness of conducting Francine, by this time his affianced wife, to the good Frau Kranich, who, convinced that she had wrongly judged her, threw her arms ardently around her recovered jewel, letting the eternal little book fly from her hand like a projectile.

"But the most singular part of the story," concluded Father Joliet, "is the letter which Fortnoye, after two or three quarrels, forced out of young Kranich when the latter had returned to Europe, full of triumph and debts, to take possession of his aunt for the rest of his life. Here it is," added the good man, opening a pocket-book. "The handwriting is drunken, but the sense is clear as Seltzer-water. The scholars tell me *in vino veritas est*, but it appears to me that truth really comes out in the repentance and headache that follow."

"My dear Aunt" (ran the letter which Charles had seen forced from the alligator after his unlucky game of dominoes):

"You have known me as the soul of candor. It is this happy quality which compels me to state (for I am something of a Rousseau) that if I ever playfully accused your pretty pet Francine of being a flirt, I knew nothing about it. The best proof is that she absolutely refused to join her expectations with mine, though I am something of an Adonis. If you believed that she and the wine-peddler had made a match, I pity your credulity and ignorance of human nature. I am certain that neither the peddler nor myself would touch the enterprise until you had shown exactly what you would (pecuniarily) do. For my part, I have act-

HOHENFELS' FAILURE.

ed throughout on the most exact and advanced scientific principles. Intending to modify the spirit-trade in America, and especially to introduce the exclusive agency of the Farina essences, I found that the sinew particularly needed for this leap was capital. Desiring to absorb your bounties toward Francine, I at first proposed matrimony. This offer was made without any enmity toward the girl, as my next move was without affection, though it seems to be resulting to her benefit. I became her accuser as coolly as I had been her lover. Passion has nothing to do with the combinations of strategic genius: I am something of a Washington. My theory of her clandestine marriage was one of the most masterly fictions of the age—a plot worthy of Thackeray. If I could have succeeded in mutilating the statue in the grave-

yard, I might have carried it, while you would have admired my act of iconoclasm with all your Puritan nature. In the momentary abandonment of my plans, owing to the machinations of my enemies, you will conceive that I am not very rich. My college-debts and other expenses I am obliged to leave for your kind attention. The main point of this letter, which M. Fortnoye has persuaded me to set down as distinctly as in my present feeble state I can, is that Francine is a pretty little maid who has never passed by Gretna Green. There! that is my *credo*, and I will subscribe to it,

"Your loving nephew, John.

"P. S. Address, with such an enclosure as your generosity will prompt, Jean K. Ffarina, sole representative and cosmetical chemist in America on behalf of the Farinas of Cologne, at New Orleans, where I am going to beat my adversaries like Old Hic—"

At this point the tipsy scrawl became illegible. "This is not a very handsome apology. Did Fortnoye accept it?" I asked, turning over the clammy and malodorous epistle. At this inquiry the crack of the door widened and Charles appeared, on fire with enthusiasm, and so possessed with self-importance that he forgot the betrayal of his indiscretion.

"I can reply to that question," said Charles. "When M. Fortnoye received the paper from the duelist he read it over and said, 'You have meant to impose on me, monsieur, with an incomplete confession. But, in return for your imperfect restoration of Mademoiselle Joliet's portrait, you have unconsciously set d o w n such a masterpiece of yourself that I am certain your aunt will see you as she never did before.'"

Charles, having thus added himself to our cabal without rebuke, took a lively interest in what followed. The proud father continued: "My son-in-law, after some business preliminaries, wrote me a handsome letter demanding what he had already effectively possessed himself of. I wrote to Francine, already returned to her duties, to be a good girl and make her husband obey her in all things."

"That may have been," said I, "what made Francine take to laughing all day and all night, as I heard she did some little time after my departure from her house. The next news of her," I pursued, "was that she had been spirited away by some sly old kidnapper. I almost suspected Kranich."

"The old kidnapper," said Joliet, laughing heartily at the compliment, "is the man now talking to you. I wanted to take Francine to her godmother. I turned the key in the door at Carlsruhe, set the geographers all upon their travels to explore new worlds, and we have been living ever since quite close to Madame Kranich, who treats me like an emperor."

It was easy now to understand why the young Kranich, as soon as he could identify me as a protector of Francine, had been thrown off his guard and tempted to attack me with his clumsy abuse.

READING THE CONTRACT.

It was not very mysterious, even, why he had wished all handsome girls to be drowned in the Rhine. For him a pretty damsel was simply a rival in trade.

Had I stopped at Wildbad with the party of orpheonists, I should have encountered rather sooner the fatal beauties of Mary Ashburleigh. It was to meet her that Fortnoye had paused at that resort, considering her introduction to Frau Kranich almost indispensable to the success of his scheme. She had no hesitation in following the protecting angel of her lost child. "My object in this journey is a happy marriage," she had told me when to my unworthy care her guardianship had been transferred. If I timorously suspected the marriage to be her own, whose fault was it but mine? My heart leaped up at the successive stages of this recital, its hopes confirmed by every additional fact: the Dark Ladye's hand was certainly free. Fortnoye, I should surmise, was not too

INTERRUPTED REPOSE.

desirous to abandon this magnificent companion at Schwetzingen; but the serpent, he knew, was left behind, in company with two or three of his and my friends: it was necessary to take the youth by the ear, as it were, and dismiss him from the country, without loss of time, to his future of counter-jumping. His dueling experience may be of some use to him among the bowie-knives of Louisiana. If his subsequent path is not strewn with roses, let him rejoice that it is at least lubricated with cologne-water.

An hour had passed, and into my room from his own adjoining one now ambled amicably my friend the baron. He greeted Joliet as an old friend. Many a smoking-match had they had in my garden at Marly. But Hohenfels this morning was in robes of state, with shoes that shone even beside old Father Joliet's, and as a concession to elegance he had abandoned his cavernous pipes in favor of cigarettes. A scroll of this description, flavored with his Cologne pastille and very badly rolled, was trying to exhale itself between his lips.

"What a genius for conversation you have to-day, my Flemming! This hour I have rocked back and forth in bed, trying to understand your observations or to cover my ears and go to rest. Your tongue has been like the tongue of a monastery-bell summoning all hands to penance." But I had hardly spoken ten consecutive words. The ears of the baron were this morning quite muffled, I think, with the abundance of his hair, which he had evidently been dressing with an avalanche of soap and water, for the topknot was as harsh and tight as a felt. He had lemon-blossoms on his lappel and lemon kids on his fists.

It was then I remembered that my bags were all in the steamer, where I had left them when surprised by Charles's indisposition. My tin box would possibly yield me a button-nosegay, but otherwise I might beat my breast, like the wedding-guest in the *Ancient Mariner*, for I heard the summons and was unable to attend in right attire. "We two must take you out in the street and dress you," said Hohenfels.

Although I had never been dressed in the street, I yielded. It was a grand public holiday, and the sounds of festivity, which had floated into my chamber with the entrance of Hohenfels, were in full cadence outside. Everybody was pouring out to the city-gate, or returning from thence, where, in honor of some visit from the king of the Belgians and count and countess of Flanders, a festival was going on in imitation or rehearsal of the grand annual *kermesse*. These festivals, retained in Belgium with a delightful fidelity to the customs of antique Brabant, would fit the brush of Teniers better than the pen of a mere bewildered tourist. Still, I will try, copying principally from the reports of Charles (who contrives to peep at everything, with an interest whose amount is in ratio with the square of his distance from his master), to give a few features of the scene, which he spread in detail before the attentive Josephine during many an evening after.

The principal fair-ground—though the

COATS vs. COATS.

occasion crammed the whole city with revelers—was just outside the gate. It was a veritable town in miniature, with a pattern of checker-board streets—Columbine street, Polichinelle street, Avenue des Parades, Place des Parades, Street of the Chanson, and the like. There were more than five hundred booths, all numbered—shops and restaurants. There were the Salon Curtius, the Ménagerie Bidel, the Bal Mabille, the Café Bataclan, the American Tavern. From one of the little costumers' shops, Charles—with a higher evincement of antiquarian taste than I should have expected—managed to bear away a pattern of wall-paper, which I afterward conferred on Mary Ashburleigh with great applause: it was Parisian of 1824, the epoch of Charles Dix, and was entirely covered with giraffes in honor of that puissant and elegant monarch. The above establishments were near the entrance, to the right.

At the left were more attractions: another menagerie, a heap of ostensible gold representing the five milliards paid by France, a gallery of astonished wax soldiers representing the Franco-Prussian war, a cook-shop with "mythologic" confectionery. Farther on, in the Théâtre Casti, was exposed the "renowned buffoon Peppino," breveted by His Majesty the "king of Egypt;" then came the Chiarini Theatre; then the Théâtre Adrien Delille, an enchantingly pretty structure, where receptions were given by a little creature who should have sat under a microscope: she was "the Princess Felicia, aged thirteen, born at Clotat, near Marseilles, weighing three kilogrammes and measuring forty-six centimètres—a ravishing figure, admirably proportioned in her littleness and *tout à fait sympathique*."

The announcements were heard, it was thought by Charles, to the very centre of the city. A low-browed animal with rasped hair was shouting, "Messieurs and ladies, come and see—come and see the theatre of the galleys! The only one in the world! This is the place to view the real instruments of torture used on the prisoners—chains four yards long and balls of thirty-five pounds. All authentic, gentlemen and ladies. You will see the poisoners of Marseilles, Grosjon who killed his father, Madame Cottin

THE JESTER AT THE FEAST.

who ate her baby. Come in, come in, gentlemen and ladies! Fifteen centimes! 'Tis given away! You enter and go out when you like. Come in! It is educational: you see vice and crime depicted on the faces of the criminals!"

In another place a malicious Flemish Figaro explained the analogy betwen *een spinnekop* and *eene meisie*, the perspiration streaming over his face; and my ancient minnesinger's blood stirred within me at the report of the pleasantries which were improvised by this Rabelais of the people, and I remembered that I too was a Flemming.

The bands belonging to the different booths tried to play each other down, forming a stupefying charivari, with tributary processions that quite overflowed the city. The house of "confections" yielded me no broadcloth of a cut or dimension suitable to my figure. But my two friends chose me a hat, a light paletot (my second purchase in that sort on this eventful journey), a scented cambric handkerchief, a rosebud, and a snowy waistcoat, in which, as in a whited sepulchre, I concealed the decay of my toilet. These changes were judged to be sufficient for my accoutrement. They might have done very well, but on my way back I paused at a lace-shop window to inspect some present for Francine. A band, with many banners and figures in masquerade, swept past, followed by a shouting crowd. My friends lost me in a moment, and I lost my way. I turned into a street which I was sure led to the

ST. GUDULE, BRUSSELS.

hotel, gave it up for another, lost that in a blind alley, and finally brought up in a steep, narrow cañon, where I was forced to ask a direction. The passer-by who obliged me was a man bearing a bag of charcoal. He answered with a ready intelligence that did honor to his heart and his sense of Progressive Geography. But he left on my white waistcoat, alas! a charcoal sketch, full of chiaroscuro and *coloris*, representing his index-finger surrounded with a sort of cloud-effect. My waistcoat had to be given over in favor of the elder garment buttoned up in the all-concealing overcoat.

The ceremonies of the day, I soon found, were to consist in an early and informal breakfast at the house of Frau Kranich; then the civil wedding at the mayor's office, followed by the usual church-service, from which the Protestant godmother of Francine begged to be excused; the day to wind up with a general dinner at a place of resort outside the city at four o'clock, the usual dining-hour in old Brabant.

The early breakfast gave a renewal of my friendship with good Frau Kranich and a glimpse of the bride, with her sweet, patient, dewy face shadowed like a honey-drop in the gauzy calyx of her artisanne cap; for she was in the simplest of morning dresses — something gray, with a clean white apron. The quaint, old-fashioned house where we met was decorated with exquisite trifles, the memorials of the mistress's old fashionable taste, but scattered over the tables also were lecture programmes, hospital reports and photographs of eminent philosophers. As I took up for a plaything a gold pen-case, well used, which rested on a magnificent old fan, the Kranich said, with just a reminiscence of her former vivacity, "You find me much changed, Mr. Flemming. I used to be the grasshopper in the fable—now I am the ant."

"I bless any change, ma'am," said I, "which increases your kindness toward this charming girl."

"Dear Mr. Flemming," said pretty Francine, "how nice and shabby you look! You will do admirably to stand by a poor girl—so poor that she has hardly a bridesmaid. I hope you are as indigent as you were at Carlsruhe." Upon this I felt very fatherly, and clasped her waist from behind as I kissed her forehead.

The lawyer, a professionally bland old man, with a porous bald head like an emu's egg, said as he was introduced, "Ah, I have heard of you before, monsieur. You are the man of the two chickens."

Joliet was so enchanted with this rare joke, laughing and clapping all his nearer neighbors on the back, that I could not but accept it graciously. For this exceptional day, at least, I must bear my eternal nickname. Was not the maid now present whose dower had been hatched by those well-omened fowls? and was not the dower now coming to use? Hohenfels paired off with the notary, and discussed with that parchment person the music of Mozart, and, what would have been absurd and incredible in any Anglo-Saxon country, the scribe understood it! Our party had to wait but ten minutes for the groom and his men. Fortnoye, in a grand blue suit, with a wondrous dazzle of frilling on his broad chest, looked a noble husband, but was preoccupied and silent. His chorus supported him — Grandstone, Somerard, my engineer and the others — in dignified black clothes, official boutonnières and ceremonial cravats: they greeted Frau Kranich with awe, and bowed before the polished head of the lawyer with the parallelism of ninepins. My little group of fellow-travelers was almost complete. The young duelist, of course, was not expected or wanted. The Scotch doctor, Somerard told me, had been obliged to fly to London, where a mammoth meeting of the homœopathic faith was in progress.

The great feature of the breakfast came on when every crumb of breakfast had been eaten. Charles and the maid cleared away the table, and the notary stood up to read the marriage contract. The reading, ordinarily a dull affair, was in this instance vivified by curious incidents. In the first place, Frau Kranich, amending the injustice her over-credulity had caused, gave her *protégée* a wedding-present of twenty thousand francs, accompanying the gift with some singularly tart remarks about her nephew: this sum was increased by the groom to sixty thousand. The second incident was when Joliet, amid the almost incredulous surprise of the whole table, raised the gift, by the addition of ten thousand, to seventy thousand francs: the money was the product of his former house and garden — that house of shreds and patches which had cost him ten francs. When it came to affixing the signatures, the notary appeal-

SQUARE OF THE HÔTEL DE VILLE, BRUSSELS.

ed to Joliet for his name. He could not sign it, being gouty and half forgetful of pen-practice, but he responded to the question as bold as a lion: "John Thomas Joliet, baron de Rouvière," throwing to the lawyer a fine bunch of papers bearing witness to the validity of the title; after which he added, no less proudly, "wine-merchant, wholesale and retail, at the sign of the Golden Chickens, Noisy."

In truth, Joliet's father had rightfully borne the title of baron de Rouvière, but, ruined by '48, had abandoned the practice of signing it. Joliet resumed it this special occasion, having every warrant for the act, but whispered to me that he should never so call himself in future, greatly preferring the enumeration of his qualities on his business-card.

Poor Francine meanwhile had looked so timid and blushed so that Frau Kranich nodded to her permission of absence. She gave one glance at Fortnoye, buried her face in her hands, laughed a sweet little gurgle, and fled. When her presence was again necessary, she reappeared, drowned in white. We went to the mayor's office, where she lost a pretty little surname that had always seemed to fit her like a glove; then to the church, an obscure one in the neighborhood of Frau Kranich's house. But at the door of the sacred edifice the elder lady said, with much conciliatory grace in her manner, "I claim exemption from witnessing this part of the ceremony; and you, Mr. Flemming, must resume or discover your Protestantism and enter the carriage with me. I must show you a little of the city while these young birds are pairing."

No objection was made to this rather strange proposal. The bride, between her father and husband, forgot that she had no friend of her own sex to stand near her. We arranged for a general meeting at the dinner.

In the carriage she said, "I brought you away because I am devoured with uneasiness. Mrs. Ashburleigh wrote me that she would certainly be here for at least the principal part of the ceremony. I do not know what to make of it. It may be of no use, but we will scour the city. These throngs, this noise, make me uneasy. I fear some accident, having," she added with a smile, "one lone woman's sympathy for another lone woman."

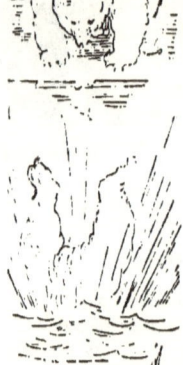

RIVERS DIVERSIONS.

I peered through the crowds at this, right and left, with inexpressible emotion. Perhaps this accidental sort of quest was that which destiny had arranged for the solution of my life-problem. To light upon Mary Ashburleigh in these festal throngs, perhaps wanting assistance, perhaps calling upon my name even now through her velvet lips, was a chance the mere notion of which made my blood leap.

When Brussels gives herself over to holiday-making, she does it in a whole-souled and self-consistent way that has plenty of attractiveness. The houses seemed to have turned themselves inside out to replenish the streets. People in their best clothes, equipages, processions, bands, troops of children, filled the avenues. Some conjecture that there might have been a mistake about the church took us to the cathedral of St. Gudule. Here, amid the superb spectrums of the stained windows, we searched through the vari-colored throngs that covered the floor, but no familiar face looked upon us. Strange to us as the old, impassive monumental dukes of Brabant who occupy the niches, the people made way to let us pass from the doorway between the lofty brace of towers to the high altar, which is a juggler's apparatus, and has concealed machinery causing the sacred wafer to come down seemingly of its own accord at the moment when the priest is about to lift the Host. All was unfamiliar and splendid, and we came away, feeling as if our own little wedding-group would have been lost in so magnificent a tabernacle. The Grande Place, on which lay the wedge-like shadow of the high-towered Hôtel de Ville, was perhaps as thronged a honeycomb of buzzing populace as when Alva looked out upon it to see the execution of Egmont and Horn. Among all the good-natured Netherlandish countenances that paved the square there was none that responded to my own.

We drove vaguely through the principal streets, and then, baffled, made our way to the faubourg in which is situated the zoological garden, toward which a considerable portion of the inhabitants was going even as ourselves. At the entrance our carriage encountered that of the bride and groom, and soon the whole party of the breakfast-table assembled by the gate, for the great coffee-rooms at which our meal was laid were close by the garden, and a promenade in this famous living museum was a premeditated part of the day's enjoyment. We entered the grounds in character, frankly putting forward our claims as a wedding-procession. That is the delightful French custom among those who are brought up as Francine had been : her father would have been heartbroken to have been denied the proud exhibition of his joy, and Fortnoye was too great a traveler, too cosmopolitan, to object to a little family pageant that he had seen equaled or exceeded in publicity in most of the Catholic countries on the globe. Francine, her artisanne cap for ever lost, her gleaming dark hair set, like a Milky Way, with a half wreath of orange-blossoms, the silvery gauzes of her protecting veil floating back from her forehead, strayed on at the head of the little parade. She was wrapped in the delicious reverie of the wedding-day. She was not yellow nor meagre, nor uglier than herself, as so many brides contrive to be. Her air of delicacy and tenderness was a blossom of character, not a canker of ill-health. Her color was hardly raised, though her head was perpetually bent. Fortnoye, holding her on his firm arm, seemed like a man walking through enchantments. Just behind, protecting Madame Kranich with an action of effusive gallantry that must have been seen to be conceived, walked the baron de Rouvière, his brave knotted hands, for which he had not found any gloves, busily occupied in pointing out the animated rarities that to him seemed most worthy of selection. The hilarious hyenas, the seals, the polar bears plunging from their lofty rocks, all attracted his commendation; and we, who walked behind in such order as our friendships or familiarity taught us, were perpetually tripping upon his honest figure brought to a halt before some object more than usually interesting. Exclamations of delight at the bride's beauty, politely wrapped in whispers, arose on all sides as we penetrated the throng: it was a proud thing to be a part of a procession so distinguished. My good Joliet beamed with complacency, and drove his little herd up and down and across and about till the greater part of the garden was explored. The zoological garden of Brussels has the beauty of not showing too obviously the character of a prison. It is extensive, umbrageous, and the poor captives within its borders have enough air and space around their eyes to give them a semblance of liberty. For the special feast-day on which we visited it the place had

THE MIMIC HUNT.

been arranged with particular adaptation to the character of the time. There were elephant-races and rides upon the camels free to all ladies who would make the venture. In addition to the zebras, gnus and Shetlands, there was that species of race-horse which never wins and never spoils a course, being of wood and constructed to go round in a tent, and never to arrive anywhere or lose any prizes. The pelicans were in high excitement, for all along their beautiful little river, where it winds through bowery trees, a profusion of living fish had been emptied and confined here and there by grated dams, so that the awkward birds had opportunity to angle in perfect freedom and to their hearts' content. In the more wooded part of the garden a mimic hunt had been arranged, and sportsmen in correct suits of green, with curly brass horns and baying hounds, coursed through the grounds, following a stag which, though mangy and asthmatic, may yet have been a descendant of the fawn that fed Genevieve of Brabant. We had re-entered one of the grand alleys, and were receiving again the little tribute of encomiums which the greater privacy of the groves had pretermitted—we were parading happily along, conscious of nothing to be ashamed of, our orange-blossoms glistening, our veil flying, our broadcloth and wedding-favors gleaming—when we met another group, which, though more furtively, bore that matrimonial character which distinguished our own.

At the head walked Mr. Cookson & Jenkinson. He still wore that species of shooting-costume which he had made his uniform, but it was decked with roses, and his hands were encased in milk-white gloves: on his hands, besides the gloves, he had the two grammatical ladies from the Rhine steamboat in guise of bridesmaids. Behind him walked Mary Ashburleigh. And emerging from the skirts of Mary Ashburleigh's dress, with the embarrassed happiness of a middle-aged bridegroom, was—no? yes! no, no! but yes—was Sylvester Berkley.

I will not expose what I suffered to the curiosity of imperfectly sympathetic strangers. I did not faint, and I believe men in genuine despair never do so. But I felt that weakness and unmanageableness of knee which comes with strong mental anguish, and I sank back impotent upon the baron, whose lingering legs repudiated the pressure, so that we both accumulated miserably upon Grandstone. My eyes closed, and I did not hear the Dark Ladye's salutations to Frau Kranich. But I awoke to see with anguish a sight that drew involuntary applause from all that careless crowd.

It was the salute of the two brides. Imagine, if you can, two great purple pansies, flushed with all the perfumed sap of an Eden spring-time, threaded with diamonds of myriad-faceted dew,—imagine them leaning forward on their elastic stems until both their soft velvet countenances cling together and exchange mutually their caparisons of honeyed gems; then let them sway gently back, and balance once more in their morning splendor. Such was the effect when these two imperial creatures approached each other and imprinted with lips and palms a sister's salute. Mary Ashburleigh, whom the throng recognized as a natural empress, was arrayed this morning as brides are seldom arrayed, but with a sense of artistic obedience to her own sumptuous nature and personality. The royal purple of her velvets was cut, on skirt and bodice, into one continuous fretwork of heavy scrolls and leafage, and through the crevices of this textile carving shone the robe she carried beneath: it was tawny yellow, for she wore under her outward dress a complete robe of ancient lace, whose cobweb softness was more than half sacrificed—only perceived as the slashes of her velvets made it evident. It was such dressing as queens alone should indulge in perhaps, but Mary Ashburleigh chose for once to do justice to her style and her magnificence.

I was leaning against a tree, stunned in the sick sunshine. I heard, while my eyes were closed, a sort of voluminous cloudy roll, and the Dark Ladye was beside me. She whispered quickly and volubly in my ear, "I tried to confide in you, but I could not get it spoken. Yet I managed to confess that my heart had been touched. It was only this summer—at the Molkencur over Heidelberg—he lectured about the ruins. 'Twas information—'twas rapture! I found at once he was the Magician. We were quietly united at the embassy this morning. And now he can leave that dreadful consulate and has got his promotion, for he is to be *chargé* here in Brussels. It is sudden, but we were positively afraid to do it in any other way, I am such a timid creature. When I saw the travelers' agent on the steamboat, I was at first struck with his manly British bearing and his resemblance to Sylvester. Then I found he had the matrimonial prospectus, and perceived he might be a link. He has managed everything beautifully. I had no idea— With his assistance you need no more mind being married than going into a shop for a plate of pudding. You must come up and be presented, to show you bear no malice."

I cannot tell how I did it, but I allowed Sylvester and the agent to grasp my hands, one on either side. Berkley, as to his collar, his cravat, his face and his white gloves, presented one general surface of mat silver. He clasped me with some affection, but his intellect had quite gone, and he said it was a fine day.

I did not rally in the least until after my fourth glass of champagne at the dinner. We made one party: indeed, Mrs. Ashburleigh had brought her husband hither in that expectation. Fortnoye vanished a minute to arrange the banquet-room; and as his wife rushed in to find him, followed by the rest of us, he snatched a great damask cloth from the table, and there was such a set-out of flowers and viands as has seldom been seen in Belgium or elsewhere. The table, instead of a cloth, was entirely laid with young emerald vine-leaves: our places were marked, and at each plate was a gift for the bride, ostensibly coming from the person who sat there, but really provided by the forethought of Fortnoye. In front of my own cover two pretty downy chicks were pecking in a cottage made of crystal slats and heavily thatched with spun glass—the prettiest birdcage in the world. On the eaves was an inscription: "The Man of the Two Chickens." It happened that the little keepsake I had found for Francine consisted of wheat-ears in pearls and gold, adapted for brooch and eardrops; so I only had to drop them in beside the chickens and the present was appropriate and complete.

I cannot tell of the effect as Mary Ashburleigh swept into that splendid banqueting-room, one long pyramid of velvet pierced with webbed interstices of light. If the largest window of St. Ursula's church had come down and entered the room, the spectacle could not have been so superb. One item struck me: the younger bride, of course, wore orange buds; but for the Englishwoman, a beauty ripe with many summers, buds and blossoms were inappropriate; she wore fruits: in the grand coronal of plaits that massed itself upon her head were set, like gems, three or four small, delicious, amber-scented mandarin oranges. With this piece of exquisite apropos did the infallible Mary Ashburleigh crown the edifice of her good taste. The two brides sat opposite each other. A small watch, which I had happened to buy at Coblenz, I managed to detach and lay on the Dark Ladye's plate as my offering. On a card beside it I merely wrote, "ANOTHER TIME!"

Who knows? Perhaps Sylvester may fill and founder as the other has done. He looks miserably bilious and frightened.

I had rather partake of a rare dinner than describe one. The wines alone represented all the cellars of the Rhine and the whole champagne country. Fortnoye, who gave the feast, entertained both Sylvester's party and his own with regal good cheer. Think not that Henri Fortnoye was the ordinary obfuscated, superfluous, bewildered bridegroom. On the contrary, assuming immediately the head of his own table, he took the responsibility of the party's merriment, and made the good humor flow like the wine. I know not how it was, but ere the meal was over I found myself joining in one of his choruses; Frau Kranich forgot her asceticism and exhumed all her youthful air of gayety; James Athanasius Grandstone promised the host to set his wines running in every State of America. But the prettiest moment was when the two brides rose and touched glasses, mutually and to the health of the company, apropos of a little wedding-song which Fortnoye had

HOMEWARD BOUND.

composed and was trolling at the head of our willing chorus.

CONCLUSION.

I have arrived at Marly, and, with the assistance of much sarcasm from Hohenfels, am getting on with considerable spirit at my Progressive Geography. When a man's Hope ceases temporarily to take a merely Human aspect, may it not suffer a fresh avatar and begin in a new and Geographical form its beneficent career? The Dark Ladye has sunk beneath my horizon, but speculations over the Atlantean and Lunar Mountains are still succulent and vivifying.

I fled, lashed by a hundred despairs and by many symptoms of headache and dyspepsia, from the wedding-feast at Brussels. Charles and the baron of Hohenfels accompanied me. It was a night-train. The spectacle of so much wedded happiness was too much for me, too much for Hohenfels. The effect was, contrarily, rather stimulating to Charles, who has made a match with Josephine, and with her assistance is now listening, the tear of sensibility in his eye, to Mendelssohn's "Wedding March" as executed by the village organ!

We passed Valenciennes, Somain, Douai, Arras, Amiens, Clermont, Criel, Pontoise—the last points of merely bodily travel that I shall ever make: hereafter my itineracy shall be entirely theoretical. We took a carriage at Pontoise, and traversed the woods of Saint-Germain. As I neared home I bowed right and left to amicable and smiling neighbors, who waved me good-day

CHARLES AND JOSEPHINE.

ARGUS AND ULYSSES.

from their doors. So did my Newfoundland, who broke his chain and leaped upon my shoulders, flourishing his tail —overjoyed to salute the returning Ulysses.

In the British Museum, among the Elgin Marbles, Phidias has carved a pile of heaped-up marble waves, and out of them rise the arms of Hyperion—the most beautiful arms in the world. Homesick for heaven, those weary arms try to free themselves of the clinging foam. Another minute and surely the triumphant god will leap from his watery couch and guide with unerring hands the coursers of the Dawn! But that reluctant minute is eternal, and the divinity still remains incapable, clogged and wrapped in the embrace of marble waves. Yet the real sun every morning succeeds in equipping himself for his journey, and arrives, glad, at his welcome bath in the western sea.

The inference I draw is: If you want a career to be eternal instead of transitory, hand it over to Art.

"HAND IT OVER TO ART."

The true moral of it all is, that we are all savage myths of the Course of the Sun. We disappear any number of times, but we rise and trail new clouds of glory, and our readers or our audiences perceive that it is the same old Hyperion back again. The youth who by the faithful hound, half buried in the snow, is found far up on the most inaccessible peaks of imagination, is perceived to grasp still in his hand of ice that Germanesque and strange device—*Auf Wiedersehen*.

www.ingramcontent.com/pod-product-compliance
Lightning Source LLC
Chambersburg PA
CBHW032001230426
43672CB00010B/2233